PRAISE FOR *Reporting the Oregon Story*

"*Reporting the Oregon Story* is an historic gem. The
knowledge Floyd McKay brings as a journalist, reporter,
and commentator adds both color and depth to the amazing
twenty-year span where Tom McCall and Bob Straub played
leading roles. Floyd's love of Oregon blends flawlessly with his
commitment to tell this story with accuracy and heart."
—BARBARA ROBERTS, Governor of Oregon, 1991–1995

"Few observers of Oregon politics from this period have had
the kind of access to the major players driving the narrative,
and few are capable of the analytical insights that Floyd
McKay offers here. We are fortunate that he has chosen to
capture what he remembers—and he remembers a lot."
—CHARLES K. JOHNSON, author of *Standing at the Water's
Edge: Bob Straub's Battle for the Soul of Oregon*

"Floyd McKay has burnished his reputation as one of the
most thoughtful and insightful observers (while a participant
himself) in an era of historic change in the Northwest and the
nation, the significance of which we are only now beginning
to fully appreciate. His account on 'reporting the Oregon
story' has intriguing new things to tell us, both about political
changes in the sixties and seventies, but also about how the
press was transformed as television became the dominant
medium through which most Americans learned of the world,
the nation, and their region. McKay is both an excellent

journalist—his crisp, clear writing is almost impossible to put down—and a scholarly observer of larger trends that spread, like ripples in a pond, through the Northwest and American life during the years about which he has written. His chapter on the domestic reaction to the war in Vietnam in the late sixties and early seventies is particularly riveting. Required reading for anyone interested in the Northwest or the years that have come to be popularly known as 'the sixties.'"

—BILL LUNCH, Political Analyst for Oregon Public Broadcasting and Professor Emeritus of Political Science at Oregon State University

"In this memoir of his years as a newspaper reporter and TV commentator, Floyd McKay gives us up-close assessments of Tom McCall, Bob Straub, Mark Hatfield, and other key leaders who shaped Oregon and helped lead the drive to protect our beaches and open spaces. If you want to understand the roots of Portlandia or how a governor could spur population growth by urging people to visit but not stay, *Reporting the Oregon Story* is an excellent place to start."

—JEFF MAPES, Senior Political Reporter, Oregon Public Broadcasting

REPORTING THE OREGON STORY

Reporting the Oregon Story

HOW ACTIVISTS AND VISIONARIES TRANSFORMED A STATE

Floyd J. McKay

*For Betsy Bergstein
a player in those good
Times!*

Floyd J. McKay

Oregon State University Press   Corvallis

Library of Congress Cataloging-in-Publication Data

Names: McKay, Floyd J., author.
Title: Reporting the Oregon story : how activists and visionaries
    transformed a state / Floyd J. McKay.
Description: Corvallis : Oregon State University Press, 2016.
Identifiers: LCCN 2015049036 | ISBN 9780870718465 (paperback) | ISBN
    9780870718472 (ebook)
Subjects: LCSH: Oregon—Politics and government—1951— | McCall, Tom,
    1913–1983. | Oregon. Governor (1967–1975 : McCall) | Straub, Robert
    W. | Governors—Oregon—Biography. | Oregon. Governor (1975–1979 :
    Straub) | McKay, Floyd J. | Journalists—Oregon—Biography. | Political
    activists—Oregon—History—20th century. | BISAC: BIOGRAPHY &
    AUTOBIOGRAPHY / Editors, Journalists, Publishers. | BIOGRAPHY &
    AUTOBIOGRAPHY / Political. | LANGUAGE ARTS & DISCIPLINES /
    Journalism.
Classification: LCC F881.3 .M33 M35 2016 | DDC 979.5/043—dc23
LC record available at http://lccn.loc.gov/2015049036

♾ This paper meets the requirements of ANSI/NISO Z39.48-1992
(Permanence of Paper).

First published in 2016 by Oregon State University Press
Printed in the United States of America

Oregon State University Press
121 The Valley Library
Corvallis OR 97331-4501
541-737-3166 • fax 541-737-3170
www.osupress.oregonstate.edu

Over the period covered in this book, many friends and colleagues provided support and guidance, but only one has been with me daily for six decades of professional journalism, with all its changes and challenges. Dixie Ann McKay remains the love of my life and constant companion. This book and all good things are dedicated to her.

Contents

Preface xi

Introduction 1
Profile Team Neuberger 11

ONE Television's Favorite Son.. 14
Profile That Old Gang of Tom's 35

TWO Saving the Rivers and Beaches.. 38
Profile Janet McLennan's Activism 58

THREE Mark Goes Rogue: Vietnam in Oregon 61
Profile Bob Duncan: More Than a Hawk............................... 80

FOUR Tumult in 1968: The Year of Change 83

FIVE Sitting in Tom's Chair.. 107

SIX Red Hat to Vortex: the Reinvention of Tom McCall 128
Profile The Odd Couple: Ron Schmidt and Ed Westerdahl.... 144

SEVEN People for . . . Friends of 147
Profile Vera Katz: From Brooklyn with Love 164

EIGHT Saving the Land.. 167
Profile The Remarkable L. B. Day....................................... 183
Profile Freshman Chutzpah: Don Stathos and Walt Brown ... 185

NINE   Holding on in Changing Times............................188
            Profile Nancy Russell: Steel in a Velvet Glove 211

TEN   Becoming Portlandia 213
            Profile Timber Jim and the Redhead 237

ELEVEN   The Legacy...239

            Afterword...245

            Acknowledgments 251

            Notes..253

            Additional Readings and Viewings 259

            Index..263

Preface

Tom McCall's centennial birthday was March 22, 2013, and I found myself sitting on a high stool alongside two unlikely partners in the celebration of Tom's birth: Victor Atiyeh and Roger Martin. They were distinguished Oregonians, but they were not friends of Tom McCall; together they extinguished his political career when he tried to make a comeback in 1978. Surely our hosts at the Oregon Historical Society knew that!

We had a pleasant evening and it was wonderful to see Vic, who had just marked his ninetieth birthday, perched firmly on that stool for forty-five minutes. He was funny, friendly, and in his element. Roger was mellower than the last time we met, and perhaps he thought I was as well. We had a good time.

How to explain the strange panel, however? Well, as I realized later, the simple fact is that nearly all of Tom's old gang is gone—including his friend and sparring partner, Bob Straub, most of his staff, and nearly all of the press who covered his governorship. History, it is said, is written by the winners. Sometimes it is written by the survivors. Vic, Roger, and I were survivors; in a year, Vic was gone.

We were players in what was sometimes called "The Oregon Story," a quite remarkable era—defined here as 1964 through 1986—a time when Oregonians wrote laws and took actions that stood out nationally and encouraged others to follow our lead. The Oregon Story has passed into mythical territory, but there were real people involved in the crafting. My fear, as survivors are harder to find each year, is that the flesh and blood will be lost and the myth all that remains. Oregonians did some quite extraordinary things in those days, and our descendants deserve to know about the events and those who crafted the story.

This book is one newsman's attempt to capture the essence of the era, relying on an aging memory, boxes of "stuff," and an unabated conviction that we created an era unique to Oregon but also important in the life of a nation. I left Oregon in 1990 after thirty-two years as a reporter in print and television and two years as a governor's assistant. My path took me from one side of the country to another and finally ended in the far Northwest corner.

By the time of my formal retirement in 2004, I had done a stint as a senior fellow at the East-West Center in Honolulu, completed a master's degree at the University of Maryland and, since 1990, served as a journalism professor at Western Washington University in Bellingham. I earned a PhD at the University of Washington; I was a certified scholar and, literally, I had moved on.

Yet the memories continued to intrude: a news story about an advance or retreat in our legacy; the death of a friend or the retirement of another; a call from a reporter probing my institutional memory. Dixie and I returned often to Portland, where our children and grandchildren live, but gradually it became rare to be spotted by someone who would work up the courage to ask, "Say, didn't you used to be on TV?" Or, worse yet, "Didn't you used to be Floyd McKay?" My image faded, but the stories and memories did not. Retirement brought the opportunity to pull out some musty clips and videotapes and ponder at leisure why that period was so glorious for Oregon and Oregonians . . . certainly for me.

Then in 2007, Oregon Public Broadcasting asked me to do an interview for a documentary on the Oregon Beach Bill. Suddenly the old habits were back: clipping a microphone on my shirt, testing for sound, trying to phrase an answer succinctly and coherently. It was going so well that we expanded into the important highway-on-the-beach at Pacific City and Bob Straub's campaign of 1966.

After all those years, I was back in the role of holder of institutional memory, or historian, if you wish. Later, I served in that role for documentaries on Tom McCall and Mark Hatfield. Many of the players of that wonderful era were gone, and I was one of the few surviving reporters. It caused me to pull together videotapes of documentaries, news series, and commentaries I had squirreled away from my KGW-TV days and have them converted to DVD format for donation to the Oregon Historical Society.

Reviewing the videos to produce a guide for researchers, memories crowded the room, and for a brief time I wanted to be back there again, young and energetic, skeptical yet hopeful. Most of all, I felt nostalgia for the actors, the battles we fought together, the triumphs and the defeats. We really did believe that Oregonians could shape our destiny as a state and a people, and that story is worth sharing.

These pages are not biographies of major figures of the era; Brent Walth (Tom McCall), Charles Johnson (Bob Straub) and Mason Drukman (Wayne Morse) have contributed excellent portraits of three of the key figures, after exhaustive research. I cite them and other works for material with which I was not familiar at the time or to guide readers to a more comprehensive treatment.

This work is largely a personal memoir; I weave my political reporting career into the narrative and quote from my writing and broadcasts. Journalism was changing rapidly during this era and my transitions and challenges may help readers understand the complex relationship between political reporters and their sources, and how it changed over time. Journalism defines our times and this was certainly true of the Oregon Story.

I've always been a bit of a packrat, and many boxes of personal files moved with me from Salem to Portland and ultimately to Bellingham. More files were created as I moved into a companion career as a Northwest historian. I would be less than candid if I didn't confess that my wife's long suffering with my stacks of boxes contributed to the impetus to finish the story and clean the garage. So here we are, cleaning the garage, sharing memories and observations of a golden era, certainly the highlight of my half-century as a working journalist and teacher.

Finally, a word for those still alive and well but referred to here in the past tense: that's not a mistake; my comments describe people as I saw them at the time, including myself. I'm so glad you are also a survivor—stay well!

Introduction

The note on the stationery of the governor of Oregon is dated simply, "Wednesday."

I found the note a few years ago, as I went through material from that era; only Tom McCall would use that wording and display that excitement about a time that we were beginning to identify as something quite special. Tom's "Oregon Message" was, by the time he left office in 1975, becoming known as "the Oregon Story." Some felt there was an "Oregon Mystique," but that implies a sense of secrecy or mystery, and one of the "secrets" behind the Oregon

Story was a brash use of publicity, the bully pulpit if you will. Tom McCall and his counterparts knew exactly what they were doing.

The story was scripted by Tom and many others over three decades, beginning in the Cold War era of the 1950s and winding down in the 1980s. A nuclear cloud hung over the world during the Cold War immediately following the hot war of the prior decade. Life was precarious, but some among us dared to strive for a better world; perhaps we could begin in our small corner. "Livability" emerged to define the goal, "environmentalism" to define the means.

Oregon became more than a small, remote state that might be a nice place to visit some time—we became a model for change, a place of innovation where it might be nice to live. The quest is universal and timeless: can a people define and control the environment in which they live or must they submit to the invisible hand of the market, the relentless forces of progress? Is it possible to build new trails and priorities and make the changes stick?

Oregon was ripe for change—not because things were so bad but perhaps because things were so good. Innovation and reform always work best when people have jobs and security. Oregon did not face a crisis as the 1960s unrolled; the state was healthy in economic and social terms and becoming a place where people wanted to live. But state and local governments were somnolent, perfectly content with the standpat Republican leadership Oregonians had elected for decades. Governor Mark Hatfield cracked the image but not the substance of the matter. His two-term administration brought more modern methods of governing and a more sophisticated approach to economic development, but little else of significance changed. Portland was controlled by old-guard Democratic leadership; you could shoot a cannon down Broadway after 6:00 p.m. and hit only teenagers "dragging the gut" in cut-down cars.

Americans strived in the post-war era for a return to normalcy— whatever that meant to an increasingly diverse nation. For some, it was a prototypical suburban rambler for mom, dad, and 2.5 kids. Others pursued a restless quest for change—new faces, new challenges, and new priorities.

Oregon's population grew by 62 percent from 1940 to 1960, primarily through wartime immigration. Many of the newcomers were young and raising families in a place they believed to be unsullied by the exploding and unplanned development driven by the age of the automobile. Oregon had fresh air and open land, beaches and mountains without "Private Property" signs. The surge, however, brought with it pressure to turn the state's assets into hard cash. More than many longtime Oregonians, the new arrivals sensed the threat to the very things that had drawn them to the Pacific Northwest.

Together with farsighted natives, they sowed seeds of change in our small corner of the nation, and by the end of the sixties a predictable one-party state had developed two vigorous political parties and genuine choices for voters. Leaders of both parties had to pay closer attention to an electorate that was dramatically changed by events during and after World War II. The next three decades would see the most significant changes in Oregon's environment since it gained statehood.

Republicans and Democrats—thrown together as much as divided by the new two-party system—found common cause at every level of government, exceptionally demonstrated in the competitive but friendly rivalry of Republican Tom McCall and Democrat Bob Straub. Their relationship epitomized the ability of Oregonians at all levels to seek common cause before dividing into rival camps. Oregon was a competitive state in political terms, which produced vigorous campaigns but urged candidates to a middle ground that could be negotiated in good faith. The term "we" prevailed over "us and them" from the capitol building to city halls and neighborhoods. Observing independently from our privileged vantage, reporters felt they were a part—a critical and sometimes obstreperous part—of the "we," a pronoun often employed in this accounting.

We stood up to the forces that would have stolen our ocean beaches and crammed the nation's best farmland with a tangle of dream homes and malls. We built a livable city and turned a freeway into a new ride we called MAX. There would be no high rises and flashing signs in the Columbia Gorge, and bottles would be kept from streams and trails. We even wrote the nation's first ban on aerosol sprays. We cheered when our feisty governor, feeling the joy, told others to come and enjoy their visit—but please don't stay. They did stay, of course, in increasing numbers.

In less than twenty short years, we were nearing exhaustion. In less than three short decades, the excitement was gone. But Oregon would never be the same again; the legacy was rooted and the challenge of maintenance had overtaken the thrill of construction. We had accomplished something really important.

When it started, there was for me the most unlikely symbol that could be conjured from the chaos of November 22, 1963, as President John F. Kennedy lay dying on a gurney in Dallas, Texas. That symbol—unrecognized by me at the time—was a stubby little man in a rumpled suit and tie, carrying a small television set into the newsroom of the Salem newspaper where I worked. Wendell Webb, managing editor and upright defender of news on the printed page, plugged it in, jerked the rabbit ears, and turned to Walter Cronkite. Without comment, he returned to his office and probably wished for a drink.

Journalists and their readers had stumbled into a new era, defined by that ubiquitous black box and the people who lived within it. Newspapers would be forced to share their coveted audiences, a television newsman would step from the black box and hold an entire state in his hand, bulky film cameras and then electronic marvels would define an age of broadcast journalism that would influence a state and give voice to a generation. The hub would be in Portland, where the complacent mediocrity of a business-dominated city hall would be overrun by the young and restless setting the cornerstones for a remarkable urban renaissance.

There was crafted in those days something we called the Oregon Story, and it was taken seriously by many who set the nation's thoughts and agenda. Two of our leaders were talked about as potential presidents; our senators' rage rattled those who blundered into and through the jungles of Vietnam. Words such as livability, sustained growth, recycling, and clean energy surged through our discussions; a phalanx of new faces overwhelmed the lobbyists and hangers-on at the state capitol, as women and young people brought a new agenda and changed the way business was done in the Club of Old Boys.

It was such a glorious time!

When it all began—if you accept my definition of the timeline—I had just turned twenty-eight and was covering local news for the *Oregon Statesman* in Salem, whose editor and publisher was former governor Charles A. Sprague. His front-page column, "It Seems To Me," was required reading for Oregon's leaders. In 1964 I would be assigned three blocks away to cover state politics at the capitol, the youngest reporter in a pressroom tucked into a back corner of the capitol basement. Just six years later I would sit in the chair that had been Tom McCall's at KGW-TV. I would spend more than two decades reporting on the Oregon Story and, like so many others, move on to other challenges—never as exciting as those years when we made, wrote, and filmed that golden age.

The way we were in that time may be impossible in the twenty-first century—at times it seemed impossible in those simpler times—but there may be lessons and certainly stories for our descendants. With gratitude and apologies to Governor Sprague's daily column, this is my "It Seems to Me" moment. The Oregon Story was written by many people, by youngsters carrying signs on a threatened beach, a fisherman with fouled gear from a noxious mill outlet, a farm family pushing back against an encroaching subdivision, a hiker with a backpack full of rusted beer cans.

The first harbingers of what was to come actually began at the federal level, in the makeup and priorities of Oregon's congressional delegation. Even during the Great Depression and New Deal, Oregon predictably sent a Republican-dominated delegation to Washington. To change that, Oregon Democrats had to cut out the rot of an aging party leadership that was content to roll over to the business establishment at every election; the surgery took place in the 1950s.

Young men returned from war eager to upset the old complacency. Howard Morgan and Monroe Sweetland conspired on a Pacific island to revive the moribund Democratic Party and turn it in a progressive direction. They found others ready to march, including a man who had served one term in the legislature before going off to war; he was best known as a journalist and writer.

Richard L. Neuberger's election in 1954 sent the first Oregon Democrat to the US Senate in forty years. Senator Wayne Morse's dramatic move from Republican to Democratic allegiance a year later completed the sweep. The Oregon Story could not have been written in a one-party system with its reliance on steady conformity. Dick Neuberger was the breakthrough for a genuine two-party system. Neuberger laid the groundwork for what would become the Oregon Story, but he was felled by cancer in 1960, at age forty-seven.

In 1973, Tom McCall was pondering a Senate race he would never undertake, and in a long, rambling interview he thought about Neuberger. "Dick Neuberger—I mean you talk about me as an environmentalist," he reflected over his coffee, "I only wish circumstances had been such that Dick Neuberger had been the senior senator and I could have been the junior senator." The cup slammed down, the lanky frame lunged forward, the finger jabbing. "Why, by god, we'd have changed America!" Well, they certainly changed Oregon.

Oregon Democrats began their comeback in 1954 with Neuberger's election to the Senate; in the same year a Portland teacher named Edith Green defeated a radio newsman named Tom Lawson McCall, who ran for Congress as a conventional Republican. By the 1960s, Democrats owned the congressional delegation and Tom McCall dropped his middle name and became a very unconventional Republican. He soon found an unlikely rival-but-partner in a Democrat named Bob Straub; they were an historic odd couple.

An even less likely pair, Wayne Morse and Mark Hatfield, gave Oregon a national reputation as the US Senate's most dedicated opponents of the Vietnam War. Both took their lumps in partisan races and Morse was unhorsed, but he mounted two more challenges and died in the saddle. In its own way, the early and fierce opposition to the war by Morse and Hatfield was part of the Oregon Story. The independence of our senators became linked to the innovative proposals advanced by McCall, Straub, and others in what we were increasingly calling "livability." Independence and livability—not a bad image to have.

Newcomers joined with activists from Portland's longtime liberal neighborhoods to create in our largest city a renaissance of sorts, merging the Oregon Story with one of a new Portland that proved to be a magnet for the young and creative. *Portlandia*—the name of an iconic sculpture and later an irreverent television series—became a chapter of the Oregon Story. Some of the players and much of their passion overlapped. Oregon was doing well economically, people were feeling good about themselves despite a national angst linked to the Vietnam War and Watergate; they could make things work, Oregonians felt. And they did.

For me, and for the main protagonists, the new era began in the campaigns of 1964, twin victories for Republican McCall and Democrat Straub. They brought energy and vision to their offices and promise of a new order for Oregon at a time when America was undergoing massive change. My remembrances are strong of an era unfolding.

This book is in part a Tom and Bob Story, an account of two quite remarkable men who came along at a time in the history of Oregon when citizens were ready for inspiration and ideas, not yet jaded by national political dysfunction, and in a mood to realize the promise of a state large enough to get things done but small enough for anyone to play a role. It is also a story of Oregonians who worked together, often crossing lines of party and geography, to build the components that made Oregon special. Legislators, city planners, farmers, and conservationists, they accepted the challenges of change. It wasn't always pretty and sometimes we failed, but the basic structure and philosophy remain half a century later.

I was forever shaped as a journalist and as an Oregonian. I loved the news the activists created and their hopes and dreams for our state. We forged friendships around common goals and danced that intricate dance of politician and reporter that is performed in every political venue, the delicate maneuvers of close contact and a decent distance that never quite reaches perfection but is quite often gratifying for both partners.

Oregon seemed to overflow in this period with big stories and I covered most of them; this accounting, however, is necessarily limited to what I call the Oregon Story. It does not include Rajneeshees or Scientologists, nuclear power, repetitive tax proposals, timber policy, and countless legislative and courthouse victories and debacles. Other writers have and will continue to explore those elements of our history.

I'll talk about Vortex, however, because that gutsy gamble by Governor McCall in 1970 created an aura of courage and leadership that helped him nail down important planks in the structure we were building. Oregonians liked Tom McCall, but after Vortex they respected—and even loved—his risk-taking and belief that Oregonians would support those risks. Vietnam will also figure here, for it defined the generation and brought Oregon Story figures into close combat.

There was an air of inevitability in 1965 around Tom McCall, the lanky, stoop-shouldered secretary of state, because the governor's office would be open in 1966 when Mark Hatfield completed his second term. Secretaries of state often ascended one floor to the governor's suite, Hatfield the latest of several who made that move. The new state treasurer, Robert W. Straub, was a less-likely candidate, a Democrat in a state still favoring Republicans, a "downstater" from Lane County, at the south end of the Willamette Valley.

Their campaigns really began the moment they stepped into their new offices on the capitol's ground floor that January of 1965. The tall man from Portland won the 1966 contest, and he won a rematch in 1970. When McCall's two terms ended, Straub picked up the Oregon Story torch and gained the governorship in 1974.

Four years later, a restive and unsatisfied McCall again challenged Straub, but his comeback failed in the Republican primary. A conventional Republican, Victor Atiyeh, defeated Tom in the spring and Bob in the fall; Oregon appeared to be tired of Tom and Bob, and perhaps the Oregon Story.

As Tom and Bob were writing their legacy at the capitol, Neil Goldschmidt was building his at Portland city hall. The Rose City was blossoming and would bloom as Portlandia. The change was driven by neighborhood activists, forward-looking planners, architects, and young political leaders who shook the gray and cautious Portland establishment to its roots. The emblem of change was the death of an urban freeway, a road to nowhere, a "Mount Hood Freeway" that would have ended forty-eight miles short of the magnificent mountain.

Ordinary citizens killed that asphalt nightmare, and others as well. The fruit of their work was a modern transit system and a European square that embodied the concept of a downtown for people. Longtime Portland neighborhoods were saved from the paving machines and over the next four decades would bloom as immigrants from all over the nation and world discovered Portlandia.

It was a glorious time to be a reporter and commentator. No such time existed before in Oregon and, in my view, none has since. My personal journey in that era began in smoke-filled newsrooms and print shops with melted lead on the floor, and ended in air-conditioned studios with bright lights and huge cameras. It was a dream for a skinny kid with weak eyes from reading by the light of gas lamps as a blizzard swirled around our farmhouse a few miles from the Canadian border in rural North Dakota.

My wartime world was defined by the *Grand Forks Herald*, a few national magazines, and radio news. We followed the news of Pearl Harbor, D-Day, and the death of a president; I knew the names of all the baseball stars and the rivalry of Army and Navy football teams. Our small dairy taught me to work and appreciate the land. Newspapering offered horizons I could only imagine—but I knew I wanted to explore.

Our family of six was part of the post–World War II rush to Oregon, where farmland beckoned in the Willamette Valley as it had a century before. I was eleven when we arrived in 1947, barely sixteen when I began writing sports news for a semiweekly paper trying to go daily in the college town of McMinnville. I went to that college, Linfield, because I could live at home and work a forty-hour week driving school buses and working in a plywood mill and a clothing store; the prestigious journalism school in Eugene was beyond my purse. Always there was writing, still mostly sports and the college paper. After six months on National Guard active duty, I began my first real news job in 1958 at the *Springfield News*, Tuesdays and Thursdays, everything from city hall to schools and

lots of mashed cars and fires along the way. I learned to be a reporter from a great editor, H. P. "Red" Hornish, a whirlwind of a man who was a Velcro strip walking down the street; news stories just seemed to stick to the young man with red hair.

The trip was fast and glorious, thanks to my bride, Dixie Johnson McKay; we fell in love at Linfield and married my senior year, her sophomore year. Dixie dropped out to help support us; I promised she would finish, and she did at the University of Oregon while I was at the *News*. In 1960 we

Floyd and Dixie McKay outside the *Springfield News*, housed in a converted dental office just off the city's Main Street, in 1958. (Courtesy of the author)

moved to Salem and the *Oregon Statesman* with our infant daughter Karen; son David was born in 1963. The adventure continued and soon we would be on the track of the Oregon Story.

I had the rare good fortune of being there when the print medium and its message were at a high point in their twentieth-century histories. For me, as well as for many people I chronicled, it was the best of times. I had the best of teachers and colleagues at every point in my journalistic journey. We moved together through a quarter-century that built the structure that is Oregon today. The story that follows is one observer's remembrance, and the subjects are those he remembers in their accomplishments and legacies but also their flaws and biases.

Profile TEAM NEUBERGER

No couple was as important to the future development of the Oregon Story as Richard and Maurine Neuberger. Dick Neuberger was an inspiration to Tom McCall and Bob Straub, among others; Maurine Neuberger inspired a generation of women entering politics, including Betty and Barbara Roberts.

Dick's victory over Republican US Senator Guy Cordon in 1954 was the first big Democratic victory in the party's rebirth. His campaign helped elect Edith Green to Congress in the same year and was a big factor in Senator Wayne Morse's

Oregon's most famous political couple, Senator Richard and Maurine Neuberger, in 1958. After Dick's death in 1960, Maurine won election to the Senate, serving until 1966. (Oregon Historical Society ba001557)

conversion from the Republican to Democratic caucus in the US Senate. Neuberger's death in 1960 at the age of forty-seven was a devastating blow to Oregon Democrats and to his widow; Maurine won the seat on her own later that year and became Oregon's first female United States senator.

Dick Neuberger, a master wordsmith, developed a national audience with his books and magazine articles on the Pacific Northwest; his followers included President Franklin D. Roosevelt and national leaders in both political parties. He was a Democrat increasingly identified as a conservationist. In that era—1930 to 1960—being a conservationist meant wise use of natural resources, in the mode of Teddy Roosevelt and Gifford Pinchot. Neuberger endorsed dams on the Columbia and marveled at their power and contribution to the economy, but he also labored for wild and scenic rivers and mountains.

He was the most prolific freelance writer in Oregon history; he first attracted national attention with a firsthand account of the growing Nazi power in Germany in a 1933 article in the *Nation*. Adolf Hitler had been in power less than a year, and most American journalists were giving him slack. Dick was the grandson of German Jewish immigrants who settled in Portland, and he held nothing back from what he saw in Germany.

Dick found time to work for Democrats in an era when Republican control of Oregon politics was absolute. In 1940, at the age of twenty-seven, he was elected to the Oregon House of Representatives and served one session before serving in the army in Alaska. He was elected to the Oregon Senate in 1948 and remained until departing for the US Senate in 1955. Maurine Brown, a high-school English teacher in Portland, married Dick Neuberger in 1945 and joined him in the legislature in 1951, elected to an Oregon House seat that she held until leaving with her husband for Washington, DC.

It was a partnership of equals, two highly intelligent and dedicated people who complemented each other in many ways. Maurine had a people touch that Dick sometimes lacked and she understood publicity. Representative Neuberger donned an apron to illustrate the process of making colored oleomargarine when the Oregon legislature banned colored oleo under pressure from the dairy lobby. As the wife of a senator, she shocked and delighted the staid Washington, DC, establishment by modeling a Jantzen bathing suit in a charity fashion show.

Senator Maurine Neuberger was a leading consumer advocate in her single term in the US Senate, and she took on the powerful tobacco lobby in a scathing 1963 book, *Smoke Screen: Tobacco and the Public Welfare*. She was the primary force behind warning labels on cigarette packages; she championed consumer protection and was a mentor for young women entering politics. Many of the young women who worked in activist causes in Oregon cited her as their inspiration, in much the manner that environmentalists cited Dick Neuberger as a force in their field.

ONE   Television's Favorite Son

My generation was born into the dark days of the Great Depression; we lost loved ones in World War II and practiced ducking under desks during Cold War nuclear drills. But we were not prepared for November 22, 1963—it was our 9/11 and our Day of Infamy, and we would always remember where we were and what we saw. The assassination of President John F. Kennedy was, for many, more than the end of his New Frontier; it was the shattering of a dream.

It changed our world in so many ways. For a young reporter still learning the ropes in the newsroom at Oregon's capital-city newspaper, the tragedy also brought a sobering realization that the familiar world of newspapering—the way we communicated since the nation was new—had a new competitor, and a grieving nation was turning in that direction.

Our managing editor shuffled into the *Oregon Statesman* newsroom that fateful day and, without ceremony, mounted on a shelf the instrument of our future. Wendell Webb, old school to his Iowa roots, plugged a television set into a power outlet and we watched Walter Cronkite weep. Walter wept with America and America turned to Walter. When Cronkite declared the war in Vietnam hopeless in 1968, President Lyndon Johnson concluded that if he had lost Walter Cronkite, he had lost the nation.

Few professional journalists took television news seriously in 1963; even the legendary Edward R. Murrow preferred radio. Earlier in the year, however, Murrow's CBS network took a huge and fateful step and doubled the airtime for *CBS News* from fifteen to thirty minutes; others followed and a headlines show became a news show.

On November 22, 1963, the former United Press print reporter Walter Cronkite was in the studio as the news of Kennedy's assassination broke. Cronkite's calm but passionate anchoring was the nation's anchor as the days of tragedy unfolded. CBS remained the news leader throughout Cronkite's career. He was rated the most trusted man in America in a number of polls. Regardless of ratings, news professionals regarded CBS as the gold standard.

Oregon was late in getting commercial television; KPTV was first in 1952. Competition for licenses was intense by the mid-1950s, when the giant Westinghouse chain bid for the license to operate Channel 8, only to be outbid by a tenacious and far-sighted Seattle woman, Dorothy Bullitt, and her King Broadcasting. Bullitt brought a new viewpoint and vigor to the nascent Portland television scene when KGW-TV went on the air on December 15, 1956.

Anchor Richard Ross had television experience in Seattle and would remain as a KGW news fixture until 1975. For many in his viewing area, Ross was the Walter Cronkite of Portland. At his side was a nervous, disheveled, and totally disorganized man with a strange accent that sometimes jarred listeners. He was not a natural for the new medium; smooth and poised he was not.

The man we came to know simply as Tom McCall had followed an up-and-down journalistic career that took him to Moscow, Idaho, and then to the *Oregonian*, where he wrote police and general-assignment stories before moving to KGW radio. Following navy service and three years as assistant to Oregon governor Douglas McKay, he returned to KGW radio and then moved into television, briefly at KPTV and then at KGW-TV.

McCall and news director Ivan Smith jumped KPTV when ordered to endorse sponsors' products on the air; KGW recruited the pair and they became part of Portland's most memorable news team. With McCall, Smith, and Ross were weatherman Jack Capell and sports anchor Doug LaMear. All spent most of their news careers at the station; all except Tom were there when I arrived in 1970.

Tom McCall was part of KGW-TV's original news team, from left: Richard Ross, Ivan Smith, Doug LaMear, McCall, and Jack Capell. KGW-TV went on the air in 1956. (KGW-TV)

Despite his growing reputation, I had little knowledge of Tom McCall. The world of a morning newspaper reporter was quite different from that of most television viewers. When local television news was on the air, morning-paper reporters were scrambling to meet deadlines, at the *Statesman* about 7:00 p.m. for day reporters and 1:00 a.m. for the night shift. I had worked both shifts, covering local government, education, police, and general assignments. Since I had not reported from the capitol, I didn't know Tom or most of the regulars assigned to the political beat.

When he drove to Salem to cover a story, Tom would work with Joey Tompkins, a sawed-off, freelance cameraman with a crew cut who was shifting from still photography to film. They were Mutt and Jeff—Joey could not have been much above five feet tall, nearly a foot and a half shorter than Tom, and they were an incongruous team walking down a hallway. Joey was still working for the station in the seventies and filmed much of my reporting and commentary from the capitol. He was one of the kindest, most decent men with whom I ever worked.

I got acquainted with Joey upon my arrival in Salem in 1960, when I worked the late shift police beat. Joey and I sometimes converged on accident scenes. One late, rainy night on a Polk County road, I found myself hassled by the sheriff, a hulking bully of a man. I was getting nowhere until Joey drove up, hailed his friend Virgil, and suggested that he give the kid a chance. It was typical of Joey; he was beloved among reporters. Even when Tom became Governor McCall, Joey called him by his first name and ordered him around if he needed a better angle. The governor was quick to obey.

Print reporters in those days were largely derisive of our broadcast cousins; our image was that of a smooth and inoffensive anchorman, a fast-talking jock and entertaining weatherman (almost all were male at that time). We were willing to recognize those with a newspaper background; Tom fell into that category.

I knew a few Portland print reporters, but was seldom in the city and its popular Press Club bar. My prior Portland experience was as a college student driving a picker bus in the summer for a large row-crop farm; we solicited the denizens of Burnside Street's Skid Road early in the morning, hangovers and all, and transported them to the bean fields for the day.[1] It was scarcely an auspicious introduction to the city that later became my home. In 1964, however, Dixie and I were raising two kids in rural West Salem and had little social life outside neighbors, family, and *Statesman* friends. We did not move in Tom McCall's circles.

My first exposure to Bob Straub was in 1958, when he spoke at a meeting that I covered for the *Springfield News*. At home after the meeting, I told Dixie I had just heard a really lousy speaker, a man with a serious stuttering problem who had no future in politics—at least in the eyes of this twenty-three-year-old reporter!

Bob was a Lane County commissioner at the time, his first elective office in a long career. He arrived in Springfield in 1947, an army veteran with a master's degree from Dartmouth, and worked first at Weyerhaeuser's new mill as a personnel officer; he soon entered the home-building business. Bob was close to Springfield's Democratic leadership, including Mayor Ed Harms and leaders in labor and public-power circles.

My editor at the *News* was a Republican and did not see a lot in Straub, who was often viewed by opponents as brash and outspoken. I really had no politics. I had been raised in McMinnville, a Republican community; Republican affiliation was typical for anyone reared in Yamhill County, and it was also emblematic of the top leadership at the *Oregon Statesman*, which I joined in 1960. Editor and publisher Charles A. Sprague was the Republican governor of Oregon from 1939 to 1943.

Sprague's front-page column, "It Seems to Me," was on the reading list of the state's political leadership in both parties. The reserved, quiet, but forceful Sprague was in the newsroom every day and would visit briefly with veteran reporters; I cannot recall a conversation with Sprague of more than a couple of sentences until 1964, four years into my *Statesman* tenure, when I was unexpectedly named capitol reporter.[2]

Salem's news swirled around the capitol and its denizens; the beat was the most prestigious in the newsroom and I was headed there at age twenty-eight, after only six years as a full-time reporter. I was struck by the confidence placed in me by the former governor.

Daily supervision of the *Statesman* newsroom was the domain of Wendell Webb, a stubby little man shortened in height by a youthful auto accident. Wendell enjoyed a bourbon and cigarette, in contrast to the abstemious publisher. He liked hard news, and his heart beat for any story that scooped the afternoon *Capital-Journal*. Competition for news and circulation was very intense in the last days of competitive daily newspapers.

The *Statesman* had a permanent base in the capitol. Salem and Portland dailies and the two news wire services had desks in a widened hallway near the basement elevator to the House of Representatives. The spot was not pretentious, but the much-visited Capitol Coffee Shop was a few strides away, and many news stories began around its tables. Paul Harvey, who was writing for the Associated Press when the old capitol building burned in 1935, was unchallenged dean of the Press Room and also presided over a round table of capitol secretaries each noon in the coffee shop. I happily inherited Paul's fondness for Charles A. Sprague, whose relationship with Paul dated to the 1930s.

Oregon's news universe in 1964 was still largely a world of print, but the once-dominant position of the Portland newspapers was shadowed by a long and bitter strike that began in 1959 and was still in effect. One result of the strike was to elevate the stature of the major downstate papers, including the *Statesman*.

Reporters were often judged more by speed with a bulletin than by depth reporting or analysis. A "scoop" of an opponent was celebrated in the newsroom more than a "thumb-sucker" analyzing the various sides of an issue. The press was respectful of the establishment and worked hard to balance quotes between both sides (more than two were seldom presented) and avoid anything that resembled opinion in news stories. I was comfortable with that, having known nothing else. Reporters gave elected leaders some slack, particularly with regards to personal conduct—we all knew which legislators drank too much, dined nightly on lobbyist tabs, or dozed off in meetings. But as long as the behavior wasn't excessive or embarrassing, it went unreported. That, too, would change.

My predecessor, Tom Wright, was a leader among the World War II veterans who built the *Statesman* newsroom to statewide prominence. Tommy had been shot out of the war with wounds suffered in the Italian campaign, where he commanded a tank-destroyer unit that suffered heavy casualties. Soft-spoken but tough as nails, he commanded respect on all fronts except one important one—that of governor Mark Hatfield and his loyal staff and supporters.

The Hatfield team was Republican. Tom and his intelligent and ambitious wife, Marguerite, were Democrats and made no bones about that. Tom had served as press aide to governor Bob Holmes, a Democrat elected in 1956 and subsequently defeated by Hatfield in

1958. Holmes' two-year stint was Oregon's only Democratic governorship between 1938 and 1974. Salem was solidly Republican and the Hatfields and Wrights ran in different circles in Salem's political and social world. Mark and Antoinette Hatfield married in 1958 in the midst of his campaign for governor; they were an elegant couple and dominated Salem's news.

Oregon's wedding of the year in 1958 was Secretary of State Mark Hatfield and Antoinette Kuzmanich of Portland. In 1960, the date of this photo, the governor and first lady were en route to the Republican National Convention. (Max Gutierrez, UPI; OHS bb011037)

I took to the 1964 campaign trail in October, carrying a notebook and a camera. I had learned the photo game from Red Hornish at the *Springfield News* and continued to take occasional photos for the *Statesman*. There were two dominant races on the ballot, secretary of state and treasurer. Attention was focused on the former; the office of secretary had produced five Oregon governors, most recently Mark Hatfield. Duties of the office were not onerous and people assumed running for governor was part of the job description. No treasurer had ascended to the governor's office. The plan was for me to spend a full day with each of the four candidates for office—Bob Straub and Republican treasurer Howard Belton and Tom McCall and his Democratic opponent, state senator Alfred Corbett—as well as cover other campaign happenings.

From the moment I stepped aboard the McCall campaign bus, "Bandwagon," on a misty October day until we were detoured by a somewhat puzzling incident, it was clear that the horse Tom McCall rode in on was a television news set in Portland's Channel 8 studio. We headed to Polk County for a breakfast in Independence and a Main Street tour and college class in Monmouth, then appearances in Dallas before heading back to Portland for an evening event. Folks accustomed to seeing Tom on television recognized the face and voice immediately but were startled when he unfolded his lanky frame. I wrote, "At 6-5 tall, he surprises most people when the real Tom McCall stands up—on television he was always seated to avoid problems of camera angle." Nearly two decades later, I would have the same experience in reverse; when I stepped out of the television set, people were often surprised that I was not larger than my five feet eight inches and 135 pounds. It was quite a disappointment for folks who had grown up with Tom McCall.

Tom was an "aw shucks" campaigner as he popped in and out of barbershops and beauty parlors, downtown stores, and a politics class at Oregon College of Education. He apologized for pushing his campaign literature as his large hand swallowed those of his constituents. "Here's a boring bit of bragging," he said apologetically, shuffling along on a frame badly injured in a 1960 car accident. Trailing in his wake, I heard comments focused more on his status as a television celebrity than on anything he said or distributed.

The campaign played on Tom's celebrity: "An old friend for a new task," was the title of one brochure. People picked up on Tom's natural affinity for ordinary folk; he was not capable of stuffiness despite his unusual accent, which hinted at a world of privilege and exclusivity.

Tom McCall's "Boston accent" was actually a unique blending of the speech patterns of his New England-born parents and the influence of his upbringing in Oregon. The McCall and Lawson families were prosperous and famous. Grandfather Samuel McCall was a US senator and governor of Massachusetts, and grandfather Thomas Lawson was a millionaire Wall Street investor and financier. By the time it all trickled down to the central Oregon ranch where Tom grew up, the Lawson family's money and privileges were gone, and the McCall family's Bostonian accent had been filtered through the cowboy towns of Prineville and Redmond.

In 1967–1968, I spent an academic year at Harvard University on a Nieman Fellowship for mid-career journalists. Governor McCall visited Boston in February, and I set up a luncheon at a Harvard Square café. My colleagues enjoyed Tom's candor and journalistic approach, delivered in his trademark accent. Afterward, the waitresses who served our lunch commented that the governor of Oregon was, "certainly tall and handsome . . . the sort of man you would expect from the West." The other added, "And such a firm, deep western voice, too!"

As much as his large body and expressive face, Tom's accent preceded him into a room. His clear speaking style, capped with the accent, was instantly recognized wherever he went. But it wasn't a Boston accent or a central Oregon accent—it was as unique as the man himself. In 1964, Tom's distinctive broadcast voice—thousands of Oregonians recognized it on contact—was just part of a persona that played well across the state.

Tom was well to the left of Barry Goldwater, the Republicans' presidential candidate, so he talked mostly about crime and corrections, as well as the elections job of the secretary of state. Tom had worked for progressive corrections and was a past president of the Oregon Prison Association, but this race would not be run on issues. His task was to solidify friendships made via television. He was at ease with most people he met; even to my inexperienced eye it was obvious that his television exposure made people feel that he was part of their extended family.

Our uneventful morning changed abruptly just before lunch, however, and gave me an early insight into Tom's character as a person and as a politician. His tour of a Dallas mill was interrupted by a phone call from his Portland headquarters, and an obviously upset candidate emerged from the mill office to cancel the remainder of the day's campaign tour. His speech to the Chamber of Commerce was scrubbed, but he positioned himself at the entry, in the manner of a greeter at a church, giving him at least some exposure to the audience. Then we pointed the bandwagon toward Portland and a news conference hastily called to respond to a statement by Alf Corbett earlier that day.

Corbett had charged that Tom switched his position on Ballot Measure 3—having to do with worker's compensation—in order to attract campaign money from business. Measure 3 was a priority for the AFL-CIO, and Tom had been active in his union at KGW; he tried harder than most Republicans to gain labor's favor. Tom was visibly angered at the idea that he would sell his position for campaign cash and went to great pains to explain himself to reporters. He was nervous, defensive, and gained nothing from the news conference, which drew little press coverage and probably changed not a single vote.

It was my first exposure to Tom the Nervous Candidate, a fellow I would meet again. Like many politicians, Tom had a thin skin and any hint that he was less than upstanding and ethical immediately drew blood; policy disagreements were fine, but anything smacking of a personal attack was verboten. Some of this dated to his failed 1954 congressional race against Edith Green. Faced with polls that showed him trailing, Tom had delivered a nasty personal attack on Edith, a speech urged on him by his Republican backers. He objected to its wording, but caved and delivered the speech, which ultimately proved to be his undoing. Edith's campaign strategists had succeeded in getting Tom's dander up, to his detriment.[3]

That the mild-mannered and gentlemanly Corbett could so easily get into Tom's head a decade later revealed how vulnerable Tom was to a rough-and-tumble campaign. Some of Tom's sensitivity bordered on paranoia, but it was more than that; he had dipped in and out of politics and news too many times. He left KGW radio twice—to work for Governor McKay and to run for Congress. He was trying to be both a journalist and a politician and the conflict made him unusually vulnerable.

Tom had no financial fallback in case of loss. His career up to 1964 was as a news reporter, a poor road to financial security. His wife Audrey was a home-economics teacher when Tom met her, but she gave up her career to raise their two sons and support his career. KGW managers had been accommodating when Tom left twice, but favors couldn't be guaranteed in the future, and Tom knew it. Ancil Payne became KGW station manager in 1965, and he told me years later that he had made it clear to Tom that there would be no more favors granted.

In 1964, Tom was gambling that he would win in November and launch a career that he hoped would take him to the governor-ship—but the uncertainty of the race made him vulnerable to even a seemingly routine charge such as that leveled by Alf Corbett over Measure 3. When the candidates debated, Tom was flustered, nervous, and vulnerable. Tom's alliance with media friends saved the day—as it often would in the future. They debated in the Channel 8 studio, and when the going got very tough, Tom's station friends arranged for a "technical malfunction" to give their former colleague time to collect his wits.

Tom's Democratic opponent was the scion of a famous Portland pioneer family, a handsome and somewhat courtly lawyer with solid liberal credentials. Outside Portland, however, state senator Alf Corbett was little known, and even the family name no longer resonated with most Oregonians. Unlike McCall, he still had the ancestral silver, but he was unpretentious and approachable. Corbett exuded a quiet competence and had an impressive legislative resume. He was fit and trim from years spent hiking and skiing, and he campaigned endlessly. I was with him on a seventeen-hour day, quite a contrast to my shortened day with McCall.

The men disagreed on few issues and the flap over Measure 3 was about as rough as it got. Yet the hill was too tough to climb for a Democrat running against a liberal Republican who was already a household name. Alf was simply running against the wrong man at the wrong time. He later held high-ranking positions in the US Office of Economic Opportunity.

If the secretary of state race was a walk for Tom—he beat Alf Corbett with a 56 percent vote—the other major race was close, featuring an upstart trying to unseat an old guard incumbent who was often called "Mr. Integrity." No one, including Bob Straub, challenged the integrity of seventy-one-year-old treasurer Howard Belton, who was appointed to the office by Governor Hatfield in 1959 and elected to a full term the following year. A Canby farmer and small-town banker, Belton was conservative and proud of it, an attribute in the eyes of many Oregonians for an office of fiscal responsibility. Belton was fit, but he was old and unprepared for the possibility that a liberal Democrat just might know more about finance than he did.

That was the case, however. Behind his liberal reputation and partisan statements when he was state Democratic chair, Bob Straub was a shrewd investor of his family money and an innovative thinker when it came to state funds. Belton followed the traditional policy of investing only in the most conservative bonds and deposits at local banks.

Straub had campaign help from Ken Johnson, who was editor of the *Capital Press*, a weekly farm paper published in Salem by Dewey Rand, a longtime Democrat. Ken was a fast man with a news release and flooded the state's newspapers with stories and letters to the editor, helping overcome the traditional Republican stance of Oregon editors. It was Ken who came up with the lasting image of the campaign: "Get our money out of the mattress," a colorful metaphor for Belton's conservative investment policies.

Secretary of State Howell Appling Jr. and other Republicans took offense to the slogan, giving it more visibility than if it had been ignored. The Straub campaign also gained traction when Republican leaders shot their candidate in the foot by instigating a raid by a state liquor-control agent on a small Eugene fundraiser for Straub, alleging that liquor was served without a license. Such events were often held by political campaigns without incident and when the Lane County Republican chairman admitted he might have tipped the liquor cops to the event, attendance at the affair became a prized bragging right, and the stunt backfired. It again gave Straub publicity and put the Belton campaign on the defensive.

Republicans had not expected an aggressive campaign for the low-visibility office of treasurer, and most thought the quiet but steady Belton would have no problem. Belton was a very low-key campaigner and most of his campaigning seemed to be done by Appling, a forceful and aggressive conservative who had also been appointed by Hatfield. Appling enjoyed a political fight and quickly took to attacking Straub, who was almost an exact political opposite.

The normally cool and shrewd Appling began using language much rougher than Straub used, terms such as "demagoguery" and "fraudulently." Hatfield joined in, accusing Straub of "character assassination" and "extremism." The quiet Belton was more restrained; his strongest criticism was that his opponent "completely disregarded standards of political decency and integrity."[4]

I caught both candidates in the Willamette Valley and the contrast was palpable, my first indication that Bob had come a long way from the hesitant and stuttering speaker I had encountered in 1958. He was no orator, but candidate Straub had a carefully honed and reasonable message and the energy to press it with the public. He had become a statewide politician and taken a lot of the state's political establishment by surprise.

The campaigns were part of a sea change in Oregon politics, with the old guard challenged within both parties as new faces and new tactics emerged. Nothing made the point better for me than a day with Howard Belton, a genuinely nice man and good public servant who had simply become obsolete.

Belton was unpretentious. "He fumbled in his wallet for a campus parking permit (at OSU) while his Oregon 3 license plate glared at the gate guard, meticulously fed parking meters, and walked an extra half-block to park on a meter with time left," I wrote. Belton's campaigning was mostly a matter of visiting with folks who were already on his side: a few employees at a small bank, Republican headquarters, and a Kiwanis Club. During a day in Corvallis and Albany, Belton met no one who needed persuasion and made no media contacts beyond an old editorial friend. Belton carried most Republican counties, but Straub won the large Democratic counties and a 51 percent vote statewide.

As with Tom, a political pattern could be discerned in Bob as early as that 1964 campaign. Bob had been through campaigns for county commissioner and the state legislature (successful) and US Congress (unsuccessful), but all his campaigns were as spare and direct as the man himself. Bob was his own staff much of the time and even when he later ran four times for governor, he always had a lone-eagle aspect about him.

He lacked Tom's easy conviviality and his joy at an outrageous turn of phrase, and he protected his privacy. Bob inspired intense loyalty among a few key people, but never had an entourage or a fan club; there was no "Straub Mystique" as later grew around Tom.

Bob Straub, unlike Tom McCall and Mark Hatfield, rode party loyalty into office. Hatfield built a formidable personal organization and McCall had a celebrity image among Oregonians; Straub served energetically as state Democratic chair. He had been inspired by the writing of Richard Neuberger, and he was part of a Eugene circle of Democrats that formed around Wayne Morse. I encountered Straub and Morse together at various times. In 1964, Straub bought one of Morse's prize Devon cattle, and it defeated the senator's own entry at the state fair, a great photo-op in the midst of the campaign.

The state fair was a big draw in the 1960s, particularly for rural families, and it was an important venue for Morse. My father, who, as a young farmer in North Dakota, had trained trotting horses for some local doctors and businessmen, loved the harness races where Morse drove his own sulky and often finished near the front. Campaigning at the fair was a must for politicians at the time, and party booths were well staffed and patronized. The later decline of the fair was perhaps inevitable as the state became more urban and new forms of entertainment gained favor, but in an earlier time it was a place where Oregonians came together.

Straub seemed to be everywhere in 1964. Young (forty-two), trim, and fit from working on his small Lane County farm and hiking, he exuded energy and worked long days. Often driving himself, he crisscrossed the state. He was in Oregon City, Silverton, and Salem when I accompanied him, and he touched factory workers, shoppers, and Democratic campaigners. At a shopping center near the capitol, a youngster asked Straub if he worked "over there," drawing a quick, "Not now, but I sure would like to" from the candidate.

That was the type of glib reply one might expect from McCall, not Straub, a man conscious of his speaking deficits and lacking the facility with words enjoyed by the broadcaster. Standing an erect six feet three, he was almost as tall as McCall, but there was nothing in his appearance to set him aside, in contrast to Tom's unique accent and his expressive lantern-jawed face.

As their campaigns unrolled, it was apparent that the pair shared a great deal in how they would approach their new jobs and regular contact—and sometimes conflict—with the popular Governor Hatfield. Both were progressive in social and environmental policy and they shared a love of the outdoors. Tom's easy victory in the 1964 secretary of state election quickly built a conventional wisdom that he was the front-runner for governor in 1966, and the spotlight easily focused on him as the two men entered office in January 1965.

A major contrast came in the important field of press relations and skill with reporters. Most successful politicians make a show of liking to deal with the media, but for many it is a pretense, and behind the scenes they deride reporters and editors as ill-informed hacks looking only for sensational quotes and headlines. Young people who enter journalism, political journalism in particular, would do well to remember the advice of Harry Truman: "If you want to have a friend in Washington, get a dog."

Tom was an exception, because he came out of the newsroom. He was helpful and kind to reporters from small newspapers and tiny radio stations; he just liked reporters, and would linger to chat with them before he would join a conversation of high-powered politicians or business leaders. He could blow his top at the press, though. I broke stories about some of his key appointments as he entered the governor's office in 1966, and he exploded at press aide Ron Schmidt, who had not been my source. When he calmed down, he congratulated me on scooping him, and life went on.

Reporters who covered state government frequented the Capitol Coffee Shop, and Tom was a Capitol Coffee Shop regular; reporters were always welcome at his table, even after he became governor. People from around the state would approach him, state workers of all ranks would get pulled into conversation, and the big, rumpled man in his working-day sweaters felt the pulse of Oregonians with an openness that was, and is, rare in public officials. He would listen patiently to a mother with a kid in a state hospital or an out-of-work janitor, then ask if he could help them deal with the government or with their lives. He was a magnet for people.

The ability to deal genuinely as well as effectively with ordinary citizens without aides to run interference is rare among high-level politicians. It cannot be faked; sometimes it improves from years in office but more often it erodes as other demands and priorities intervene. I had the good fortune of knowing every governor of Oregon from 1960 to 2014, either in office or before, and only Tom McCall had the unique combination of empathy, understanding, and patience to deal with ordinary citizens in this manner. I sensed it in only one other governor of this era, Barbara Roberts, who I knew prior to but not during her governorship.

No person achieves high office without learning to deal with media; regardless of how shielded they are by press aides and gate-keepers, they live in a glass house, and reporters have faces pressed to the glass. Almost without exception, reporters will spot false camaraderie on the part of a politician. Reporters always played a game of sorts with McCall, wanting to lure him into a quotable comment or a heads-up on a forthcoming story, but also not wanting him to blurt it out if other reporters were present. So we talked around a subject and then, if we smelled a lead, we would scuttle around to his office afterward, hoping to take it one step further.

Bob Straub had reporter friends, both in Eugene and Salem, but he lacked the personal magnetism to become a media star, nor did he cultivate that status. My own friendship with Bob was built more on proximity—we were neighbors in West Salem—than on any calculated effort by either of us. Bob was a private person who respected reporters and was honest in dealing with them, but cultivating those relationships was certainly not a priority.

Tom's easy manner with reporters was both calculated and natural for a man whose professional career was spent in newsrooms. He was known at KGW as a convivial colleague, expansive over drinks, and a defender of press rights and privileges. During the Watergate era, a group of reporters and editors worked to establish a "reporter's shield," allowing reporters to guarantee confidentiality to sources; Tom worked with us, one among peers trying to shape the legislation. Later, he happily signed the new law.

Much has been made of Tom's media connections, and there is no question that he gained from those associations and his own knowledge of what made a news story and a quote that would be impossible to resist. We all gave Tom latitude because he was one of us in his heart and because he was so open in dealing with reporters. I once described Tom as someone "walking around inside out," because his personal feelings and travails were in the open for all to see. He could be candid to almost an embarrassing level.

Tom had one overpowering broadcast advantage: his unique voice and delivery. But it was more an advantage for radio than for television, where his craggy face and large ears might have invited caricature in a lesser man. He was not a natural on camera, but his serious approach to the news, his presentation of analysis as well as hard facts, and his skill as host and interviewer on the weekly *Viewpoint* program brought him an immediate following.

Tom came to television much as the broadcast icon Edward R. Murrow. Both had grown up in rural communities, attended state colleges, and worked in radio before television. Murrow was, in the words of one of his associates, Ed Bliss, more a crusader than a reporter, and Tom was that as well.

As I began to settle myself in my new assignment at the capitol, I was intrigued by the emerging personal and political rivalries that surrounded the men who held Oregon's top three offices. Together, the governor, secretary of state, and treasurer made up the Board of Control and the Land Board, meetings of which brought them face-to-face about once a month.

The Land Board, written into the 1859 Constitution, supervised state-owned forests and grazing lands and had a role in wetlands and estuaries as well. The Board of Control, created in 1913, supervised the state's prisons and hospitals. Together, these institutions were big lines in the state budget and impacted a lot of Oregonians. They were of particular interest to my Salem readers because all of Oregon's prisons and hospitals at that time were required to be within Marion County.

Although both boards had small professional staffs, the directors were political appointees and many of the decisions were fraught with political implications. Hatfield served on the boards six years with Secretary of State Appling and four with Treasurer Belton, and he had appointed both of them to their offices. The three Republicans preferred to work out differences privately, and public meetings of the boards rarely drew an audience because the action had been carefully scripted in advance.

That came to a screeching halt in 1965 as McCall and Straub took office and demanded open meetings. Such a position might be expected from Democrat Straub, but Hatfield and McCall were of the same party. Closed meetings were an anathema to former newsman

McCall, however, and Hatfield had no choice but to open the deliberations. He brought to the meetings a steely and cutting approach to the newcomers, and he was particularly hard on McCall.

I started going to all the meetings, and soon others would drift into the room to see the show, which was at once embarrassing and revealing. Hatfield was always well prepared, and he knew the history and precedent of every item. His colleagues were new to office, working with a new and limited staff, and they got no quarter from the governor.

Tom brought a reporter's habits to the table. He gathered up documents as if on deadline, scanned them quickly, and left for the meeting. Bob, successful in business and a former county commissioner, was more disciplined and always better prepared. Hatfield jumped on this, pinning Tom down on detail, ridiculing him when he seemed lost or confused.

The room's atmosphere was electric at times, as Tom and the governor went at each other in an unequal contest. Mark Hatfield was a notable and much-publicized teetotaler, and his abstemious ways were part of his appeal to many Oregonians. Tom enjoyed his martinis and a late evening with friends. When an issue that dealt with liquor came before the Board of Control, the governor would be particularly pointed in his views of alcohol, clearly implying that if Tom were better disciplined personally, it would help him in his work.

Bob at first let the two Republicans spar, but gradually he came to Tom's side, rebutting some of the governor's missiles and voting with Tom against Hatfield. Tom and Bob began feeling comfortable with each other personally, while both hungered for the governor's office in 1966, when Hatfield's two-term limit would be reached.

Oregon's political history has its share of intra-party rivalries, certainly including that of Democrats Wayne Morse and Richard Neuberger, which seriously split the party in the fifties. The Hatfield-McCall rivalry was less obvious on the surface but just as nasty backstage; if it had ever resulted in a showdown in a Republican primary it would have been bloody.

It didn't result in that showdown largely because McCall was one of the world's most nervous campaigners—as we saw in his 1964 campaign. He was particularly vulnerable to a challenge from a fellow Republican. Having watched the two men at close range, I believe that Hatfield would have prevailed and left McCall depressed and determined to leave politics. Tom knew how vulnerable he would be in a bare-knuckle contest.

Tom and Mark were totally different personalities, although they backed many of the same liberal-to-moderate Republican causes and candidates. Both were heavily influenced by strong mothers, although Hatfield was an only son and McCall had four siblings. Hatfield was a genuinely religious man and deeply antiwar, based in part on his experience as a young navy officer entering Hiroshima at the conclusion of World War II. McCall was secular in taste and outlook. He was as gregarious as Hatfield was controlled. Dealing with the press, Hatfield relied heavily on his savvy press aide, Travis Cross; McCall forged his own press relations, leaving the capable and loyal Ron Schmidt to clean up any messes. They married different types: Antoinette Hatfield was fiery, opinionated; Audrey McCall was quiet, nonpolitical.

McCall was as unpredictable as Hatfield was calculated in his approach to politics. Hatfield was a popular professor of political science in his years at Willamette University; McCall could not handle the routine and discipline of teaching a single class at Oregon State University, which he attempted briefly after leaving office. They were a rumpled mackinaw vs. a buttoned-down shirt, a manuscript with footnotes vs. a notepad with scrawled handwriting.

Governor Hatfield ran a tight ship, as I discovered early in my stint at the capitol. The 1965 legislature was my first—and his last—and in preparing for it, I managed to come up with the sort of news scoop that my editors loved.

Secrecy was a big deal in the governor's biennial budget, and very few details were released before the budget was mailed to legislators the day before it was to be publicly released. The idea was that it would be in the mail, but nobody would see it prior to the governor's news conference. However, Salem senator Cornelius Bateson got his mail at a local post-office box; when he cleared the box that evening, it contained one of two budget documents, containing all the detail for state buildings, equipment, and long-range plans.

Democrat Bateson was no friend of Hatfield's and he slipped me the document in time for the *Statesman*'s late-night deadline. State budgets are of particular interest in Salem, because they impact the local economy. We printed the story in the morning, shortly before Hatfield was to release his budget. When I got to the capitol for the announcement, the press corps regulars had chairs with their names and a copy of the budget. My chair was in a corner, turned to the wall! It was a joke with a bit of an edge. My editors loved the scoop.

All three top officials would campaign again in 1966 and their encounters were always with that date in mind. Mark Hatfield was building a campaign for the US Senate and Tom

Candidate Filing Day, 1966, brought together Secretary of State Tom McCall (left) and Treasurer Bob Straub in the first of their two contests for governor. (Oregon Historical Society ba008949)

McCall and Bob Straub were reaching to take Hatfield's seat in the myrtlewood-paneled executive office. They would need to pass muster with the 1965 legislature and then face the voters again. The first was a piece of cake, the second not as easy. Before 1966 was finished, we would be knee-deep in the Mekong Delta.

McCall and Straub brought similar conservation values to the table as they prepared for their important confrontation in the 1966 race for the governor's office. A simmering showdown on the Oregon Coast, however, threatened those shared values just as the candidates were settling into their new capitol offices. It was the first of several big chapters in the Oregon Story and one of the few where the two men would be in sharp disagreement.

Profile THAT OLD GANG OF TOM'S

"Legendary" and "iconic" were only two terms to describe the original news team at KGW-TV, five men who immediately became the team to watch on Portland television. Tom McCall was the only member who had moved on when I started at KGW-TV in 1970, but he remained part of the gang, and when he encountered the other pioneers there were always stories and laughter.

Television in 1956, when Channel 8 went on the air, was a matter of viewer loyalty; families huddled around black-and-white sets, tuned into a station, and spent the evening. Technology was rudimentary and much of the show was live; at first, everyone was a reporter as well as an anchor. Most television news pioneers came out of radio; that was the case with four of the five KGW-TV pioneers. The exception was meteorologist Jack Capell, who worked for the US Weather Bureau in Portland following his graduation from the University of Washington.[5]

Tom McCall was unusual because, in addition to radio work, he spent several years as a newspaper reporter. Richard Ross began in Spokane radio, Doug LaMear began covering sports on an Albany radio station, and Ivan Smith started on KMCM in McMinnville, where I was in high school in the 1950s. I remember Ivan's smooth baritone voice; KMCM was a pretty low-budget operation then and later, and Ivan moonlighted as a projectionist at the local drive-in theater. Two decades later, I came to appreciate Ivan's judgment, his sense of loyalty and ethics, and his warm and welcoming wife, Thelma; Dixie and I had some good times with them before they retired and moved to the Oregon Coast.

The pioneers, with the exception of Doug, had served in World War II; Jack wrote a short book about his experiences, which included Normandy beach on D-Day. The pioneers in my years with them were fiercely patriotic and a bit conservative, but they knew their audience, and Portlanders felt like they were part of the family. Doug's forays into the region's fishing rivers were closely followed, and Dick was a first-rate ambassador to local organizations and causes.

Jack Capell was one of the toughest men I ever knew. He was diagnosed in 1972 with primary lateral sclerosis, a disease similar to ALS (often called Lou Gehrig's disease), but he refused to give in, and his audience continued to rely on him, even when his report was largely prepared by his loyal and supportive wife, Sylvia, and his two sons. Jack finally retired in 2000.

Jack's legacy was "calling" the Columbus Day Storm of October 1962; working with the crude forecasting tools of the day, he went out on a limb and warned listeners that a huge storm was on the way, well before officials in the US Weather Bureau were making such a dramatic statement. He was one of the few certified meteorologists among weathermen in the 1950s, and his serious, well-researched forecasts set the standard for years.

Dick Ross was the prime anchor until he left for KATU in 1975. By that time, Dick had become increasingly uncomfortable with the younger reporters, who wore their hair long, dressed casually, and almost without exception opposed the Vietnam War and the Portland establishment figures that Ross respected. There was some mockery of Dick's proper manners and demeanor, which he sensed and resented. He had paid his dues and no one was ever smoother and calmer on the air, but times were changing faster than he was, and his 1975 move seemed to work for all concerned.

When I departed a decade later, only Doug and Jack remained of the original five, and Jack was a shadow of his former self. I had actually spent more airtime with the pioneers than Tom had spent, but our experiences were vastly different and I was never part of the "old gang."

In the fifties, the pioneers were jammed into cramped quarters in an old building and literally rubbed shoulders daily; they were young, full of spirit, and they bonded as a group and had a lot of fun. By my arrival in 1970, KGW had a new building with lots of space and a larger news staff of younger people. At thirty-four, I fit midway between the generations but did not share the wartime experience or early-TV stories of the pioneers. We worked together but did not play together; I learned a lot from them and respected what they had done for Channel 8. They were true pioneers and real professionals.

TWO   Saving the Rivers and Beaches

We are defined by glistening and powerful waters: the Columbia on the north; the Willamette, its valley teeming with crops and people; and the Pacific Ocean, playground, fishery, and gateway to Asia. The Oregon Story simply had to begin on water; it defines us, and it was the original lure for the pioneers of the previous century.

In the mad rush for post-war normalcy—and even prosperity— Oregonians by 1960 were polluting our water and air, and our unrivaled beaches were already in danger of "No Trespassing" signs. Trash was everywhere. Much of what unfolded in the two decades from 1964 to 1986 began with our understanding of how important rivers, streams, and beaches were to Oregon—and how we had neglected our stewardship of these priceless resources.

Tom McCall planted a television camera on the banks of the oozing Willamette River in 1962 and showed the filth and degradation to an awakening Oregon audience. Bob Straub planted his hiking boots on a hill above a pristine Oregon beach in 1966 and declared there would be no asphalt highway on those sands. Iconic images planted in the minds of Oregonians as we opened what would become the Oregon Story.

McCall's 1962 documentary, *Pollution in Paradise*, opened the eyes of Oregonians to the neglect of the state's heartland river, the Willamette. It was foul, a sewer running through the state's major cities and best farmland. Fish were dying. It was unsafe for swimming, let alone drinking; you could run a boat on it—but don't fall in!

Seen half a century later, Tom's film is still evocative, a vintage reminder of the power of the emerging television medium. *Pollution in Paradise* wasn't slick; it was shot on film with bulky cameras and sound equipment. Sound bites were long and there were no electronic visuals or editing tricks. But it was solid, and it secured Tom's journalistic credentials and gave him a leg up in his 1964 campaign for secretary of state.[1]

Oregon was not a pioneer in environmental protection in 1962, but a core of hardy hikers, backpackers, river rats, and immigrants escaping the increasing degradation of other places began to call attention to our remaining natural resources and the indifference of many Oregonians to their value. Some in this group had read works by Aldo Leopold, Wallace Stegner, and John Muir. More than any one publication, Rachel Carson's *Silent Spring* in 1962 laid out a challenge to the earth's environment that demanded attention.

Pollution in Paradise marked Oregon's entry into the fast-growing movement that soon marched under the banner of "environmentalism." Tom McCall and Bob Straub began talking about environmental issues in their 1964 campaigns for state office and the audience that watched *Pollution in Paradise* formed part of McCall's base of support.

Bob Straub was a natural recruit to the environmental movement. His father was a prominent San Francisco attorney but the family lived in an idyllic rural setting south of the city where Bob worked in apricot orchards and spent a year felling timber in the Sierras to pay for his education at Dartmouth College. While there, he met a young Smith College woman, Pat Stroud, in 1940 on a trail near New Hampshire's Mount Moosilauke. The couple shared a deep interest in the outdoors; they were married in 1943 while Bob was in the army. After the war they decided to move to Oregon, in large part because of the state's natural beauty.

Over the fourteen years that Tom McCall and Bob Straub dominated Oregon politics they were seldom on opposite sides of an environmental issue; the partnership of rivals drove the state's agenda

from 1964 to 1978, and the only environmental losses they suffered came when they were too little or too late in making common
cause. More than any other individuals, Tom and Bob co-authored
the Oregon Story.

It didn't start out that way—very early in their 1966 campaigns
for governor they were at each other's throats and, as the race
moved along, the rhetoric increased. State highway engineers had
long wanted to straighten Oregon's twisting Highway 101 along the
coast. In 1965, the State Highway Commission approved a plan to
straighten a stretch north of Neskowin; the plan involved placing
Highway 101 on sandy beaches at Nestucca Spit and Pacific City.

Passions heated up and Tom McCall and Bob Straub quickly
became key players in the dispute. There was another heavyweight
at the table as well: Glenn Jackson, widely considered the state's
most powerful private citizen at the time. Jackson was chairman of
Pacific Power, but his influence went far, far beyond the utility giant,
which was in its own right one of the state's power players. One of
his roles was chairing the Highway Commission. A small man with
intense eyes, Jackson quietly smoked his pipe and blended into a
crowd. But no one ran for major political office in Oregon without
gaining his support or worrying about an opponent doing so.

The Highway Commission was arguably the state's most powerful
statewide appointed body, and governors took great care in selecting commissioners who could be helpful to their careers. Jackson
was originally appointed by governor Mark Hatfield and was easily
returned by McCall and later by Straub; he served twenty years.

The chairman was a powerful advocate of modern highways, and
the I-205 bridge over the Columbia is named in his honor. Oregon
highway engineers were powerful and single-minded, and they produced good roads on budget and on time. But in the eyes of critics—
and I became one of those critics—they were in love with straight
lines. A road from Point A to Point B should have as few curves
as possible. Jackson was not an engineer, and his usual instinct
was to follow their lead. In turn, his colleagues on the Highway

Commission, also appointed by the governor, followed Jackson. Disputes were dealt with privately before the public commission meetings.

There was no one Tom McCall solicited more avidly for advice and support. Jackson's endorsement influenced much of the state's Republican business establishment and its campaign donations. McCall was too liberal for Jackson's personal taste but he saw a future governor when he agreed to support Tom in 1966. He asked only one favor—not for himself but for the Highway Commission—to support the commission's efforts to relocate Highway 101 along sections of the Oregon Coast. The grateful candidate agreed and boxed himself into one of the few cases where he was outflanked by Bob Straub.

Widely recognized as Oregon's most powerful private citizen, businessman Glenn Jackson was already chairman of the State Highway Commission in this 1962 photo. (Oregon Department of Transportation)

The 1965 Highway Commission decision to relocate and straighten Highway 101 on the Nestucca Spit had escaped attention from inlanders. A public hearing at Tillamook drew opposition from a few owners of beach houses, but not until 1966 and the onset of the gubernatorial campaign did it get statewide attention. On March 8, 1966, the commission reaffirmed its 1965 decision to build on the beach, and the handful of beach-house objectors suddenly got the attention of my newspaper, among others. The engineers were eager to move, and the timing could not have been worse for them; they ran into big-time politics. The beach highway drew my attention early in 1966, perhaps because the area was familiar to folks from Salem, an easy drive of less than an hour. I spent hours at the Highway Department, poring through files and looking at

maps for a two-part series that ran in the *Statesman* May 8 and 9. I
opened the series with this description:

> The peaceful beaches of South Tillamook County, with their clean sand
> and protective rock formations, have largely been bypassed by the great
> "coastal rush" of the last twenty years. With the exception of a long-es-
> tablished retreat at Neskowin for the socially prominent of Salem and
> Portland, and a small cluster of beach houses at Pacific City, time has
> passed the area by, leaving it essentially undeveloped. Proposed relo-
> cation of the present tortuous route of Highway 101 will change all
> that—regardless of which alternative is selected—and therein lies the
> current argument about the site of a relocated 101 from Neskowin to
> Cape Kiwanda, north of Pacific City.

My research told me that the concept of the beach highway
dated to 1945 and had never been challenged. The beach route was
"straighter, cheaper to build, and requires less right-of-way purchase
because some is in state ownership," I noted. In 1962 the state purchased land on Nestucca Spit for a future state park—the park also
included a grant of federal land that would later be a critical factor
in deciding the issue.

As I looked at maps, at one point I took a ruler and laid it across
the line of bays and estuaries from Neskowin northward. My
non-engineering eyes saw the perfect storm: a straightened Highway
101 running across and through beaches, bays, and estuaries in the
name of a "scenic drive" at lower cost. The idea was staggering to
contemplate; the Neskowin-Pacific City struggle would need to be
fought all the way up the coast, I feared.

Tillamook County officials and local business owners had long
campaigned for a faster Highway 101, and they loved the straight
lines of the highway engineers. Even at Pacific City, the peaceful
beach where dories were launched into the surf, the highway advocates ruled—except for that pesky band of folks with beach cabins.
They got in touch with Bob Straub, and his campaign seized an
issue that resonated with his natural environmental instincts. Straub
began speaking out against the beach route.

Bob Straub needed a popular issue to counter his rival's enormous statewide name familiarity and popularity. Glenn Jackson handed it to him on an asphalt platter; Bob wasn't aware of the promise Tom McCall had just made to Jackson to get his endorsement, but it was a gift to his campaign.

Janet McLennan, an activist for liberal causes and a dedicated Straub supporter, rounded up a passel of Portland friends and Straub backers and took them on Mother's Day to Porter Point, north of Neskowin. Complete with handmade signs and a few reporters and cameras, they expressed their opposition to a highway that would drop from Porter Point on a major bridge, landing on Nestucca Spit at Pacific City. "Beaches are for Kids," the signs proclaimed. Afterwards, they roasted wieners and had a picnic, despite brisk winds and showers. A handful of highway advocates showed up with countering signs, and Straub was hung in effigy by his detractors.[2]

The *Statesman* editorialized following the Mother's Day march; this was a major statement for my newspaper, considering Charles A. Sprague's lack of enthusiasm for Bob Straub. By this time, however, Sprague was beginning to reduce his traditional heavy workload, and news editor Wes Sullivan was writing some editorials. Wes was a beach guy—the family had a cabin south of Lincoln City on the Siletz River. Wes wrote the editorial, but it's likely that he cleared it with Sprague. The editorial noted:

> Ideas of beach use have changed markedly since the Pacific City route was originally proposed. Twenty years ago it might have been acceptable to run the highway along the beach. With the population boom, however, we have begun to realize the true value of undisturbed beachfront. The population pressure of future generations demands that we do not disturb more miles of beach by running cars and trucks along it. Another important factor has entered the picture since the first plans were drawn. Nestucca Spit is now state park land. To run a highway through the middle of a state park would be unthinkable.

We were not the first editorial voice in the fray; in April the *Oregonian* came out against the beach route, urging citizens to protest to the Highway Commission. Other inland editors also got on board, trying to counter the voices of Tillamook County business and political leaders. Our combined forces began to take a toll on beach-highway supporters, in particular Tom McCall. Tom's pledge of support for the beach route had picked up Glenn Jackson's important support in the governor's race, but the cost was beginning to mount for Tom. In Salem, at the headquarters for the highway department, engineers read the *Oregonian* and the *Statesman*, as did Jackson.

Two months after the Mother's Day march, Tom cranked out a news release he hoped would "put an end to a series of publicity shenanigans." Laying the blame at the feet of beach-property owners, he labeled as "totally untrue" the idea that the highway would be built on the beach and claimed that it would "enhance recreational and scenic values for the benefit of many." His news release was pap, and he knew it; the "shenanigans" continued and an exit would be necessary.

An exit ramp was being prepared, and Jackson himself began the retreat. At a June 2 Highway Commission meeting, he engaged with Straub and promised to reconsider, professing that the commission was "honestly confused" about a proper route. "The statement by Jackson was the first indication in months that the commission may be willing to back away from its 1965 decision to run the nine-mile highway down the beach," I reported.

That took some of the heat off the 1966 gubernatorial election, but a year later, after McCall's election victory, the Highway Commission again approved the beach route. Straub was irate. Governor McCall responded: "The spit route will afford a continuous majestic view of ocean and hills in an area between Lincoln City and Tillamook where the motorist scarcely sees the surf and beaches. Far from restricting access to the beach, it will provide convenient public access to beaches—most of which can now be reached only by vigorous hiking, boat, or sand buggy." Once again, he misstated the facts.

Straub described the ruling as "a sad decision and one that will last for all time. I am sure Oregonians will regret it in the future. And it raises the question: Which long, straight beaches will be converted next from public playgrounds into highway roadbeds?"

The decision did not "last for all time." Straub personally lobbied US Secretary of Interior Stuart Udall, a noted conservationist, after Straub learned that federal lands had been given to the state under an agreement that prevented a highway in the planned park on Nestucca Spit. Udall sided with Straub and Governor McCall declared the beach route a dead letter, telling one reporter, "If I ever catch a highway engineer looking even cross-eyed at a sandspit, there will be the devil to pay."

And yet the beat went on . . . highway engineers simply moved their stakes inland a sufficient distance to avoid the federal land— but still intrude on a portion of beach. A hearing was held November 29 in Tillamook and all the old wounds reopened. No decision was made and the issue went behind closed doors. Quietly, Governor McCall told Chairman Jackson to back off; the beach highway's official death notice didn't finally come until a statement by McCall in December 1969—just as McCall and Straub were opening another campaign against each other. At the time of McCall's brief statement in 1969, I noted that conservationists still must keep their eyes on the engineers: "There has never been an official announcement on the planning of Highway 101 north of Pacific City and Cape Kiwanda. But sources close to the highway commission say the use of sandspits and ocean beaches to the north is an alternative favored by some engineers."

In March 1970, after everyone thought it had been settled that beaches were for kids, I learned that highway engineers had their eyes on Nehalem Bay, also in Tillamook County. Like the earlier highway relocation, it would open a relatively isolated stretch for more and faster traffic, including a fill along three miles of estuary.

I had become increasingly interested in estuaries, that magic transitional zone between saltwater and freshwater where so much of our marine life is nurtured. On March 8, I wrote in my weekly *Statesman* column:

> Against this backdrop and amidst public awareness that the heritage of nature is being stripped from our hands, the State Highway Division's plan to fill and bridge the lower end of Nehalem Bay is well nigh incredible . . . Highway engineers have worshipped so long at the shrine of the straight line that they cannot—or will not—hear the cries of outrage from a public finally awakening to the tragedy of spreading asphalt and fill over our vanishing natural heritage.

The Nehalem plan was quickly dropped; Governor McCall, now in the midst of his 1970 race with Bob Straub, certainly remembered the furor that had been raised over the Neskowin-Pacific City beach highway. He ordered a halt to highways in estuaries, a decision that had important implications for the precious coastal environment. Only a week later, my column expressed appreciation for McCall's executive order but warned that all of Oregon's major estuaries are within port districts.

Port districts, with rare exceptions, are primarily concerned with economic development rather than the more exotic but less profitable business of ecological protection. The two major dangers to estuaries are pollution and filling. The state does have power to control pollution, through the Department of Environmental Quality. But its powers to control filling are almost nonexistent.

Less than a month later, I left the *Statesman* for KGW and, for the time being at least, turned to other matters. Filling and desecration of estuaries continued to plague the state; Tom's executive order kept highways off the fragile lands but the boomers and hustlers continued to push.

The effort to keep Oregon's beaches safe from highways had one major hero, Bob Straub; his persistence continued long after his 1966 gubernatorial effort was defeated. At times it was a lonely struggle waiting for the media to alert inland Oregonians to what their coastal neighbors were ready to support and engineers were willing to build. Two decades later, governor Neil Goldschmidt dedicated the Nestucca Beach Park in Bob's name; it was an overcast, drizzly day but it honored one of the truly important efforts in the Oregon Story.

Oregonians assumed they owned the beaches, thanks to governor Oswald West's farsighted announcement in 1913 that the ocean beach was a public highway. It had been used as such in horseback days before a modern road system was built. West convinced the legislature to declare beaches as public highways and most Oregonians simply accepted a right to access the entire beach.

For anyone who grew up in the Willamette Valley, a weekend trip to the coast was an adventure on the cheap. As teenagers, we crammed into our lowered, dual-piped cars and headed for the sand, a roaring bonfire, and some illicit beer and, for those fortunate enough to have a steady girlfriend, some necking to and from. No one, absolutely no one, not even the most conservative of our parents, ever had the notion that we didn't own the sand and have the right to it forever.

Oregon's beaches were priceless, but by the 1960s developers began to envision a price: if they could control access to the sand, they could sell that exclusivity to tourists and homeowners alike. In March 1964, my editors sent me on a reporting trip from Brookings to Astoria to examine the state of the coast. Their frugality assured winter rates at motels; I didn't need to defend a boondoggle in rainy and windy March. But it opened my eyes and I began my three-part series:

> It doesn't take an old-timer to remember when Uncle Claude and all his family could pull off narrow old Highway 101 most anyplace, throw a blanket over an arm, take the picnic basket, and troop off to the beach.

> The beach is still there, but in many a case Uncle Claude now has a retirement home on the site, and to get to the sand you must stop at a jam-packed state park or a motel with beach access. About the only thing on the Oregon Coast that hasn't increased in the past few years is the coast itself—and one day the irrepressible expansion will catch up with the immovable object. And while that day may be distant, there's already plenty going on to worry coastophiles who remember all that

uncluttered beauty. For the coastal businessman who must live largely off tourist trade, however, a renewed surge in developments now under-way is welcome and coastal operators are becoming skilled promoters. Not content to spend the Oregon rainy season knitting and recalling last summer's crowds, the smart operator on the coast several years ago began to seek a better year-round dollar. His success, if not spectacular, has been steady. There are still boarded-up cafes on the coast in winter, and you might get your hand stepped on picking up a loose quarter in Seaside in January, but the winters aren't as economically hard as they used to be.

Those businesspeople were onto something even if, like many other Oregonians, they were still wed to wider, straighter, and faster highways—even across beaches and estuaries. There was a perva-sive fear that politicians would prevent them from the main chance, the opportunity to develop beach property.

It didn't take long for the prospect to emerge.

William Hay, owner of the Surfsand Motel, proclaimed that his property extended all the way to the wet sands of popular Cannon Beach. He built a fence to make his point. People complained and state lawyers discovered that Hay had a case: Governor West's famous beach highway law could be interpreted to mean the pub-lic only owned the wet sands—not the wonderful dry sands where children and dogs loved to run and play. Warning signals went off in Salem as preparations were made for the 1967 legislative session, governor Tom McCall's first.

A "little housekeeping bill" would fix the problem. That descrip-tion of a routine, noncontroversial measure is one that legislators and reporters are wary of hearing; frequently the measure at hand is much more, sometimes very much more. That was the case of House Bill 1601, introduced in the 1967 legislature by the Highway Department to correct a bit of a misunderstanding at Cannon Beach. Developer Hay had gotten backing from others hoping to cash in on the increased popularity of the Oregon Coast. They in turn got backing from coastal legislators and Republicans from rural dis-tricts who worried about attacks on private property.

Most legislative reporters, including myself, paid little attention; there were many other important measures in McCall's first session. The first warnings of trouble came from Associated Press reporter Matt Kramer, a veteran who was popular and respected in the Capitol Pressroom. Matt began spending time in the House Highways Committee chaired by a retired banker from Grants Pass, Sid Bazett. Sid was under siege and Matt Kramer soon had plenty of company as reporters flocked to the committee. Backroom intrigue is a certain lure for reporters bored with budget bills and tendentious oratory, and House Bill 1601 had the obvious additional lure of becoming a big story.

It was an interesting test of character and will. Sid Bazett was a quiet man who normally voted conservatively, but he was no backwoods guy. His banking career was in San Francisco and he and his wife, Marge—they looked so alike, both with pure white hair and immaculate dress and demeanor, that we called them the Bazett twins—had retired to Grants Pass; but they had broader visions and tastes. Sid latched onto House Bill 1601—which Matt Kramer was now calling "The Beach Bill"—and took it for his own.

Republican leaders were not amused. In particular, the powerful majority leader Bob Smith, of Burns, was not amused, and he had leverage over other Republicans on Bazett's committee. Deadlock resulted; coastal Democrats and rural Republicans had their hands around the neck of the Beach Bill. Bazett fumed over his pipe and complained about his party's leadership of Smith and Speaker F. F. (Monte) Montgomery of Eugene.

Smith and Montgomery were a potent team—each served as speaker for two terms—but their styles were different. Bob Smith was blunt-spoken, sometimes intimidating to the uninitiated, and he enjoyed a good political fight. Monte sold insurance and had the instincts of a good salesman: can a middle ground be found where both of us can win? It became apparent that Monte wanted to find a way out of a battle that could short-circuit other things he wanted to accomplish, like running for secretary of state.

For the first time since *Pollution in Paradise*, television made a big political impact; KGW station manager Ancil Payne unleashed a hard-hitting editorial urging viewers to contact legislators and save the beaches. Forty thousand letters and calls cascaded in, by Bazett's count. With McCall, Straub, and thousands of citizens now aboard and others rushing to join, the tide was turning.

What resulted was a classic example of publicity and media hype, citizen pressure, showmanship, legislative maneuvers, genuine bipartisanship, and even statesmanship. Governor McCall was master of ceremonies, orchestrating a grand media event complete with helicopters, scientists, and—of course—television cameras, as he dramatically drew a line in the sand to be protected for all time. He was in his element and loving it.

The governor barnstormed the northern Oregon Coast via helicopter, attracting a news scrum; beachwalkers were agog at such a

Governor Tom McCall squints through a transit as he surveys the Oregon beach in 1967 during the height of the Beach Bill controversy. Rep. Sid Bazett of Grants Pass is at left and Robert Schultz, an Oregon State University engineering professor, is at center. (Leonard Bacon, *Oregonian*)

show. Tom "dropped in" at Cannon Beach, and his assistants began putting up markers, transits, and other paraphernalia while the governor walked over to scowl at William Hay's intruding barriers. Tom knew a news visual better than most, and he marched from a dry-sand marker down to the surf, contrasting his line in the sand with that of Republicans; it reminded me of those old silent movies with the hero rushing to rescue a damsel from the clutches of a villain.[3]

It was all very effective, and when he returned to Salem, the governor was master of the issue and had very effectively erased any lingering stain from his Nestucca Spit highway debacle.[4]

In addition to being wary of "a little housekeeping bill," those who follow legislation learn that the devil is always in the details. One word, even one punctuation mark, can change the meaning of a measure; recall the 1913 beach-highway law. Drafting legislation is a narrow craft mastered by few.

With the governor's office now joined by Speaker Montgomery in seeking some sort of compromise, a pair of young lawyers who would go on to statewide and judicial office combined their talents to produce the final legislative product. Democratic minority leader Jim Redden was from Medford; Republican Lee Johnson from Southwest Portland. They shared a very helpful trait: both genuinely enjoyed a good laugh, and that could relieve tension. Redden was known for his quick comebacks in debate, often with a humorous edge, and Johnson was known to make fun of his tendency to look as if he had slept in his suit. He was also a notorious moocher of cigarettes, although his family's timber fortune made him one of the richest men in the legislature.

Speaker Montgomery, now solidly on board, came up with an answer to a serious problem in the Beach Bill: he suggested zoning to protect the public from encroachments such as fences and walls that fall upland of the line defined by the governor on his beach tour. Any structure would need a state permit. Redden and Johnson and McCall and Montgomery put aside party or personal differences and came up with a bipartisan measure that easily passed both houses and was immediately seen as an iconic victory for the state.

A memorial marker for Matt Kramer, whose articles helped shift public opinion to preserve the beaches, stands at the trail divide between Short Sands Beach and Cape Falcon in Oswald West State Park. With the exception of the whimsical Mill Ends Park on Naito Parkway in Portland, dedicated to *Oregon Journal* columnist Dick Fagan, Matt's memorial may be the state's only public monument to a working journalist. It's a lovely touch, much in the image of Scotland or Ireland, where poets and authors are honored above generals and masters of industry.

The Beach Bill required some amendments by the 1969 legislature, easily handled. Bitter battles of 1967 put aside, a big chapter in the Oregon Story was written.

On December 19, 1969, the Oregon Supreme Court upheld the Beach Bill in a 6–0 decision by justice Ted Goodwin. Goodwin relied heavily on the historic Blackstone commentaries in English Common Law relating to customary use of the land, in this case the Oregon beaches. "The record shows," Goodwin wrote, "that the custom of the inhabitants of Oregon and of visitors in the state to use the dry sand as a public recreation area is so notorious that notice of the custom on the part of persons buying land along the shore must be presumed." In 1972, US District Court judge Gus Solomon, writing for a three-judge panel, upheld the Oregon ruling.

Judicial imprimatur of the Beach Bill helped salve the wounds from a serious defeat for Oregon's coastal playground, a mistake that must be shared by political leaders and the Oregon electorate. That would be the 1968 vote that rejected Measure 6, an initiative promoted by Bob Straub to increase gas taxes by a penny per gallon for four years to create a $30 million bond issue to purchase beach lands and access. It failed by a 59–41 percent margin, a shortsighted decision by the Oregon electorate.

Voters were fooled by dirty-tricks expert Ken Rinke, a professional strategist and lobbyist whose dark tactics were widely feared.

Rinke worked with a bankroll of over $81,000 ($477,000 in 2015 dollars) from national oil companies and came up with the slogan, "Beware of Tricks in Number 6." I commented later that "the wary voter 'bewared himself' right into voting against a measure that might in retrospect be his best, if not last, chance to tie up public rights on the beaches."

The bipartisanship and cooperation that made the Beach Bill possible simply broke down in Measure 6 and Straub was hung out to dry; his allies gathered signatures to put it on the ballot but had neither manpower nor money to counter Rinke's trickery. Governor McCall initially opposed the measure, arguing that if money was needed to purchase access, it was up to the legislature.

Measure 6 needed the governor, plain and simple, but he rode to the rescue too late to influence the results. Tom came around several days before the election, but his rationale was muddled and he failed to make a difference. Ken Rinke had come up with a slick slogan that capitalized on an old axiom of ballot measures: if in doubt, voters will vote "no," particularly if a tax is involved.

Oregonians showed a different mood in 1970, passing by a two-to-one margin an initiative to protect scenic rivers and trails. The measure was clearly stated and—most importantly—no tax money was involved. It was a freebie good deal; people loved it.

The 1970 Scenic Waterways Initiative was sponsored by Democratic senator Don Willner of Portland and Republican representative Stafford Hansell of Hermiston. The liberal lawyer and conservative hog farmer co-sponsored a package of progressive legislation in the 1969 Legislature, and gained passage of most of their agenda—except the state network of scenic rivers and trails. A coalition of hiking and conservation groups took it to the ballot. Eventually parts of twenty rivers, small and large, were protected under the initiative measure.[5]

Willner and Hansell were one of several odd couples of that time, legislators willing to cross party lines for common goals. Hansell went on to play a major role in both the McCall and Straub administrations; Willner ran unsuccessfully for US Senate in 1974, losing to Wayne Morse in the Democratic primary.

Staff Hansell was a genuine fiscal conservative, a tough vote on Ways and Means, which he chaired several sessions. Blunt and brief, he had enormous credibility inside and outside the legislature. I once saw him back down a rough-looking group of bikers who were flexing muscles on the state capitol steps to protest a mandatory helmet bill.

Don Willner was hyperactive, a ranked tennis player for his age, just too intense to be a good campaigner. He reserved a large portion of his law practice for pro bono work and took on, among others, Collegio Cesar Chavez, a Latino project that never gained traction.

Despite success on the beaches, the fate of the Willamette River was somewhat of a mixed bag. Both Tom McCall and Bob Straub wanted to rebuild the Willamette as something other than a sewer for mills and cities, and Tom had already established the high ground with *Pollution in Paradise*. Big corporations that owned the mills and plants along the river tried to slow the river cleanup, but most Oregonians supported a cleanup. It would cost taxpayers money to install modern sewage treatment along the river, but the costs were stretched out over many years and reckoned a good investment by homeowners, developers, and those who loved the river.

Tom's emphasis on the Willamette began with his inaugural message in January 1967 and a much-publicized move in April when he appointed himself as chair of the State Sanitary Authority, the agency charged with river cleanup; longtime chair Harold Wendell died of a heart attack, and the new governor seized the reins. Shortly after making his point, he turned the job over to former legislator John Mosser. The legislature approved a big increase in the budget of the Sanitary Authority with bipartisan support in both houses.

The State Sanitary Authority had been a weak agency with a weak budget during the Hatfield administration. It was not that Hatfield was opposed to cleaning up the Willamette or other polluted sites, but his priorities were on economic growth, education, and a streamlined government. Hatfield was not an outdoorsman and did not have many aides or department heads who fit that label; it was one of the contrasts between Hatfield and the two governors who followed. Tom McCall and Bob Straub presided over budget increases in several environmental agencies and named high-profile board members and staff to oversee the efforts. Their priorities were writ large upon the state.

Ironically, the earliest and most innovative environmental proposal of the era, put forward by Straub and quickly endorsed by McCall—the Willamette Greenway—ran into a buzz saw of opposition and ultimately fell far short of the original goals.

My West Salem neighbor, Ralph Grenfell, was a biologist with the Oregon Game Commission (later the Fish and Game Commission) and a World War II sailor who had been the helmsman on landing craft in the South Pacific. An expert boatman, Ralph was assigned to pilot a riverboat one summer day in 1965. I well remember the trip, for the other passenger in the small boat with Ralph and me was Bob Straub.

The Willamette's upper reaches were familiar to Bob from his years in Lane County; he was not a fisherman, but he knew the river and its tributaries, the McKenzie in particular. Bob wanted to see up close the Willamette River from south of Albany to Salem, as a Land Board member charged with responsibilities on rivers but more, I calculated, as a politician looking for new territory. His boatman lacked political leanings but had a deep and abiding concern for Oregon's natural terrain, whether on land or water.

Ralph was a quiet man but brutally honest and blunt. He let Bob know what he thought of the river—that it was polluted from paper mills and sewers, including the huge Kraft mill at Albany, that fish were in danger and the riverbanks were a mess. Bob took it all in, asked questions, and thought.

Bob's knowledge of and interest in the river and his search for a good political issue caused him to work with Karl Onthank, a University of Oregon professor and environmentalist. Together, they

fleshed out a system of parks and access points that Straub chris-
tened the Willamette Greenway. Onthank later shared the plan with
McCall, who endorsed the idea within hours of its announcement
by Straub.

It was a shrewd move by Tom, immediately blunting the edge of
his opponent's issue and eventually allowing his higher visibility and
publicity skills to neutralize it completely. That was typical of Tom;
his superior communication skills and popularity allowed him to
enter a field already underway, generally with the approval of those
who got the ball rolling, and quickly take command—and credit. It
was frustrating for Straub, but over the long run the unusual partnership of Tom and Bob was a key to the Oregon Story.

Tom's reputation for getting credit for another person's idea was
not limited to big-ticket items. Anyone who knew him well could
regale a listener with tales of Tom coming out of a conversation or
meeting with an entirely egocentric version of what had taken place.
It wasn't even deliberate, most felt, it was just "Tom being Tom." It
could have serious implications, however; Tom went into a meeting
in 1958 with governor-elect Mark Hatfield and emerged thinking
Hatfield would appoint him secretary of state. He even drafted an
acceptance speech; when it didn't happen, a breach was opened that
lasted for years.

The Greenway, despite its support by both Tom and Bob, would
battle farmers and developers for years in the legislature and
emerge much less grand than its sponsors envisioned. It was a priority in Tom's 1967 inaugural message, but legislators allowed only
$800,000 to begin acquiring land and even that would require local
investment by cities and counties along the river. The governor's
attention turned to beaches, taxes, student unrest, and a host of
high-profile issues. Straub moved his investment bills as state treasurer, and easily won a second term in 1968.

When he was elected governor in 1974, Straub returned to the
stalemated Greenway and attempted to reverse an action of the
1973 legislature that prohibited the use of condemnation to purchase
Greenway land. He failed, but eventually some eighty-three parcels

totaling more than thirty-eight hundred acres were acquired along the river and several state and local parks are linked to the Greenway. It was far short of Straub's original vision, but it was not insignificant.[6]

The limited sweep of Greenway access was a big disappointment for Bob, and it also revealed Tom's pragmatism as he endorsed the Greenway but did not involve himself in the emotional debates that ensued. Two very different Republican women were instrumental in limiting the Greenway: state representative Norma Paulus, an ambitious and talented Republican from Salem; and Liz VanLeeuwen, whose family farm was situated on a key Linn County river site. VanLeeuwen later rode her anti-Greenway notoriety into a House seat where she was as conservative as Paulus was liberal.

They were riding the crest of farmers' fears that the state would condemn farmland for parks, and they drove the 1973 prohibition and expanded it into general opposition to the Greenway. Some of the legislative hearings took on a pitchfork mentality, with plenty of venom released on city dwellers allegedly leaving a mess on the riverbanks and in general carrying on as a public nuisance.

Although he supported the concept, Governor McCall expended little political energy to make it happen. The Greenway was more emotional with Governor Straub, and he ignored counsel (from McCall, among others) warning that he would create an unnecessary donnybrook with farmers and get nothing for his efforts in the end.

McCall could see what Straub did not: Oregonians by the thousands thronged the state's beaches, but the Willamette was the domain of solitary paddlers and fishermen, all but empty most of the year. Beaches were for play; the Willamette was for farming, industry, and public water treatment and disposal. Cleansing the Willamette had massive support, but access was another matter if it cost money or threatened private property rights.

There were lessons from the rivers and beaches. One of them was the immense power of Tom McCall to carry a big project or idea; when he took over the Beach Bill and became its public face, the battle was over. No one else could have done that. By the same token, Bob Straub had showed his strength and persistence in the long fight against highways on the beach. He won, but it was difficult against McCall and Glenn Jackson.

The rivals locked horns, joined forces at times and went to the mat at others. The eventual score was one win apiece. Bob Straub forced highways off the beaches. Tom McCall drove the Beach Bill campaign—and earned the credit. Together, they were formidable and could win most battles; they could have carried Measure 6 if they had joined forces at the beginning. Operating separately, McCall was more effective, with his ability to marshal public support. It required enormous effort and dedication for Straub to carry a big issue by himself.

An activist for environmental issues, civil rights, and other progressive causes, Janet McLennan led the march against a proposed highway on the beach at Pacific City and later was a prominent advisor to Governor Straub. (Robert W. Straub Collection, MSS 1, Western Oregon University Archives)

The national turmoil and angst of the 1960s often surrounded the polarizing Vietnam War. Oregon once again figured in the national headlines as hawks and doves tangled in a battle that drew big names and stamped the state as a place of independent thinkers and voters. It began in 1965 as American involvement in Southeast Asia escalated, and it reached a fever pitch in Oregon as Mark Hatfield's term in the governor's office ended and he sought a seat in the US Senate.

Profile JANET McLENNAN'S ACTIVISM
Janet McLennan didn't invent community organizing, but

she certainly was one of its major practitioners during this era in Oregon. By the time she emerged as chief organizer of citizen efforts to kill the beach highway at Pacific City, Janet was already a veteran of citizens' movements across a host of progressive issues. She worked for civil rights as well as conservation causes and she headed the successful 1964 effort to repeal Oregon's death penalty.

She and her attorney husband Bill lived in the leafy Eastmoreland area adjacent to Reed College, a hotbed of young liberals who could be found on the Reed campus or in Portland law offices. The well-educated wives of these men were not content to bake and sew—but many professional jobs were closed to them.

Janet was a quiet, slender woman, not given to outbursts or speechifying, and she built a network of friends active in the revitalized Oregon Democratic Party of the 1960s in Oregon. Many of these activists brought their liberal politics from other parts of the country. One of their underrated skills was balancing their activism with raising a family as well as supporting a husband forging his career. Long before we learned about soccer moms, most were mothers with children to shepherd while pursuing politics. Janet was an expert at involving her kids and their friends in her campaigns, putting the patina of fun on what was really very hard work.

Research into many of the popular citizen efforts of this period frequently reveals women leading the petitioning, the marches, the volunteering; still shut out of the inner circles, they were doing the "grunt work" and doing it very well. Some would later wind up in elective office or working for politicians—Janet became a key advisor to Governor Straub and was consulted on every policy decision he made in the area of natural resources and a host of other subjects as well. Representing Governor Straub, she took on the rancorous fight over field burning in the mid-Willamette Valley and emerged with respect from both sides.

Janet was tough and straight talking; Straub and others listened to her quiet, well-researched opinions. Although very early in her career she had tried without success for a legislative seat, she was content to be a staffer who made a difference. She was also studying law and was licensed in 1972; Janet went on to chair the Oregon Board of Forestry and hold top positions at the Bonneville Power Administration.

Others among the corps of primarily female organizers finally got their chance to use their education in professional careers as doors began to open. Many of the signal accomplishments that made up the Oregon Story owed much to Janet McLennan's counterparts in other campaigns; indeed, this ramping up of citizen activism was itself part of the Oregon Story.

THREE Mark Goes Rogue: Vietnam in Oregon

As the 1965 legislature convened, Tom McCall and Bob Straub were sizing each other up from opposite ends of the capitol and Mark Hatfield was winding down eight years in the center office. There was no Tom and Bob show yet, no Oregon Story, but national politics was beginning to pull Oregon into the political spotlight.

It was a good learning session for me; very little of consequence took place, allowing me to meet the players and learn the process. Governor Sprague advised me to learn the budget and learn taxation—the rest would follow. It did. The action was with the "big three" as they prepared for 1966 amidst their sparring in Board of Control and Land Board meetings.

The ink was hardly dry on the final bills passed by the 1965 legislature before Governor Hatfield was on an airplane to Minneapolis for the annual meeting of the nation's governors. Mark was all business at these sessions; not a man for the cocktail parties, he would have done his homework and on his list would have been the explosive subject of the war in Vietnam. Hatfield left Oregon as a rising star of the Republican liberal wing and an odds-on favorite to be elected to the US Senate the following year. He returned a rising star of opposition to the Vietnam War, an unlikely partner with Democratic senator Wayne Morse, and an open target of President Lyndon Johnson and the hawkish wing of the Democratic Party.

It was quite a trip.

The president spoke to the nation on July 28, and the nation's governors listened in Minneapolis. "I have asked the commanding general, General Westmoreland, what more he needs to meet this mounting aggression," a somber-faced president announced, "and we will meet his needs. We cannot be defeated by force of arms. We will stand in Vietnam."

It was escalation, and it had been building since Johnson and Secretary of Defense Robert McNamara engineered the Gulf of Tonkin incident a year earlier, prompting a congressional resolution giving the president authority to use force in Vietnam. Oregon's Wayne Morse was one of only two senators voting against the resolution, and he took the lead in opposing Johnson's policies. Governor Hatfield immediately issued a statement from Minneapolis:

> I regret the steps of escalation of the war. I am pleased there is a move toward involvement of the UN in the quest for peace. I would call attention to the departure in language and in spirit from the many, many statements of McNamara, Taylor, Lodge, and others as they have returned. Until now the public posture was that the situation was about to improve, the boys would be home for Christmas, and things were looking up.

> President Kennedy, in September of 1963, told us that, in the final analysis, it is the war of the Viet Nam people—they are the ones to win or lose it, while we could send equipment and men as advisers, the people of Viet Nam are the ones to win it. Today we are told it must be our boys who must win it—not as advisers but as combatants.

Hatfield punctuated his terse statement by voting against a governors' resolution in support of the president; only Michigan governor George Romney joined him, and Romney reversed his position the next day after governors met with the president. Hatfield did not waver; leaving the White House briefing, he said he was "even more concerned than before regarding the cause of peace as it relates to our action in escalating the war."

Mark Hatfield was not an impulsive man. His words and actions were as meticulous as his three-piece suits. It was an act of courage on the part of a man whose steady rise was calculated and careful, from a legislative seat at age twenty-eight to statewide office for ten years. Hatfield was a star on the Republican stage; in 1964 he delivered the keynote speech at the Republican National Convention. He maintained solid credentials across the party's political spectrum nationally and in Oregon, and he enjoyed support among many Democrats. There was no good tactical reason for him to jump into the emerging Vietnam debate as he prepared to run for the Senate in 1966. Hatfield rolled the political dice that week in July 1965 and a promising young state politician became an increasingly vocal and persistent national voice against the war. In some states that would have been a reckless move; even in Oregon it was still very risky.

If Hatfield's articulate and crafted statements against American escalation came as a surprise to national political and media leaders, it did not surprise those who knew the backstory of Oregon's most prominent Republican. Mark Hatfield was raised in Dallas and Salem by a railroad blacksmith and a schoolteacher, devout Baptists. Their son was dutiful in church attendance but soon rejected the institutional trappings of religion and turned to his own faith-based worldview, a humanist philosophy combined with hard-nosed political skills that created an unusual and successful political persona.

Hatfield's views on war and peace were profoundly affected by World War II, where he commanded a landing craft in the Iwo Jima and Okinawa invasions, escaping injury as comrades fell around him. He became an informal chaplain for the dying and wounded and would later tell a biographer:

> (The war) brought me close to death . . . it gave me a perspective of life being but a vapor. You see it and you don't see it . . . The fact that I was sort of an acting chaplain aboard our ship gave me an understanding . . . that the Christian faith was something more than a formal worship service; it was very personal and something very individual.[1]

Hatfield's Navy unit entered Hiroshima a month after the city was obliterated by our first nuclear bomb, and the horror and devastation left an indelible impression that ultimately led to his stand on Vietnam. His ship also made a port call in Vietnam, but the Hiroshima experience struck the marrow of the young officer's conscience. Mark was not a pacifist, but he became deeply antiwar.

His cynicism regarding religious affiliation grew quite naturally in later years as the Christian Right began to dominate the Republican Party and it became politically fashionable to be "born again" or evangelical. Hatfield was evangelical, but he often directly confronted the evangelical right, its radio and television preachers and political hangers-on. Perhaps because I had been raised in a Baptist home similar to his and had also lost respect for institutional religion, I could relate to Hatfield's deep-seated religious and moral views.

In 1965, Mark Hatfield was Oregon's child of destiny, but the more he spoke against the president and his Vietnam policies the more he risked his future. He was laying the groundwork in 1965 to challenge Senator Maurine Neuberger the following year, but few who knew Maurine expected her to seek a second term. She came to Washington as the spouse of Senator Richard Neuberger, elected in 1954; when he died a few months before the 1960 election, Governor Hatfield bypassed Maurine for the short term and named instead a placeholder, conservative Democrat Hall Lusk, an Oregon Supreme Court justice. Maurine won the seat, but gradually became tired of the Senate without Dick; in 1964 she married a Harvard psychiatrist, prompting the ambitious Hatfield to primly refer to her as "Mrs. Solomon" rather than by her senatorial title. His rather obvious patronizing of Senator Neuberger was an indication that Hatfield was already in campaign mode for a Senate race in 1966.

Hatfield had remained coy about his senatorial plans, waiting to see what Maurine would do, and shortly after the 1965 National Governors' Conference he indicated an interest in returning to college teaching, while admitting that he was "a political animal" and enjoyed that life. When Maurine Neuberger decided not to run, Hatfield quickly drew a tough opponent, Democratic congressman Bob Duncan, who immediately tied himself closely to the White

Oregon Congressman Bob Duncan had the blessing of President Lyndon B. Johnson in Duncan's 1966 Senatorial campaign, where he defended LBJ's Vietnam War policies. (Oregon Historical Society bbo13593)

House and President Johnson's war policies. Senator Morse convinced Howard Morgan, a former chair of the Oregon Democratic Party, to enter the Democratic Primary as an antiwar candidate against Duncan.

Mark had already picked the horse he would ride, and as 1966 opened, Hatfield was a candidate and his strategy was clear. Several days after he announced, I sat down with him and asked what issues would dominate both his campaign and other congressional races that fall. Without hesitating, he proclaimed, "The issue of peace and war is uppermost in every person's mind." He was already ratcheting the rhetoric to another level, telling me the US must not commit to a ground war in Asia, which he felt would lead to "the inevitable next step—conflict with Red China and World War Three." As the campaign picked up speed, the tone and volume of the rhetoric on both sides was raised; at one point Duncan warned Oregonians that if the battle was lost in Vietnam, inevitably we would be fighting "in the ryegrass fields of the Willamette Valley." The Cold War was still hot in 1966 and China was on voters' minds; Asia dominated the headlines.

The increasingly unpopular Vietnam War was polarizing the American electorate, particularly within the Democratic Party. That was doubly true in Oregon because of Senator Morse's strident language raised against the president of his own party. Morse put himself right in the center of the 1966 Senate race and his relationships with Duncan, Morgan, and Hatfield got tangled up in the yearlong campaign. Vietnam created an uneasy alliance between senator and governor; the men had a considerable history, and it had not been good. Relations were proper but far from cordial.

Morse had been newly minted as a Democrat in 1958 and anxious to build his party credentials when he tried to derail the young Republican's campaign for governor. In the final days of the campaign Morse charged that Hatfield had lied in testimony he gave when, as a teenager, he was the driver of a car that killed a young girl. The man Morse hoped to help, governor Robert Holmes, disavowed the statement and the state's political and media establishments rushed to Hatfield's defense. Hatfield won that election handily, but deep scars remained. Morse and Hatfield managed to find some common ground after the 1958 debacle, largely through the intervention of Glenn Jackson, but the alliance was uneasy at best.[2]

Hatfield and Morse came to the Vietnam question through vastly different doors. Morse, a law professor, believed the Constitution demanded a declaration of war before the president could order attacks such as that authorized by the 1964 Gulf of Tonkin Resolution. Hatfield was not a lawyer; he was educated as a political scientist, but was increasingly devoted to the study of history as well as his abiding efforts to humanize institutional Christianity. If Morse was a maverick, Hatfield was an independent but, most of all, a humanist.

On the fiftieth anniversary of the 1964 Gulf of Tonkin vote, I served on a panel discussing a play based on Morse's unsuccessful opposition to the Gulf of Tonkin Resolution. It was a jarring reminder, and it opened old wounds in audiences that included many Vietnam veterans. There was still heat in their voices and in some cases an emotional, almost irrational, lashing out against the politicians, generals, and news media that sent them to Vietnam to be killed or wounded for no justified reason. There was nothing to say in response; we just let it roll. The anger amounted to a purging that was probably healthy but left everyone exhausted.[3]

Morse's resolute stand in 1964 made him an early hero of the antiwar movement, which was already gathering steam, but it also stiffened the resolve of his many Oregon detractors; they would finally descend on the senator in 1968. Morse was a true maverick, powerful and often effective in debate but a loner in the Senate, a man lacking a sense of humor and susceptible to plays on his giant ego. He was a loose cannon; he could fire without warning — Hatfield knew that better than most.

Before Oregonians could get to the main event of 1966, Democrats had to deal with the primary election contest between Bob Duncan and Howard Morgan. Morgan certainly opposed the Vietnam War and he was well known to Democratic partisans — less so to the general population. He was not a happy warrior in 1966; he was a one-issue candidate who had previously campaigned for Duncan as he rose to prominence in Oregon. I met up with Morgan in McMinnville shortly after he announced his candidacy. He confided his reluctance to enter the race and split the Democratic Party he had done so much to revive in Oregon. "Someone had to do it," he said of his decision to challenge the president's Vietnam policies. His campaigning was remarkably low-key, in the manner of a professor attempting to educate students about the complexities that were making Vietnam into an American quagmire.

There was little subtlety about his opponent. Bob Duncan was a former speaker of the Oregon House and had served two terms in

Congress from southwest Oregon's fourth district; he had worked as a seaman and was a World War II Navy pilot who still flew occasionally. Duncan was informal and easy with people, one of those natural legislators, a good man in committee and a speaker you wanted on your side on a tough floor vote.

Morse Democrats were the heart of the Morgan campaign and proved difficult for Duncan to recover in the general election. As the Democratic primary neared with a Duncan victory almost certain, Morse announced that if Morgan lost, his (Morse's) support would go to Republican Hatfield, solely on the issue of Vietnam. Morgan did lose, by nearly a two-to-one margin, and it was clear there would be a donnybrook in November. Hatfield doubled down on his Vietnam bet; in July 1966, at his final National Governors' Conference, he was the only governor to vote against President Johnson's conduct of the war.

Morse did not leave the field of combat after the primary. The 1966 race revealed yet another version of Oregon's political divisions, now tied to the increasingly acrimonious debate over Vietnam. Republicans, typically more loyal to party than Democrats, largely stayed with Hatfield, although there were defections by conservatives when Hatfield first surfaced as a prominent war opponent.

Democrats suffered multiple self-inflicted wounds and all seemed to turn around the brilliant but cantankerous Morse. Democrats had celebrated in 1952 when Morse left the Republican Party that had been his home since he was elected to the Senate in 1944. While serving as an Independent from 1952 to 1955, he helped elect Richard Neuberger to the Senate. Oregon's two Democratic senators were pivotal in Lyndon Johnson's ascension as Senate majority leader, and LBJ gave Morse a seat on the Senate Foreign Relations Committee, a platform Morse used to torment Johnson in later years.

But the Morse-Neuberger honeymoon was short and soon the pair began to bicker and then to spar openly. The feud became increasingly nasty and in the fifties it split the party—not along the old liberal-conservative lines, as both were liberals, but along lines that involved personal friendships, patronage, and campaigns. So in 1966 many Neuberger backers supported Duncan despite their dislike for his hawkish position on Vietnam.

The close race opened Hatfield to more press contact; he was generally good with reporters and very telegenic, but his natural caution caused him to leave most of his press contacts to Travis Cross, his longtime friend and press and political mastermind. Although I first met Hatfield in 1958 when he was running for

Pfc. Floyd McKay, on National Guard duty, interviews Secretary of State Mark Hatfield in 1958 at Fort Lewis. (Courtesy of author)

governor, it was an occasion he was not likely to remember. I was at National Guard camp at Fort Lewis, Washington, serving in a public-information unit when the candidate, wearing his secretary of state hat, came to visit the troops. I, the rookie reporter, asked some version of the old rookie question, "Sir, what is the purpose of your visit?" and wrote something innocuous to send to Oregon's small newspapers.

Hatfield was a war veteran and easy with guardsmen; he was handsome and "Oregon's most eligible bachelor" until his marriage that summer to the equally striking Antoinette Kuzmanich in a glitzy Salem ceremony that combined the city's social and political elites. Oregonians in the 1950s seemed to care about having a First Lady who looked the part. Travis Cross, the master of image, was pleased at how his boss was looking in 1958.

Ultimately, the personal organization that Mark Hatfield had built over his time in office may have turned the tide on the solid 55 percent Democratic registration margin that existed in Oregon in 1966, aided in part by immigrants from California and other parts of the nation discovering Oregon. As a college student, Hatfield had worked in the office of secretary of state (later governor) Earl Snell, a master of constituency relations—cards and letters on birthdays, extra efforts to single people out in a group—and the budding politician learned the importance of personal relationships. Mark developed a notecard system that he used on trips, with information about people he would meet; combined with his very good memory, the system served him well in elective office. In 1966, he also called in chits from his two terms as governor; Howell Appling Jr., Hatfield's appointee as secretary of state, was no peacenik but he rallied troops in conservative Klamath Falls with a recitation of Hatfield's Republican credentials.

Oregon continued to favor candidates of the liberal Republican brand; they were in the vanguard of environmentalism and held statewide offices, whereas many Democratic leaders were in less-visible congressional offices in Washington, DC. Hatfield benefitted from the bitter split between Morse and Duncan and also from growing opposition to the war on the part of Oregonians. He ultimately defeated Duncan by only 14,017 votes; it was the closest of the many elections he fought over a forty-six-year career in public office. Duncan and Hatfield never faced each other again, but Morse and Duncan tangled in Democratic primaries in 1968 and 1972, and Morse and Hatfield were opponents in 1972.

Hatfield's 1966 win was big for the antiwar movement, and he quickly pushed his advantage in Washington. He was still establishing himself in August 1967 when I visited his Senate office on my way to begin my academic year as a Nieman Fellow at Harvard; perhaps my lack of a notebook and pencil allowed a long and open

Tension is evident on the faces of Senators Mark Hatfield (right) and George McGovern (left) as they enter the Senate chamber on June 17, 1971, for the critical vote on their end-the-war legislation. Senator John Stennis (center) led the effort against the amendment. (AP Photo: Henry Griffin)

conversation that was the best I ever had with him. A student of political history, he was a schoolboy in a candy shop, and because the Senate was in recess he was able to tour me through private areas normally closed to all but senators. As we approached one historic area, a guard challenged the senator; he was still a Senate newbie, despite a national reputation built on Vietnam. His energy level was high and he was making the connections that would lead in 1970 to the McGovern-Hatfield Amendment to end the Vietnam War.

When I next spent real time with Hatfield I was in a new role, accompanied by a camera crew. Ancil Payne, newly installed as King Broadcasting president, asked me to do a documentary on Hatfield in the fall of 1971, before the senator's campaign for re-election was formally announced. After that announcement, we would have been required to give equal airtime to anyone who filed for the office, no matter how serious their candidacy. I told Ancil it must be about

Vietnam, the senator's seminal work at the time. The McGovern-Hatfield Amendment had lost, 39–55, in 1970, but it sent a strong message to both the White House and to young protestors in the street that there was a core vote in the Senate to end the war.

By the time I began my research for the Hatfield documentary, I had also plunged into the emotional maelstrom of Vietnam and discovered the depth of feelings among Oregonians. My first year at KGW had presented so many major topics for commentary that I limited Vietnam references. But I was sure the war was a mistake, and in 1971 as the tragic slaughter of villagers at My Lai played out, I "came out" on Vietnam and it ignited reaction. The military trial of Lt. William Calley, whom the generals had declared responsible for the murder of twenty-two civilians, produced a verdict of guilty, with a life sentence. He was the only soldier charged, and I saw hypocrisy:

> And so we have disposed of Lieutenant Calley. This pathetic little man whom the Army made an officer and a gentleman. But what now of Captain Medina? And what of the chain of command with its free fire zones and body counts? What indeed, of us, the American people? It's impossible to avoid the question of whether in judging William Calley we are not really judging ourselves.

> The question nags, and I think it's what really bothers Americans about the trial of Lieutenant Calley. His ordeal has forced Americans, many for the first time, to look deeply, and consider what we have done in the name of fighting Asian communism.

> Make no mistake, that's why we went to Vietnam. We did not go there to defend freedom. There was no freedom to defend. There is none now. There will be none when we leave. We sent our Calleys, and hundreds of thousands of young men who neither understood nor believed in any mission beyond survival.

> We—the American people—defoliated the lush jungles. We napalmed the villages and killed the young with the old, the child with the mother in the name of defeating godless communism. We turned daughters of gentle Buddhist families into prostitutes. We turned sons to petty thievery

and the black market. We dropped more bombs on the villages of an Asian farming nation than on all the cities of Europe in World War Two. Over one million South Vietnamese civilians—our allies—have been killed or wounded, often by our bombs and shells. Nearly fifty thousand brave Americans share the graveyards of Southeast Asia.

At home, we have created a division equaled in our history only by the Civil War. We heard no truth and called it a credibility gap. Our children were raised with pictures of death and horror and we wonder why they shun our values.

One President pledged American boys would not go; and half a million were sent. Another President pledged to end the war and expanded it into two more nations. A delicate, ancient culture is decimated in one corner of the world. An open, trusting, and believing society is crumbling at home before our very eyes.

Lieutenant William Calley killed people in an insanely misguided effort to do what he thought was demanded of him. To what jury will we plead our insanity?

Looking back, I wonder why it took me so long to step forward on Vietnam. I think it was a combination of trying to stay with topics where I knew I had enough facts and expertise to pose as an authority and the process of feeling my way in a new media form. Reporting exclusively on regional politics, I had not written about Vietnam, nor did I know much about Southeast Asia prior to 1967 and my study at Harvard. But I did know it would continue to be an Oregon issue in 1968, and I set out to educate myself. I followed lectures on the topic and monitored classes in Chinese history from John Fairbanks and Japanese history from Edwin Reischauer, leading lights in their field; they helped me understand the region. A lot of education was also coming from the streets in 1968. When the US Senate held its Fulbright Hearings, largely because of Morse's insistence, I read most of the voluminous testimony, and the more I learned, the more I worried that we were making a serious mistake in Vietnam (I discuss 1968 in Chapter 4).

Audience response to my "Calley commentary" in 1971 was swift and overwhelmingly supportive at both the KGW switchboard and in my mail. For the first time, I was forced to resort to a form letter to reply to most correspondents, although I sent individual letters to people I knew or who made a special effort in their letters. The commentary was printed in several places and read from some church pulpits. I heard from Rev. Theodore Hesburgh, the president of Notre Dame, who was becoming active against the war.

It was my first real indication that I could go beyond the rather cautious analyses of my first year and dive into topics that were emotional, even divisive. Several people within the station expressed support; Keith Lollis, program director, commented in a note, "Your stature in the public eye has increased a thousandfold by this one commentary and should be extremely helpful in the long task of gaining public confidence and trust. Keep it up." Of special interest to me was a note from ZeeZee McCall, the governor's niece and our personnel director: "Excellent analysis on Calley and the war—you articulated beautifully what most of us had been thinking all day." That was probably not true of her Uncle Tom; he was a staunch defender of the war, where his son, Tad, was serving. Families across America were split as the war continued.

I was struck by how many viewers embraced KGW as part of their family, and I think in some ways the Calley commentary brought me into the fold. Nearly all letters were handwritten, such a sharp contrast to hastily composed and sent e-mails that I would receive four decades later responding to my columns in the *Seattle Times*. I wonder if the process of handwriting forces one to think a bit longer or more deeply than is the case with instant messaging.

The Calley analysis was a turning point, and I began to be more assertive in my views both of the war and the Nixon administration in general. More than a year later, on May 11, 1972, with escalation of bombing in Southeast Asia and street violence in major cities, including Portland, I turned loose a commentary that literally shut down our switchboard and produced dozens of requests for copies and reprints. It was in similar vein to the Calley commentary and it concluded:

> We have been at this ghastly business fulltime now for seven years. We have been lied to by two presidents and a host of generals. We have been fed a public relations gimmick called Vietnamization. Only to find that the war has now become a struggle to salvage the pride of one more American President.
>
> We have had our intelligence and patriotism insulted by a Secretary of Defense who talks about quitters and bug-outs like a high school back-field coach.
>
> Millions of Americans threw no rocks at office buildings today. But we, too, cry out in anger and frustration against a war we never wanted and cannot justify. As one American citizen to one American President, wipe the blood off my hands!

It was the strongest piece I ever did on television, and when I finished and turned to anchor Dick Ross, I was sweating. My official title was news analyst, but we had begun using the label "commentary" on pieces that went beyond analysis. I had ventured deeply into that field. When I returned to the newsroom, my colleagues greeted me with applause, and my phone was already ringing off the hook. We ran the commentary again at eleven o'clock and on the next day's noon news.

I felt strongly about what I said, but I also worried that I was moving very far into the field of personality, and for a time I reverted to more analysis and less commentary. I wrote one viewer, who wondered about reaction to my Vietnam comments:

> You're right, I have received some of what you call considerable abuse. However, the reaction to the Vietnam comment has been running roughly three to one, in favor of the comment. The problems of television news commentaries are unlike those of newspaper columnists. It's a personal medium, but we always have to be careful not to use the personal nature of the medium very often. The Vietnam comment is probably the most personal comment I have made and it seems to have hit people that way.

I had hit a nerve; one viewer suggested that I "put my umbrella of appeasement where it will do [you] the most good"; another suggested that I should "obtain a position writing fairy tales for a class of preschoolers." Another handwritten note commented, "That fellow who calls himself your news annalist (Floyd Somebody) had no right this evening to call our President a lyer," and others suggested exotic locations where I might be sent. But I was warmed by many more supporting letters, mostly handwritten and some obviously from people who were agonizing over the war and its effects.

Whether this type of aggressive commentary helped or hurt our audience numbers was beyond my knowledge, and station management never attempted to have me tone down to appease angry viewers. I think viewers in those days had a station loyalty, primarily to anchors, sports, and weather people. I sometimes joked that I captured my audience while they were trapped between weather and sports—and there was an element of truth in that.

I was still becoming accustomed to working with film; I'd always gone on stories by myself at the *Statesman*, and print reporting was simple stuff compared to putting together thirty minutes of film. The 1971 Hatfield documentary was filmed in large part in Washington, DC, where anti-Vietnam tensions were rising and security was tight. The senator and I were on common ground regarding Vietnam, but we had sometimes been wary of each other in the past. I would need cooperation from Mark and his staff but complete independence in my movements.

We filmed the informal Wednesday Club, a small group of liberal Republican senators who met weekly for lunch. Among Hatfield's colleagues on Wednesday were senators Ed Brooke, Jacob Javits, Clifford Case, and Lowell Weicker, the heart of a Republican liberal caucus in the Senate. We filmed the senator and family at their suburban home outside Washington and their Oregon home at Newport. Our crew traveled with Hatfield to college campuses in three states: Youngstown (Ohio) State, Eastern Washington University, and Linfield College in Oregon, my alma mater.

What I found most interesting was the reaction of students to Hatfield's message, and their search for someone in high places who understood their angst. The three campuses were not Kent State, but Hatfield had also spoken on campuses with more radical students. He communicated and empathized; we later learned that while we were in Washington some of his staff were actively working to build links to more militant wings of the antiwar movement, trying to tamp down rising frustrations. It was done outside the reach of our cameras.

Vignettes remain from that experience. In Youngstown, an old steel city already beginning to rust away, we rode to the airport in a van. My film crew was up front with equipment bags and cases, and in the back a bemused United States senator was wedged in between two rather substantial ladies in pink formal gowns on their way to a lodge convention. The dignified senator struggled to keep from smiling and our camera was packed firmly in its case, so we just had to savor the moment.

The title of the thirty-minute documentary, *The Very Personal War of Mark Hatfield*, reflected what I had observed of the man and his crusade during just seven years. It was, indeed, a lonely seven years in many respects, and it alienated him from some longtime supporters. There was even disagreement at home, as we learned when filming a family dinner; the formidable Antoinette was not very dovish.

In most of the political documentaries I did for KGW over the years, I tried to show the personal side of my subject. News reports, including my own, gave voters as much issue-oriented content as most could digest. A documentary could look more into the person behind the campaign slogans and dogma, but it was always a balancing act to be fair as well as candid.

Mark Hatfield was not a man to bare his soul; it was one of his many differences from Tom McCall. To my knowledge Mark had no close friends among the working press. That was unusual in Washington, one of the most incestuous places in the world, where veteran reporters and writers move in circles that include top-level elected and appointed officials. My encounters in 1967 and 1971 were perhaps as close as any working reporter had been to the inner man, but there was so much more to know and so few chances for the type of access I had on those occasions. The senator acknowledged a natural caution that contributed to his image as a private man in a public office:

> I've always been somewhat aloof from the political social side, which has created a problem sometimes. People thought I was aloof and therefore not easily communicated with . . . sometimes problems arise in which if you don't drink you're not quite in the same spirit, or the mood of the whole meeting or the whole affair, and it causes a little difficulty. And I suppose I felt a little bit sensitive on that.

> The news media, it has been charged, and probably to some degree true, that it has not been the warmest or the best or the most open type of relationship . . . I delegated much of that, maybe too much of that kind of relationship to Travis (Cross). Although I think he handled it ably and well . . .

> I had always been rather sensitive too to the politician who ground out the press releases as publicity and political promotion. And therefore I sort of reacted the other way, that we had our share of handouts so to speak, or of press releases, but if I would call up a member of the press or the journalistic profession, say "Let's have lunch," or "Would you like to have a cup of coffee?" I always had the feeling that the first thing in his mind was, he wants for me to write an article or he wants some publicity. And therefore I always thought, well they get enough of that from other politicians. If they want to find out something they can call me. And out of that was created some of my problems.

The concept of a mere reporter calling Governor Hatfield without going through Travis had never occurred to me—or to anyone else, I suspected. Hatfield's phone was guarded by the formidable Leolyn Barnett, no lover of reporters. The governor's press office under Travis was the best in the business and certainly not reluctant to cultivate reporters, but it was not the governor who did the cultivating. Hatfield was correct in his surmise of how the media would react. When Mark moved to the Senate, Travis remained in Oregon; media relations suffered badly and were sometimes nonexistent.

Despite his high profile on Vietnam and growing Senate influence, I cannot recall a time when Hatfield appeared on the Sunday network television news panels. That was surely his choice, for he would have been an excellent "get," to use media parlance. He never agreed to appear on *Viewpoint*, the Sunday show I moderated for seventeen years—or any of the other Portland shows, in my recollection.

Press relations were just one of the many differences in style and personality between Republicans Hatfield and McCall. Hatfield always dressed impeccably and looked ready for a public appearance, even as he worked in his office; McCall rambled around his office in loose sweaters, often without a tie, appearing like a man who had lost his glasses. Hatfield gardened; McCall fished. Hatfield acquired a large and impressive collection of Lincoln artifacts and browsed Washington's bookstores to add to his American history bookshelves; McCall was a reader but not a collector, and only a casual student of history. Perhaps the greatest contrast between Hatfield and McCall was party loyalty. Tom on several occasions endorsed Democrats—notably Bob Straub—but Hatfield stuck with the party that brought him into politics. He was loyal to the end: my last conversation with Mark was at lunch in Portland in 2004; I chided him on his support for President George W. Bush's re-election, which seemed totally contrary to Mark's views on war and peace. He defended his choice, although with less than his usual vigor.

My 1971 documentary was more than a description of Senator Hatfield's Vietnam crusade; it also reflected his approach to public life. Increasingly, in later years, his rise to power in the Senate and challenges in his personal life served to isolate him even more from the public as he nestled ever more deeply into the cozy Senate establishment. In 1971 Mark Hatfield had come a long way, but he still had a long way to go.

That was also the case for Vietnam as an issue defining Oregon in this era; it was certain to bring out both the best and the worst in everyone, as the rhetoric heated and people took to the streets. The tangled web of the 1966 Senate race became even more complex as Tom McCall inserted his large presence into the debate in 1968. Oregon was a small state where personalities easily overshadowed issues. Oregonians—and a sizeable national audience—watched as four experienced and capable politicians carved each other up over old grievances and the deepening tragedy of Vietnam. Perhaps it was a distraction from creating the Oregon Story, but it was also part of the story, a state of independent politicians unafraid to speak their minds because they knew their constituents demanded nothing less.

As we were defining ourselves as a state with a special place for environmental activism, young people were taking to the streets and Morse, Duncan, Hatfield, and McCall would revisit Vietnam. Young Bob Packwood had little to say about Vietnam but a lot to say about Oregon's senior senator, in a race that again brought national attention to our small state. In 1968 almost anything could happen; it produced perhaps the nation's most traumatic politics since the Great Depression.

Profile BOB DUNCAN, MORE THAN A HAWK

Bob Duncan's place in Oregon political history will be as the man who lost to both Mark Hatfield and Wayne Morse in bitter races for the US Senate, a hawk flying without success in a state that favored doves in the case of the Vietnam War. He deserves a better remembrance.

Duncan was one of many post-war immigrants who chose Oregon to start a career. A Navy flyer, he took a law degree from the University of Michigan and headed to Oregon with his wife, Marijane. Bob joined the Medford practice of William McAllister, a former legislator and future chief justice of the Oregon Supreme Court. Duncan was known as a trial lawyer who was fast on his feet and quick to find the vulnerability of an opponent.

He was gregarious and quickly gained stature in the Oregon House; elected in 1956, Duncan was speaker in the 1959 and 1961 sessions. He was elected to Congress from southern Oregon's fourth district in 1962 and was quickly spotted as a future leader; but President Johnson convinced him to run against Hatfield for the Senate in 1966, when Vietnam was expected to dominate the campaign. Bob was on the wrong side of history and it cost him three senatorial races, two in Democratic primaries against Morse in addition to his 1966 loss to Hatfield.

Thrice a loser, Duncan moved his law practice to Portland and in 1974 won the third district (Multnomah County) seat vacated by Edith Green. Bob was welcomed by congressional colleagues and patched up his differences with Senator Hatfield; he gained good committee seats but was never comfortable with the young liberals in the Portland half of his district, many of whom were dedicated opponents of the Vietnam War. He played a critical role in a major chapter of the Oregon Story, converting federal highway funds from the Mount Hood Freeway—which he originally backed—to Portland's new light-rail system.

Beyond Vietnam, Duncan was a solid liberal vote on social issues, but the rapidly changing third district rejected him in 1980 for Democratic newcomer Ron Wyden, opening Wyden's long career in Congress.

Bob carried a bit of the combativeness of a former Navy boxer, took chewing tobacco in his cheek and made no bones about it, and was seldom seen without his Clan Duncan necktie. Still wearing a fifties-style crew cut, he was a "man's man," but he married two strong women in his life. Marijane Duncan was the mother of their seven children and Bob's equal partner until her death in 1990. Later, Bob married Katherine Boe, widow of former Oregon Senate president Jason Boe, and they settled into domestic life at the Oregon Coast and Portland.

We enjoyed their company on several occasions thanks to our mutual friends Tom and Marguerite Wright. Duncan was a source of great stories and more complicated than he appeared in the bombast of three electoral campaigns dominated by the Vietnam War. But he was a genuine "hawk"; even years after he left politics, Vietnam was not a topic one raised in a social evening with Bob Duncan.

FOUR

Tumult in 1968: The Year of Change

Entire books have been written about one of the most tumultuous years in American history since the Civil War: 1968, the year when almost everything went badly.

It was the year Lyndon Johnson lost Walter Cronkite, America lost Martin Luther King Jr. and Robert Kennedy, a generation of young people lost their political innocence, democracy was crushed in a police riot in Chicago, and we elected as president a man who claimed to have a secret plan to end the Vietnam War.

People less famous than King and Kennedy died in the violence: 16,899 Americans were killed in Vietnam that year, the highest casualty count of the war. Senator Wayne Morse was a collateral casualty of the war; he was humiliated by defeat at the hands of a young Republican state legislator, turned out just as the nation began to share his views on Vietnam. Senator Mark Hatfield saw his antiwar and liberal voting record turned against him at the Republican National Convention by leaders of the Southern strategy that would elect Richard Nixon. The Oregon State Prison exploded in rioting and fire in March, on governor Tom McCall's watch.

We looked long and hard for those who fared well in 1968. Winners were hard to find in the turmoil. One certainly was Bob Packwood, the thirty-six-year-old who brought Morse's twenty-four-year career as Republican, Independent, and Democrat to its close.

On a personal note, it was a seminal year, perhaps the most important of my career. I spent the 1967–68 academic year at Harvard

University on a paid Nieman Fellowship, the most prestigious in the nation for mid-career journalists. It was a first trip outside the Northwest for my young family (Karen was seven, David was four), and it was a great year for me. It was an exciting opportunity for someone from a small paper in the Pacific Northwest, who graduated from a little-known college and had no major prizes or awards to his name.

After a trip of nearly four thousand miles, we proudly drove down Storrow Drive in Cambridge with a chair and a mattress lashed to the top of a Rambler station wagon. The four of us looked as if the Joad Family had taken a wrong turn and driven east. I was the perfect candidate—if the Niemans had been in the NFL—for "most improved player." Everything was a learning experience, and all of us learned. For a farm boy from North Dakota, Harvard was another world.

Niemans were members of the Faculty Club and given top-drawer treatment everywhere. My cup overflowed when I was able to take my father, a farmer, millworker, and maintenance man, to the Faculty Club, where he was quick to observe that horsemeat was on the menu, a remnant of World War II days that remained to satisfy a handful of aging savants. Dad, an accomplished horseman who had farmed with draft horses, preferred the beefsteak and wondered at the odd tastes of supposedly intelligent professors.

We arrived back home in Oregon on the day Robert Kennedy was killed in Los Angeles. Wayne Morse had just squeaked through the Oregon primary; Bob Duncan nearly got revenge for Morse's role in Duncan's loss to Mark Hatfield in 1966. The feud would come home to roost in November. We barely had our bags unpacked before politics resumed bubbling; the *Statesman* asked me to begin writing a weekly political column, and I checked back into the capitol.

Across State Street from the capitol, a historic Oregon university was about to have the distinction of placing two alums in the US Senate at the same time. Bob Packwood had been a student of Mark Hatfield when Hatfield taught at Willamette; Mark was also a graduate of Willamette. When Packwood upset Senator Morse and joined Hatfield in January 1969 in the Senate, they made up one of the youngest state teams in the venerable body.

It was a busy year for both Hatfield and Packwood, as well as for the harried Senator Morse, who realized much too late that the young Portland legislator was not only a serious candidate but a very savvy one as well. Morse was hard-pressed to beat an angry Bob Duncan in the Democratic primary with 49 percent of the vote. Phil McAlmond, a gadfly and a hardliner on Vietnam, picked up 4 percent; if his vote had gone to Duncan—the most likely recipient— Morse would have lost his party's nomination. As it was, his nomination was damaged goods. Packwood, meanwhile, had no serious opposition and spent most of the summer fundraising and honing his considerable political organizational skills.

Morse, at sixty-eight, was showing his age, even on good days. He stubbornly stuck with campaigning tools that were under siege from younger politicians such as Packwood. Traveling with him one day in Willamette Valley towns, I reported:

> Oregon Senator Wayne L. Morse does his best to live up to his image as an institution . . . and it is a mixed blessing in a political year when institutions are not all that big . . . He carries it (the campaign) as he has always carried it—in the time-honored tradition of the grand platform speaker, the fiery voice of independence, and the moral indignation that has its roots in the great Populist and Progressive tradition of the West.

> As he moves across the state he has represented for a quarter-century, Morse eschews the tactics of the new breed of politician. He is prone to forty-minute lectures in the day of the five-minute pep talk, discusses an issue at exhausting length with one person while a dozen pass ungreeted. He would be embarrassed traveling in an emblazoned campaign bus.

I joined Morse in Portland for a day's campaigning, riding with him in the rear seat while his wife, Midge, was up front with Ron Abell, a reporter friend who had joined the campaign. Pulling out my small tape recorder, I asked Morse an introductory question to break the ice. Half an hour later we were driving through Newberg

and Morse was still talking—without stop—on my opening question. While Morse shook some hands, I badgered Abell: "He won't
stop, even when I try to break in," I implored my friend, "This will
be a disaster." We climbed back in the car, I asked another question and got a short, tidy reply; on it went, the senator helping me
(and himself). At Dallas, I asked how Ron had pulled it off. "I told
Midge," he smiled. The senator's wife was one of the few who could
influence his behavior.

Life with the senator in 1968 revolved to a great degree around
those close to him, and it was a very bad year. Morse lost two trusted
aides who had been with him most of his long career, Bill Berg and
Charlie Brooks. There was simply no one else—except Midge—
whose advice he trusted. Brooks' wife was dying of cancer, and Berg
died of cancer on September 28, a week after an *Oregonian* poll
showed Packwood had
drawn even with Morse.

The saddest thing in
following Morse was to
see how much he relied
on his ability as an
orator; if he had been
watching his audience,
he should have seen that
eyes were glazing and

Even with friendly audiences,
Senator Wayne Morse
lectured in old-school
campaign style in three
Senate races from 1968
until 1974. (Wayne Morse
photograph collection,
PH131, box 1, folder
3, Special Collections
and University Archives,
University of Oregon
Libraries.)

heads nodding. There was nothing wrong with Morse's mind, but he was running another generation's campaign. Morse was raised in Wisconsin and his hero was the fiery progressive, Senator Bob LaFollette, one of the great stump orators of the time. Morse earned a master's degree in speech before taking his law degree; when he was younger he had the ability to turn an unruly crowd of detractors into reluctant supporters. Instances of this were part of his reputation in Oregon. When pushed, he fell back on his oratorical skills; in the Senate, his long speeches and occasional filibusters had become a hallmark, often viewed negatively by colleagues.

Ron Abell had a fine reportorial mind, and I agreed with his later assessment that in 1968, "Wayne Morse won a primary election he couldn't possibly have won and he lost a general election he couldn't possibly have lost." Morse's constituents had changed and so had a new generation of political candidates; neither trend was in tune with Morse's old-school tactics. I noted that Morse had support from older traditional Democrats and young, angry antiwar voters. But the middle ground belonged to Bob Packwood.

Many of the female activists who engaged in the Oregon Story causes of the time were Democrats. Packwood realized that Republican women were just as ready to participate. He worked hard to build a personal brand (an odious term we were beginning to hear). Just as Morse would have been aghast to ride in a motor home with campaign slogans on its side, Packwood would never have passed up the opportunity to ride in a roving billboard. A month prior to the election, I wrote:

> An interesting, and crucial, question in the current campaign is how much mileage Packwood can get from his volunteer army of suburban housewives, teenagers, young executives, and others attracted to his banner in the past few years. . . Packwood says he has fifteen thousand (lawn) signs planted hither and yon, and it's a believable statistic. The significant part of the statistic, however, isn't the signs but the fact they represent fifteen thousand people scattered across the state who are sold on the candidate . . .

Packwood has attracted this following of volunteers with a couple of basic appeals, but one is all-important: he gives them something to do. People in our increasingly affluent society have more time on their hands than ever before, and not all are content to spend it on motorboats and riding lawnmowers. Suburban women, with a maze of gadgets to do the housework, have a yearning to use the college training that an increasing number of them have acquired. Their vast store of energy, plus that of teenage youth whose interest in politics has been aroused but who can't identify with older, more established politicians, is the pool that Packwood has been drawing on for six years.

It was not that Packwood relied entirely on tactics—he had issues as well, although he basically punted on Vietnam, calling for a rather vague "land reform." Vietnam hawks already knew how to vote; they didn't need him to point the way. He was against gun control and for law-and-order; students who occupied buildings at Columbia University were "kooks" and should be "put in the pokey." Following Packwood on a busy day, I described an encounter in Newberg with an older voter who greeted the candidate: "So you're the one! Well, you've got my support—I'm a Democrat but I can't vote for that Morse."

Bob Packwood was in a way the ideal candidate against Morse. He was largely unknown and easily dismissed by the veteran senator,

Challenger Bob Packwood and Senator Wayne Morse survey a packed house at the critical Portland City Club debate in 1968. (Max Gutierrez, UPI; OHS bb011878)

which gave Packwood running room to do what he knew best—organize and execute a flawless campaign. He prepared relentlessly, and it paid off in a pivotal debate at the Portland City Club shortly before the election, in which youth bested age and sent Packwood on his way to a narrow victory over Morse.

Bob Packwood created his own brand: People for Packwood. The form was widely imitated and in the 1960s kept Republicans in control of the Oregon House for four sessions. It took its author to the US Senate.

When I was assigned to the state capitol in 1964, Bob was already making a mark, particularly among Republicans whom he had recruited and coached. Packwood was all politics all the time; in the House he focused on legislation that would help his party, and he cultivated reporters and provided good copy. He could sum up an issue in short, pithy comments that played well on television, but he could also sit with a print reporter and dissect complex legislation. He was smart and good on his feet, but at times he seemed machine-like in his drive for success.

Packwood's brilliance—and toughness—was epitomized by the institution that he created to set himself aside from the garden-variety politicians of the day. The Dorchester Conference began in a modest Lincoln City hotel in 1965, created a stir at the time, and fifty years later was still going with Packwood in attendance. Packwood organized the first Dorchester as a showpiece for moderate Republicans to contrast themselves to Goldwater-style Republicans. It was also, of course, a showpiece for Bob Packwood.

With its open nominating system and history of electing independent thinkers, Oregon is not a party state. Packwood walked a tightrope in this environment—he wore the GOP label and voted the party line on most occasions, but he distinguished himself on a few newsworthy issues to build support for future campaigns. In the midst of the 1965 legislative session, he invited about two hundred Republicans to the old Dorchester House for an informal meeting, ostensibly to chart the party's future.

Bob Packwood, founder of Dorchester, was a constant presence for fifty-plus years, joining table talk and summing up ideas at the conference that took him to the US Senate. (John Patterson, Dorchester Conference)

Among those not invited was Republican chairman Elmo Smith, a former governor who epitomized the party's old guard. Governor Hatfield and Secretary of State McCall were invited, but only the latter attended. Tom loved a good party and there was partying at Dorchester, but there was also a lot of serious discussion around the tables and networking that would benefit both Packwood and McCall. I was a new reporter on the block and Dorchester introduced me to people I would deal with for years.

In the years that I covered Oregon politics, I seldom missed a Dorchester Conference. The early Dorchesters gained attention both in Oregon and nationwide and had no trouble in attracting frontline national figures as speakers. When Bob Packwood defeated Wayne Morse in 1968, I linked his victory to Dorchester in an article published in *The Nation* titled "The 'Kaffeeklatsch' Constituency":

> Packwood discovered as early as his first legislative campaign in 1962 that for great masses of middle-class Americans, political participation can be an end in itself . . .

Dorchester's format was elastic. People talked about what was on their minds, guided only by general subject areas. The politically conscious husband or wife brought the uninitiated mate and new interests were kindled to replace family finance as an after-dinner topic. Everyone took part. The debate and discourse flowed from workshop to dinner table, from the crowded bar to a closing session at which Packwood and his lieutenants tried to pull together a Dorchester view of the world.

Would anyone remember, a year later, what resolutions had been passed, what issues searched, what answers trumpeted to a perplexed world? The cries of the ever-circling gulls would drown the words before they left the conference hall.

Not so easily lost, however, would be the vibrancy of participation, the warm glow of earnest talk and new friendships, the laughter shared at an amateur-hour musical comedy. It mattered little if Dorchester urged withdrawal from Vietnam or the negative income tax or whatever. It mattered little, even, if Packwood later took opposing views. But it mattered a great deal to be there, to take part, to be involved. Dorchester was a "be-in" for the suburban middle class . . .

By 1968, his Dorchester gatherings had attracted more than one thousand participants, and the more zealous were ready to fill key spots in Packwood's well-planned campaign. They spread across the state like a chain letter, each hand reaching for another, pulling it into the circle. In November, the circle closed.[1]

Packwood was in his environment in small groups, and his skill stood out. There was a studied intensity to the man, a grasp of politics and an eagerness to share that intensity with others. Bob was not a person given to small talk—even about politics.

His ambition was palpable, but ambition is not a sin in politics. Packwood was elected to the Oregon legislature in 1962; he saw the growing vulnerability of Senator Morse in that election, as Morse won by a less-than-convincing margin against Republican Sig Unander, a silk-stocking son of the Portland establishment. Packwood drew a target on Morse's back, not realizing how scarred that back would become as a result of the Vietnam War.

Packwood kept his eye on the media at all times. By the 1967 legislative session I had built a modest reputation in a crowd of more-experienced newsmen. Unexpectedly, Bob wondered if Dixie and I would join him and Georgie for an overnighter at a friend's Road's End beach house, and a chance to watch his political pitch to a local Jaycees group. The Jaycees were a big part of the Republican base at that time and I thought it would be interesting, so we loaned our children to their grandparents and drove to the beach. It was a learning experience.

I watched as Packwood worked the small sympathetic group of Jaycees, and it left an impression. A trained debater and public speaker, he used pauses strategically, each pause followed by an appeal crafted to unite his audience in a common cause. "Together we can do what we cannot do separately" became a mantra in his campaign. It was an indelible contrast to the formal approach of Morse and other traditional political figures.

As our evening progressed, Packwood eagerly brought out a Monopoly board; I had grown up with family board games but never considered them a serious adult pursuit. Bob played like a man possessed, quickly wiping me off the board. I decided that standing between him and a train he was trying to catch could be hazardous. Later, he asked if I would be interested in joining the campaign team he was forming. I was not sure if the offer was serious, and Dixie blurted that I was a Democrat. Ever efficient, Packwood had checked the voter-registration rolls at the Polk County Courthouse; I had not taken the time to change my registration, but I had begun voting Democrat in most races. That pretty much put an end to anything serious, and, in any case, I was a finalist for the Nieman Fellowship at the time and would not have left journalism for politics.

Over the years, Packwood and I pursued one of those symbiotic relationships common in our field. Particularly after I moved to KGW, he sought me out when he was in Portland, and when I was in Washington we would meet, once at his suburban home. Bob was well connected and quite candid on political matters. He shared his concerns about the quality of President Reagan's thinking process well before it became a media item; he had good insights on national politics and, when I was preparing to go to the Middle East in 1982, he provided top-level contacts at both the Israeli embassy in Washington and in Israel itself.

My only quid pro quo was unusual: his aides noticed that Bob was often quite expressive when we talked, so they asked me if I would allow his photographer to snap shots of him during one of our meetings. It was a bit unusual, carrying on a conversation over the click of John Patterson's shutter, but it produced some good information for me and some good shots for him. I'm not sure it was a good idea, but at the time I saw no ethical breach.

Packwood's single-minded dedication to his cause was illustrated at the 1968 Republican National Convention in Miami Beach, the first of ten that I would cover for print and broadcast. Bob didn't seek a delegate position, but he was a presence, filling his campaign coffers by convincing donors that he could defeat Wayne Morse. A high priority for Republicans that year was picking up a Democratic seat and taking revenge on a man who had walked out on the party sixteen years before.

Oregonians voted for delegates of their party in the primary election and dozens ran for the eighteen positions. Hatfield narrowly received more votes than McCall. Despite this, Tom thought he had a promise that he (McCall) would have the usual governor's role of delegation chair. He was wrong, and the Hatfield forces cut him down ruthlessly two days after Hatfield's announcement that he would support Nixon. Hatfield, acting on an outside chance that Richard Nixon would select him as his running mate, had made his peace with Nixon on June 20, an uneasy peace but one that allowed liberal Republicans to envision a ticket balanced with an articulate and attractive young senator who might appeal to women and young voters.

"It was all over so smoothly and nicely that you hardly noticed that Gov. Tom McCall had been neatly snubbed—not a spot on any

convention committee or an office in the delegation," I wrote for
the *Statesman*. It was classic backroom politics, of the type Tom
never mastered. There was precedent for this type of hardball politics. Republican conservatives had used it in 1952 to punish Senator
Morse. The place on the GOP Convention's Platform Committee
that Morse sought went instead to a young state legislator named
Mark Hatfield. It was one of several events that year that led to
Morse leaving the party.

Governor McCall gamely kept a smile on his face but, behind
the façade, Tom was seething at the put-down by his old rival, and
I have no doubt that it was a major factor in his denunciation of
Hatfield and Morse the following week. Having gritted his teeth
and backed Hatfield when he had no choice, he vented his spleen
when he had an opportunity to undercut the senator's chances for a
spot on the national ticket. A politician who was beaten in the back
room could always go public, and Tom was never reluctant to take
that route. He was not an adept backroom operator; he was, however, adept at making a point.

Tom exploded on July 28, at a Republican state meeting at
Gearhart, and it came out of the blue, as Tom's thunderbolts frequently did. The governor had introduced Massachusetts governor John Volpe, and at the conclusion of Volpe's speech was slated
to present the visitor with a gift. Instead, he launched into an
unscripted, rambling denunciation of Oregon's dovish senators and
pleaded that Republicans endorse a strong stance on Vietnam.

Tom's foreign policy was not nuanced—it was personal, centered
on family. Tom and Audrey's firstborn, Navy ensign Tad McCall,
was en route to Vietnam, assigned to the dangerous riverboats. His
fiercely proud father expanded his natural protective instincts to
cover not only Tad but Lyndon B. Johnson's war as well. Tad was
on the firing line and by extension that brought Tom into America's
deepest trauma, the Vietnam War.

Speaking off the cuff—always a danger with Tom—he delivered
the most deeply personal and biting remarks I ever heard him make.

I had a small tape recorder and transcribed his outburst. It was a doozy:

> I want to say about a favorite son . . . I don't know what your resolution is on Vietnam, but we have a favorite son who became an ensign last Friday in Newport. And he is our favorite son! I tell you . . . even though I have been a Rockefeller supporter, that I'll feel safer if Dick Nixon were President of the United States standing behind that boy than if Mark Hatfield or Senator Wayne Morse were President of the United States.
>
> I think Nixon or Reagan can stand up better for those boys and I'll feel safer. I want to look at that resolution today, and I hope it wasn't a yellow, chicken kind of a resolution we had in 1966.
>
> When you've got a boy of the age and he's over there, then you begin to count the cheating and the weaseling when it comes to what do you have to say about Vietnam . . . so that I can say to that guy I saw without any feet in that hospital in Saigon, we sent you over there not because you were going to be engaged in an immoral and rotten mission but because we felt that security and freedom needed protection.
>
> And let me tell you one more thing and I believe this, and I suffer every night over Vietnam. And now I've got one that can't come back because he's going to the most dangerous duty you can engage in in Vietnam. Let's pray for them and think for them. You've got a great idea to get him home—get him home. But stand united behind him until you can get him home.
>
> And this is what we haven't done. We've been a weaseling, two-faced party for our boys . . . For God's sake, I've been there—in Vietnam—and if you want to find out what is going on in the world and what the attitude of Americans is in the world, look to those young people of dedication who think they're saving freedom, who think they're saving self-determination over in Vietnam. And once we argue that [*sic*] out of the fact that they're doing that—then God help us as the protectors of peace throughout the world.

Tom was referring to his part in a delegation sent by President Johnson to Vietnam in 1967 to observe the first elections in South Vietnam. The president knew of McCall's hawkish views and was acutely aware that Morse—a serious thorn in Johnson's side—would be running in 1968. McCall and his associates got the usual Pentagon dog-and-pony show in Saigon, but he and Eugene Patterson, editor of the *Atlanta Constitution*, managed to split from the group and fly to the Mekong Delta to do a little investigative reporting. Reporter Tom made a genuine effort to assess the election's fairness, using interpreters to question voters, but the fix was in and the assessment by McCall and his associates of a flawed but fair election served only to bolster the president's position at home.[2]

Governor Volpe turned to the person at his right and asked, "Did he just say what I thought he said?" He did, and he meant it. Senator Morse replied to Tom's outburst in Gearhart with a brief statement: "Our boys in Vietnam will be safer if we get out." Senator Hatfield declined to comment. The next day, McCall told me he was "a little sorry about my outburst last night—but it was straight from the pump, sort of a heart seizure!"

Although the Vietnam outburst was widely portrayed as another "just old Tom" remark made after a few martinis, there was calculation in the governor's remarks, delivered only three days before the Republican National Convention was to convene. Senator Hatfield was on the short list for vice president if Nixon was nominated; Mark determined to keep Tom away from microphones and in the background at Miami Beach.

After his Gearhart tirade, McCall was a lonely man in the Oregon delegation at Convention Hall. He was assigned a seat in the middle of a row, far from roving reporters, where it was uncomfortable for as large a man as Tom to stumble across colleagues to reach an aisle. He moved himself to a vacant aisle seat in the Michigan delegation, where he held occasional court with reporters, but he produced pretty much of a blank sheet in news accounts, unusual for Tom.

Hatfield's endorsement of Nixon was, in Mark's later words, a "practical political decision"; Oregon law required the delegation to vote for the winner of the presidential primary for two ballots and it also looked as if Nixon would have the nomination by then. "Once you've been had, you might as well take advantage of it," quipped Nelson Rockefeller. That is exactly what Mark and his backers were doing; "I Like Mark Hatfield" buttons began to appear, causing me to remark that they were "a handy item to promote a non-candidacy." One did not run for vice president, but one was prepared.

Hatfield ran afoul of the emerging Southern Strategy, despite being championed by Billy Graham. He was just too liberal for Republican loyalists, and Nixon chose the relatively unknown Maryland governor Spiro Agnew for the ticket. Tom, who had been on good behavior throughout the convention, rushed to endorse Agnew. His friend Ted Agnew, he told me, was a liberal in the McCall mode. As Agnew later became the spearhead of Nixon's anti-media campaign, Tom reckoned the man had changed, and he had a couple of explosive confrontations with his former buddy.

I asked Hatfield in 1971 if he had pondered what would have happened if he had been chosen and ultimately elected in 1968. He thought a minute and replied:

> I have thought about it. I would be less than honest if I didn't say that. One of two things as I see it. One, there would have been a relationship in which I would have had complete freedom and perhaps had some influence . . . or I would have been one of the most unhappy isolated men, in the corner, the political corner so to speak, that have ever been in the position of vice president.

Was he sorry about being passed over? I asked. He thought a bit more. "Frankly, I feel that was one of the greatest things that ever happened to me, that if I had been in the consideration, that I wasn't chosen." He laughed, and it appeared genuine.

He went on to describe the lengthy and agonizing process he went through to get Nixon's approval for the seconding speech he made for him in Miami Beach. Nixon advisers were vetting the speech and wanted Hatfield to stress Nixon's religious background and also the issue of peace:

> I asked, "Well, what are his religious convictions to which I can make reference?" "Well, you know, his mother was Hanna Nixon, who . . ."

and I said, "Yes, I knew Hanna Nixon, she was a fine Christian lady, a fine practicing Quaker and so forth and belonged to the Quaker church out in Whittier." And I said, "I am not seconding his mother, I'd like to know what his views are." . . . Well, we obviously dropped that question pretty quickly because there wasn't anything of substance that anybody could give me. Well, I wrote it with the main emphasis on peace . . . We were to meet back and go over it that afternoon before that evening—this was all in the same day.

As the hours ticked by, Nixon's advisers went back and forth, toning down the speech until, Hatfield believed, little of substance remained:

> We reached some sort of agreement through argumentation and debate. It was haggle, haggle, haggle over whether or not it was going to offend one group by attracting another group. Now I don't mean you have to kick somebody in the shins or the opposition, to prove your position with those you are trying to communicate with. But it was very obvious that we really just were not in a good working relationship with the convictions that I held and what the strategy of the campaign was to be . . . I think this idea of doing things so as to keep all options open reaches almost to a point of two things: one, indecision or, number two, decisions that are so totally camouflaged, so totally fuzzy and confused that you really have not communicated and brought along the people.

Two years after Hatfield's comments, Vice President Agnew resigned in a plea deal to avoid prosecution on extortion, bribery, and tax evasion. If Hatfield had been selected in 1968 in Agnew's place, he would have become president in 1974 when Nixon resigned in the face of impeachment.

Mark Hatfield was a practical and very tough politician, but if he had been in the Nixon White House he would almost certainly have been shielded from Watergate by Nixon's inner circle. His sense of moral justice would have prevented him from keeping silent as the burglars and phone-tappers went their criminal way—at least that's my analysis. Would he have resigned if he discovered the scandal, and brought the house down, or would he have waited for it to collapse around the president, opening the office for himself? Or would he have gone with John Dean to warn Nixon that a cancer was growing on the presidency? How impossible it is to predict the fates of presidents, senators, and nations.

Beyond the excitement and tensions of the vice presidential selection, Miami Beach was showing a preview of politics to come, a glitzy and choreographed Republican image of happy American youth rallying around the flag in contrast to the ugliness that was already building toward the Democrats' convention in Chicago. Miami Beach was not my sort of town. It was kitsch, "a city that has to be seen to be unbelieved," in one of my dispatches from the city. "In one of the lounges, the walls are lined with reproductions of major art masterpieces, all done to the exact same size and appearing for all the world like a blown-up collection of postage stamps."

That convention was my first, to be followed by nine more, including two more in Miami Beach. By the time of the 1984 conventions, the last I covered, they had become meaningless because of the spread of primaries and reforms following the riotous 1968 convention in Chicago. Television came to dominate, but did little real reporting—the conventions had become a backdrop for well-coifed anchorettes and their serious-looking male partners, loosed from their studio sets for a week to play reporter at a convention with nothing to report. The spread of celebrity journalism could be charted by looking at how local television stations played the conventions. Promotion was the name of the game, and my heart was no longer in the game.

If Miami Beach was a fantasy world, Chicago 1968 was just plain ugly; tear gas wafted around the convention hotels, and disillusioned youngsters—I called them "Gene McCarthy's government in exile"—clustered around the Chicago parks, easy targets for serious troublemakers and Chicago cops all too eager to bash some skulls.

Most of the minor-league press rode a press bus from downtown to the stockyards convention hall, deliberately routed through Mayor Richard Daley's home neighborhood of blue-collar bungalows. The first day, we were greeted with "Welcome to Chicago" signs and waves from the mayor's faithful. Over the next three days the cheers turned to boos, obscene gestures, and placards urging all of us to go home, some implying that home was somewhere near Moscow.

I reported on Wayne Morse's impassioned speech for an anti-Vietnam resolution, one of the best (and shortest) the old warrior ever made. But speeches were drowned by violence, and fear was everywhere. Phil Hager of *Newsweek* and I were in a taxi when it missed a sign or barrier, and we found ourselves the only vehicle on a wide street, while overhead a military helicopter swung down and tailed us until we could find an exit. Another *Newsweek* friend, a slight, balding man in his fifties, took a nasty gash to the head from a police baton; other reporters were gassed.

Thousands of well-armed and muscled police and soldiers confronted unarmed and not very muscled young protestors, most of them scared to death, as Chicago delivered what subsequent investigations called a police riot. I inhaled a heady cocktail of tear gas and marijuana smoke but escaped wounds and bruises. As the convention wound up with the nomination of Hubert Humphrey and Edmund Muskie, I joined a massive crowd gathered to hear Gene McCarthy in Grant Park. "One could not help but feel threatened by the ring of four-deep National Guard troops surrounding the group," I commented, suggesting that the massive show of force was excessive for the relatively small number bent on violence. I concluded:

> The tragedy of this city and its armed-camp appearance is much deeper than the cracked skulls and fat lips. The tragedy is in what it has done to the spirits of Democrats here and those watching across the nation. The anger created by the tight police security, the constant shoving, orders being given, restriction of free movement has spilled over onto the convention floor. It played a large part in the bitterness seen during debates and floor fights. It spilled out in angry booing of Daley himself.

> If there has been any good come out of this exhibition of muscle, it might be that for most delegates and observers it provided a first chance to get

an inkling of what black Americans are talking about when they speak of police harassment and the threatening and intimidating feeling one has when there are officers everywhere and the right of free movement is a perishable commodity.

When I returned to Salem, I found a lot of folks in deep denial. One of the local Rotary clubs asked me to talk about the convention, and I was on my way to our battered old Studebaker Lark when my boss, Charles A. Sprague, caught me and asked if he could ride along. He said he needed to make up a missed Rotary meeting, but I immediately thought, "Oh, no, this cannot be good." To add to the moment, my passenger door was broken and I had to sprawl across the seat to release the door for my boss.

We bounced along together, with me worrying about his reaction to my speech. As we entered the restaurant, an ABC network television crew showed up, following Bob Packwood. They wanted to film a Packwood speech, and he was hoping for an audience, but the Rotarians declined my offer to speak at a later date, so I addressed my publisher, a network crew, and a future US senator, as well as the local businessmen. I made no bones about the police behavior I'd witnessed and my fears for democratic government, and my comments drew several sharp retorts from the Rotarians, who were sure that hippies and yippies got what they asked for. The network crew had been in Chicago and gave me a thumbs-up, however. On the ride home, Sprague said he had liked the speech and agreed with its general tenor. Not long afterward I got a small raise, and linked it to his ride in my battered old car with the creaking springs and rusty passenger door.

If Bob Packwood was cruising in 1968, Tom McCall also got a big break in the election of Clay Myers as secretary of state, the position to which McCall had appointed him in 1966. Clay easily defeated Democrat George Van Hoomisen, the Multnomah County district attorney, in the fall, but the really significant victory came in the primary election. Governor McCall's most serious competition within the Republican Party was House speaker F. F. (Monte) Montgomery of Eugene. Clay Myers walloped Monte in the primary and, for Tom, that quashed concern about a serious Republican challenge in 1970. Treasurer Bob Straub was already gearing up for 1970 and easily won re-election over an unknown named Ancil Page, most of whose votes surely came from television-viewer confusion. (Ancil Payne's Beach Bill editorials on Channel 8 gave a whole new cachet to an unusual name.)

The Democratic self-destruction parade marched through Oregon again in 1968 and as the year ended Republicans owned both US Senate seats, two of the three top statewide elective offices, and both houses of the Oregon Legislature. Senator Morse bitterly contested Packwood's razor-thin election margin and threatened to take it to the floor of the US Senate. But it was done, and an Oregon icon exited just as the nation was joining his position on Vietnam. He had done it to himself with his isolation from the realities of a new style of politics and his stubborn insistence that his reputation and oratorical skills could make up for the absence of a campaign strategy.

The strategy Bob Packwood created would affect Oregon politics for many years. Packwood protégés won across the board in 1968, and Republicans seemed entrenched statewide. Personal participation became as important—perhaps more important—than issues in many campaigns. Writing in December 1968, I quoted newly elected Attorney General Lee Johnson, one of Packwood's associates. "I'm not so certain how important issues are in any race," said Johnson, who spent $132,685 on a skillful marketing campaign to defeat incumbent Robert Y. Thornton, who spent $17,000. Lee Johnson's campaign mirrored Packwood's, and Bob Thornton was even more out of touch with campaign tactics than was Wayne Morse. In sixteen years, he'd never mounted much of a campaign; the office was so obscure that few good lawyers even considered joining it.

Nearly half of Johnson's money came from a cousin who was in business in Las Vegas and Freeport, Grand Bahama Island, in the Caribbean. A 1967 *Life* magazine article, co-authored by former *Oregonian* reporter and Pulitzer Prize–winner William Lambert, presented in graphic detail the control of the island's business and politics by casinos and mob interests. Mark Johnson and his company, Zia International, were not mentioned in the *Life* article, but Zia had a close relationship with Wallace Groves, a financier and ex-convict prominently mentioned in the *Life* article. The situation was ironic: Lee Johnson was running as a crime-fighter, in a campaign largely financed by money earned in Las Vegas and Freeport, Grand Bahama Island.[3]

Lee was rich, and a scofflaw of sorts—his driver's license was suspended twice for fourteen infractions he incurred from 1961 to 1969, seven for speeding. In office, he professionalized what had been a low-key operation under Thornton, and at least two assistants later became appellate judges. Johnson permanently changed the image of the agency, raising its profile within state government.

After the dust settled on the 1968 election and Johnson beat back a lawsuit filed by Thornton, I used the campaign in an April 20 *Statesman* column to call for an enforceable disclosure law to deal with large individual contributions such as those hidden by Johnson in an out-of-state committee. I was also becoming concerned about the increased "Packwoodization" of Oregon campaigns, and in the column, I concluded: "Bringing a great many new faces into some aspect of politics is a good thing. But the danger is that, for the uninvolved, there may be a tendency to confuse the size and zeal of a candidate's army with his skill and ideas as a legislator. If this is to be the trend, we have no one to blame but ourselves, for political trends are usually set by those who are smart enough to figure out what the voters will buy." The column won an award from Oregon Newspaper Publishers Association as the best of 1969.

My concern was vindicated in 1972, as Treasurer Straub finished the two terms allowed under Oregon law. Straub left the office in remarkable shape; he was clearly the most influential and successful treasurer in state history. The Oregon Investment Council he championed and managed was earning excellent returns for Oregon public-service retirees, and Bob had formed a close relationship with the council's president, Republican Roger Meier, an heir of the Meier and Frank Company.

One of the informal rules Meier and Straub agreed upon was to avoid firms that weren't transparent about exactly how they were making their money. This was basically the "sniff test" that veteran reporters sometimes relied upon in sizing up a public figure. Straub and Meier studiously avoided the aggressive lobbying of Portland financial firm Capital Consultants because president Jeff Grayson failed their sniff test. The State Investment Council wasn't among the many victims of Capital's ruinous collapse in 2000.

Despite the improved reputation of the office, the 1972 campaign to succeed Straub drew a disappointing field, and I found myself applying my own sniff test to an ambitious young man named Craig Berkman.

Bob Packwood's campaign formula spawned a host of wanna-bees in this period, using tried-and-true tactics that had done so much for their originator. It brought some really excellent talent to the legislature and local office—the Republican-controlled Oregon House from 1965 through 1971 had several—but the formula elevated image over substance in many cases. None stood out like the 1972 candidacy of the thirty-year-old Berkman for state treasurer.

Berkman was a champion self-promoter who somehow managed to get himself named one of America's "Ten Outstanding Young Men" by the national Jaycees organization, and the Oregon chapter put up a bunch of billboards to tout Berkman's accomplishment. When he announced in February, I saw it as the ultimate in hype: friends had talked him into the race (of course), his attractive young family showed up to happily applaud. I was underwhelmed by the puffery. One of the things I tried to avoid, especially in my early years on television, was outright opposition to a candidate. But Berkman just didn't pass my reportorial sniff test; he looked like the ultimate plastic man and he was proposing to manage the state treasury.

The more I looked into his background, the more I feared a con job was in the works, and a week before the primary election I described the campaign as "a smooth billboard and advertising blitz planned with the aid of a national campaign consultant." The candidate had only lived in Oregon three years as an adult, his performance at two jobs was at best marginal, and he was using family money (he had married into a wealthy Seattle contracting family) to finance the campaign. There was little "there" there, and what was there was not impressive. I was pretty much alone before the May Republican primary—several editors bought the Berkman line—and Berkman eked out a close win over Representative Don Stathos, a very sound legislator from Jacksonville.

Democrats nominated Alice Corbett, a perennial candidate and former legislator who relied on a familiar name (although she was not of "the Corbetts" of pioneer fame) but contributed nothing to the process. A Berkman-Corbett choice for such an important position was unthinkable. The Oregon Supreme Court subsequently declared Corbett ineligible to take the office of treasurer because of a previous election-law violation. At a special convention, Democrats selected Jim Redden to replace her. Redden had no financial expertise but he was a fine lawyer and one of the best legislators at the state capitol.

Redden was a favorite of reporters, who loved his droll humor, and that, plus a mounting feeling that Berkman wasn't all that he pretended to be, produced a flurry of news attention, overshadowing Berkman's slick advertising. Having done the early spadework on Berkman, I watched others follow, and by the time it was over, Berkman was done. Redden's natural calling was the law—he was attorney general (1977–1980) and later a federal judge (1980–1995), but no one worried about the keys to the safe when he was treasurer.

Berkman proved to be the con man that I sniffed in 1972. After years of bilking investors of millions of dollars, he was sentenced in 2013 to six years in federal prison for fraud. Before leaving Oregon in 2008—avoiding angry clients—he ran unsuccessfully for the state senate and governor. He tried to become chairman of the Republican National Committee and settled for heading the Oregon Republican Party from 1989 to 1993.

I don't mean to place the blame for Berkman on Dorchester or on Bob Packwood; I have no idea whether Berkman was a Dorchesterite. Dorchester became less important in Republican circles in later years. Packwood consistently maintained that the purpose of Dorchester—still running in 2015—had been to reform the Republican Party, rather than elect him to the US Senate. He was elected, but the party began moving in a direction opposite to that of many original Dorchesterites, most of whom were moderates. Even moderate Republicans became more conservative—the entire GOP spectrum moved to the right after 1980, even in moderate Oregon.

Dorchester could not maintain its original edge and after ten years lost its ability to generate young electable Republicans. The paint was peeling on the lawn signs and suburban housewives were active on other fronts.

The 1968 election that ended Wayne Morse's political career and brought Bob Packwood to the national stage was the last I covered as a Salem newspaper reporter. For the 1970 campaigns, which featured a re-run of the McCall-Straub gubernatorial matchup, I was on television and learning a whole new way of covering elections and almost everything else. I was sitting in Tom's chair at KGW in Portland, wondering if it would fit my slender frame. At times it was a near thing.

FIVE

Sitting in Tom's Chair

Early in 1970, I was visited in the capitol newsroom by Norm Heffron, the news director at KGW-TV, Tom McCall's old station in Portland. I knew the station because of Tom, but I didn't know Norm or anyone else at the station and I didn't watch much television. Morning newspaper reporters are seldom home for a five o'clock news show, and in any event I had plenty of news in my head by the time I drove home to my family.

Norm was a tall, slender, crisp sort of fellow, cut in the Edward R. Murrow mode, even to the constant cigarette (smoking killed him at an early age, as it had Murrow). Before becoming news director he had held Tom's old job of news analyst for a year or so, and hewed a liberal line. He was quiet and contemplative, an intellectual lacking a good people touch.

Norm was looking for an assignment editor—the TV version of a newspaper's city editor, assigning reporters and photographers. I didn't see it as a very interesting future, and I asked if a replacement for his news analyst job had been selected. He said it had not, and I said I might be interested. I surprised myself with that inquiry. I had never considered broadcast journalism; print types looked down on broadcast colleagues as shallow and fixated with appearances. But I was worried that I would stagnate in Salem, and the death of Charles A. Sprague the previous year meant uncertain times ahead for his newspaper.

Sprague was the senior statesman of Oregon journalism. Owner of the *Statesman* since 1929, he had written a page-one column until shortly before his death. We were certainly not friends, but I could talk to him and I knew he respected my reporting. But for his death, I might not have entertained KGW's opening, but I suspected—correctly—that his son Wallace would not hold the paper long before selling. Wallace worked in New York, and his wife considered Salem a provincial backwater.

Dixie and I had talked about my leaving the *Statesman* after Sprague's death, and some of my Nieman friends suggested I consider political writing in the nation's capital. But we were Northwesterners, raising two kids and with family roots in Oregon. Washington, DC, seemed very distant, and even Portland was a big step. Dixie in particular loved our West Salem home and neighborhood. We had built the house ourselves, working with two friendly elderly carpenters, and our sweat was on every doorknob and banister.

But I was restless and intrigued by KGW, in part because of Tom McCall. Norm Heffron said he would discuss the analyst opening with station manager Ancil Payne. I met Ancil for the first time after I joined the KGW staff; he became my defender and my friend, and when I later moved to Bellingham, I would drive down to Seattle for lunch and his rollicking humor and insights.

Television was totally new territory for me; I had appeared a few times on the news panel of *Viewpoint*, the discussion show Tom McCall originated. *Viewpoint* became mine, and I hosted some eight hundred programs over the years, with future presidents, governors, and leaders from the worlds of environmentalism, education, and social issues as guests. But I was not hired primarily to do *Viewpoint*—I knew I could do that. My prime role was on the nightly news—and I had no idea whether I could do that.

Despite what was surely a ghastly on-camera audition, I was told to report to work well ahead of the May primary election, where I would play a key on-camera role. I received no instruction in dealing with the camera, writing for television, or reporting for the new medium—it was sink-or-swim time, and I foundered for a while. I had my thick glasses tinted so the cameras didn't make the lenses look like Coke bottles. I arrived with the typical newspaperman's disdain for pretty faces in television, plus a male aversion to putting on makeup.

My camera audition revealed that I had a beard akin to that of Richard Nixon, and I would do well to address the problem, as Nixon had failed to do when he debated John F. Kennedy in 1960. Nixon waved off makeup artists and applied dime-store makeup himself; it began to run when he started to sweat under the harsh studio lights, making him look sinister. For the next seventeen years I applied a layer of "Ross Number Two," named for Richard Ross, our prime anchor. Nordstrom's knew it by that name.

It took me no time to understand that tinted glasses, makeup, and proper attire would be as important in my job as selecting the proper phrase or asking the key question. Early in my tenure at KGW, I was described by *Oregon Journal* columnist Doug Baker as having "the appearance of a small-town mortician." So much for trying to appear serious! To add to the difficulty, a series of job shifts took place shortly after I was hired. Payne moved to King Broadcasting's Seattle headquarters and was replaced in Portland by Forest Amsden. Forest and I shared a newspaper background and a liberal but pragmatic political viewpoint. In the same shuffle, Norm Heffron joined Payne in Seattle as news director, and Amsden hired Ed Godfrey from a Miami station as KGW news director.

Godfrey and I were as different as two people could be, and he hated news commentary; he disliked fielding calls from angry viewers and he disliked long on-camera dissertations. Ed was a broadcast guy, not a former print reporter. We had nothing in common other than an employer and the fact that we were a bit over our heads: his managerial experience was limited, and my television experience was nil.

Ed was charged with improving our ratings—the common charge when a station changes news directors—and he brought in the first of a series of consultants from Frank Magid, an Iowa-based consulting firm. Consultants were all the rage in local television at the time, but King had been slow to join the trend. The ubiquitous experts had transformed television news in such key markets as San Francisco and Los Angeles; their emphasis on fast-moving short stories and feel-good features was already changing the culture of the industry—in my view, not a positive change.

Consultants had no use for commentary, particularly from someone still learning how to behave on camera, and the already thin ranks of news analysts and commentators were being reduced across the nation. But King was different, and commentary was a company tradition on King's Portland, Seattle, and Boise stations. Forest Amsden and Ancil Payne stood behind commentary, and Godfrey was forced to accept my existence.

Godfrey deserves credit for making me more effective by insisting that I cut down the length of commentaries. At first, I sometimes went beyond two minutes—an eternity for a medium that sells soap in fifteen-second commercials. Ed pushed me hard to get under a minute and a half for 5:00 p.m. and a minute if I taped a piece for 11:00 p.m. It made me a better writer. One of the things anyone must learn in moving from print to broadcast is to write short, declarative sentences with as few punctuation marks as possible. Colons, semi-colons, and dashes simply don't transition to verbal presentation (some may recall a hilarious old Victor Borge skit in which he "pronounced" punctuation).

Keep it short, keep it direct, and make only one or two points in your commentary. I learned by watching the good broadcast writers in our newsroom. My writing was crisper and clearer because of what I learned on television; a good many writers could benefit from these lessons, learned under the pressure of adapting to a new medium.

I was helped enormously by good access in Salem. I could get the governor when I needed him, and I had excellent legislative contacts in both parties. Rather than trying to immediately plunge into the politics of Portland, I decided to continue concentrating on the legislature and state government and to ease my way into the big city. Events overwhelmed that plan, however—1970 was not an ordinary year.

Even though he had been gone since 1964, Tom's aura still hung over the newsroom. Tom, along with Richard Ross, Ivan Smith, Doug LaMear, and Jack Capell made up the original team, and KGW dominated Portland television in the fifties and sixties. As the new guy, arriving in the midst of Tom's re-election bid in 1970, I felt a lot of scrutiny and it was not always favorable. If there really was a "Tom's Chair," I was never shown there; it would certainly have been too large for the latest pretender to the throne.

Dick Ross, the primary five o'clock anchor, was always professional on the set, but there were times when his normal cheerful delivery tightened as he followed one of my commentaries; my on-air performance was ragged and Dick was also more conservative in his politics. It was a tense time for Portland, with protesters on the streets and even invading the studio. One night an unruly, long-haired young man got into the studio while the news was being broadcast. Ross and LaMear left the set and tackled him, holding him until help arrived. When Tom sponsored the Vortex rock festival, his normally conservative old buddies sided with him. He had paid his professional dues and was close to the old-timers on the staff, both in the newsroom and on the production side.

King Broadcasting had launched a gentrification program for its news staffs, hiring as many Ivy League graduates as possible, usually lacking formal journalism training. It made for an interesting dialectic, with the youngsters rubbing up against the pioneers, and it didn't always work. My rural Oregon roots combined with my recent year at Harvard made me a hybrid of sorts and I could relate to both camps.

But many of the best reporters—and future network stars—were Oregonians. Jim Compton joined us on his way to NBC as a foreign correspondent; he later returned to King as my counterpart in Seattle. Ancil was proud of discovering Ann Curry, the future *Today Show* host and intrepid NBC reporter, when Ann was breaking in as a reporter on a Medford station.

KGW was an NBC affiliate and many of our stories aired on the network; crews from the network regularly stopped in, particularly during election season. I was with David Brinkley the day Chet Huntley died in Montana in 1974, and David graciously allowed us to run my commentary on our five o'clock show before his own thoughts appeared at six o'clock on NBC. My Nieman Fellowship colleague Cassie Mackin had become an NBC reporting star before her tragic death from cancer in 1982, and we saw each other during the political season. The network crews were professional and worked well with our crews. When I was in Beirut in 1982, I worked out of the NBC office and used their drivers to navigate the militia roadblocks.

In addition to daily commentaries, the station also wanted me to do documentaries. Prior to the May primary, photographer Eric Johnson and I did a half-hour on a proposed new state constitution, probably the dullest-ever topic for television. I was learning the limitations of my new medium. My Salem contacts prepared me well for my second documentary, a half-hour program on the 1970 governor's race, featuring the personal sides of Tom McCall and Bob Straub, utilizing my knowledge of the men.

One Sunday in Central Oregon, we scheduled a shoot with Tom at the family ranch near Redmond. The entire McCall family was there, Tom's mother as well as his two brothers and two sisters. This was an extraordinary gathering, as the entire family rarely got together, scattered as they were over Oregon and California. The McCall spouses avoided the imperious Mother McCall and none of them showed up for this made-for-TV production. The weather was great, the rustic setting very telegenic, and we pulled up to the ranch house with great expectations, prepared to unload our gear.

Suddenly the governor darted around the corner of the house, obviously agitated. "Don't pack your gear through the front door," he cautioned. "Follow me, and we'll sneak around by the side and keep you out of sight."

What the devil was happening? Hal Lesser, Ralph Ahslen, and I—and Tom—carried cameras, recorders, lights, and power cords as unobtrusively as possible as the hulking governor guided us up a back stairway and into the attic, full of childhood antiques from various McCall children. Mother McCall, he explained, also had a camera crew on the premises—a photographer from Redmond was taking pictures for her second book; there was no question as to who had first call on all the choice spots in the house. It was my introduction to the wackiness of the McCall family, and to the strange combination of love and competitiveness that ran between mother and her famous son.[1]

Filming on the first floor when Mother was on the second, and vice-versa, we then followed Tom and his brothers out to a staged assault on area pheasants, then set our equipment to film the family at dinner, the five children sans spouses. The dinner featured good-natured sparring between Tom and his mother, frequently with cutlery waved grandly in the air to make a point. The McCall siblings, all of whom were known to have strong opinions, rarely intervened as the governor and his white-haired mother vigorously asserted their views and personalities. The thought ran through my mind that we might wind up with film of Mother stabbing the governor with fork or knife as she played grandly to the camera.

As dessert approached, Tom's sister Jean disappeared into the kitchen and emerged with six slices of apple pie, placed on individual plates. Mother McCall erupted, "That's my apple pie! I baked it and I want to slice it and serve it!" A major crisis visited the table. The diplomatic Jean collected the pie plates, returned to the kitchen, and re-emerged with the pie in its original container. Dorothy beamed, re-sliced the pie, and handed it around the table. "And the cheese stands alone," muttered Jean as the rest rolled their eyes and dug into dessert.

Dorothy was given to picking up the telephone and calling her son—and anyone else whose ear she wanted to bend. The story of Dorothy's 1968 call to the White House to ask President Lyndon B. Johnson to relay a message to Tom to call his mother became a legend. She actually reached the president, who sent a telegram to the governor to call his mother. Tom kept his home phone number secret from his mother; it was a strange experience for me to have an unlisted number that the governor's mother lacked, but that was the nature of their relationship. Dorothy was notorious for calling Tom at work. Station colleagues recalled Tom fielding calls as he was frantically trying to finish a script, shouting, "Mother, I've got to go!"

Dorothy McCall once called Bob Straub to complain about his comments to Tom during a debate, awakening the early-to-bed Straub from a sound sleep. Bob was Tom's opposite socially. It was not unusual for him to begin yawning and stretching if a dinner party lasted past ten o'clock. If guests were slow to take the hint, he would start for the bedroom, leaving Pat to usher guests out the door. Bob was a light drinker; Tom was into his third martini by ten o'clock, enjoying robust conversation and jokes with no sign of worry for the morning ahead. He worked morning-newspaper hours as a young man and had enjoyed making the rounds of reporters' hangouts after the paper closed.

The Straubs lived less than a quarter-mile from our house on Orchard Heights Road, in an old farmhouse they had extensively remodeled. They loved the farmhouse and it made for good film in our 1970 documentary.

Bob and Pat enjoyed small groups gathered around the kitchen woodstove while Pat stirred up the dinner. Pat came out with an organic cookbook, *From the Loving Earth*; it reflected her culinary views—simple and nourishing, organic but not gourmet. Since it was well before the day when "organic" was a byword in many houses, the cookbook looked rustic and had a plain-folks appeal. Few cookbooks at that time had recipes for zucchini frittata, kale with sour cream, or fried parsnips. It was quite a contrast with the other governor's cookbook on our bookshelf, *ReMarkable Recipes* by Antoinette Hatfield, full of calories.

Pat came from a Philadelphia banking family and met Bob while she was a student at Smith College, the exclusive women's college near Dartmouth, where Bob did his undergraduate work and a master's in business. They were attracted by a common interest in the outdoors.

Pat was a class act in denim; she could hold her own with intellectuals or with farm wives, but she kept herself in the political background.

The Straub farmhouse overlooked open fields and peach orchards. Pat raised chickens, to which she became attached—Dixie once helped her splint the broken leg of a banty, while the little bird squawked its protest. Bob was attached to unruly German shepherd dogs, one of which bit a state policeman assigned as security; even close friends approached the house gingerly.

Dixie and Pat shared a love for gardening and, as mothers will, they talked about their children. Our son, David, born in 1963, had been diagnosed dyslexic, at that time a mystery condition with dire outcomes; the Straubs' son, Billy, was dyslexic and Pat sent Dixie to see Portland teacher and tutor Dorothy Blosser Whitehead, who used a tutoring method that seemed to work. Dorothy became Dixie's lifelong friend and mentor when Dixie changed her career path and became a learning specialist. We owed thanks to Pat Straub.

We would occasionally have dinner at the farmhouse, and I recall vividly an evening with San Francisco longshoreman philosopher Eric Hoffer, a close friend of the Straubs. Hoffer and Bob entered into a friendly but heated debate over the relative values of big cities versus natural or rural areas, with Hoffer taking the side of cities and Bob arguing for places resembling Oregon's open spaces. I cautiously sided with Hoffer, for reasons I cannot recall but which seemed reasonable at the time. Perhaps it was my "Eastern year" in Boston.

Close on the heels of our 1970 "Tom and Bob" documentary came the 1971 legislature, and it nearly did me in. I learned a lot of lessons about television, mostly the hard way. It was the final gasp of the old Senate Coalition, the ruling expediency of Republicans and conservative Democrats. Once again, Democrats had a majority in the Senate but couldn't hold sixteen votes to elect a president. It took the Senate thirteen days to do that, with Portland Democrat John Burns moving over to the coalition to break the stalemate.

Oregon's Senate in my two decades in the Capitol Press Room had in varying degrees three political parties: Republicans, "regular"

Democrats with an urban bias, and "conservative" Democrats with a rural or small-town bias. This was particularly true in the Senate but it also prevailed at times in the House. Republicans in both chambers were always more disciplined and could usually make a slim majority prevail. Will Rogers was correct when he said, "I belong to no organized political party; I am a Democrat." More than once I saw it demonstrated before my very eyes. The Senate coalition of Republicans and conservative Democrats ruled from 1961 through 1971. It was a potent political arrangement, shutting out urban liberals in favor of senators from small towns and rural areas.

Joey Tompkins and I set our camera in the Senate each day and tried to milk a story out of the stalemate; it was usually pretty sour milk. My stubborn insistence on standing by to film the great moment when the Senate stalemate was broken was a sure sign that my head was still in newspaper mode, and it added to my difficulties with Ed Godfrey. Godfrey wanted visually interesting stories, not a deadlocked Senate, and that thirteen days seemed like a year. Ed came down to Salem a couple of times during the legislative session, wanting me to introduce him around to key players, but he seldom had anything to say when we sat down with a key legislator or official, forcing me to carry the conversation in a very stilted environment. It was just strange, but in retrospect I realized that he had been a photographer, not a reporter, and lacked interviewing skills. Ed Godfrey was gone by 1980; he settled in for a long career at a station in Louisville. We were too different to be friends, but Ed and I had learned to get along and he supported my interest in documentaries, perhaps as a way to get me off the air for a brief period.

For several years after we moved our family to Portland, I tried to cover the legislature in addition to doing commentary, but by the end of the seventies it had become too difficult and I increasingly relied on capable colleagues Dan LaGrande and Stephanie Fowler to provide the hard news. The job of news analyst was both the best job in Oregon journalism and the most frustrating. The very nature of television abhorred stories without pictures, and sometimes politics was akin to watching paint dry. The ideal way to present analysis or commentary was to follow a reporter's story laying out the basic facts, leading into my analysis (so, what does this mean?) or commentary (here's what I think about that!). This formula tied up a camera crew covering what was often a non-visual story. So Godfrey and I were in constant conflict, made worse by his aversion to callers demanding my scalp or other body parts.

Joe Tompkins, Salem's leading freelance news photographer for four decades, decked out in his custom-made television kit for a day at the Oregon legislature. (Courtesy of author)

For many years, I kept on my office wall a framed note, scrawled on rough paper dated May 14, 1974, and signed with a giant X. It read: "Floyd McKay Democrat Abortion: You sure are a miserable, un-American radical son-of-a-bitch!!" I have no idea what prompted the outrage, but it made for a great story to tell after someone introduced me in glowing tones at a speaking engagement.

King Broadcasting liked the idea of news analysis, and I held the job longer than anyone in either Portland or Seattle. We treated analysis like an editorial-page column, as the view of the analyst, not the station. As long as Ancil Payne had my back at King headquarters, I knew he would resist the inevitable calls from offended politicians for my dismissal. He always did, probably in a lot more cases than I knew. Ancil had done some political work as a young man and he had friends in both parties—and he could charm the socks off a lamppost.

Preparing my on-air work, I wrote the script on my typewriter (I didn't use a computer until I left KGW in January 1987), using the phone, interviews, visits in and outside the office, and a personal filing system that I had started in Salem. No one saw my script until I dropped it in the producer's box before airtime. I sent a copy to Ancil in Seattle.

This was real journalistic freedom—and responsibility. There was no one to blame for a mistake—it was on my head. Local television at the time had a handful of positions similar to mine, and if you didn't mind stepping on sensitive toes, sometimes those of your friends, it was a wonderful life.

The job's freedom was also its most frightening aspect. In my newspaper jobs my copy always went through at least one editor, and questions of fact, style, or just simple grammar were instantly called to my attention. No one looked over my copy at KGW or had the experience or background to question my facts; Google was a far-off concept. There was virtually no editing for content in the entire television newsroom.

I heard news directors challenge reporters on their on-air appearance, their walking standups, or even their choice of attire, but seldom heard challenges to the factual content of their stories. Errors were seldom corrected on the air unless they were so egregious as to demand a retraction; the medium was not formatted for corrections or retractions. The primacy of image over content was obvious and it increased during my years in television.

It was during this time that the station also flirted with a cartoon commentary; as far as I know it was unique on local television. William Sanderson came to us from the *Oregonian,* where he was a reporter and backup cartoonist, a better talent than the aging Art Bimrose but politically a bit too liberal for the paper. Sandy drew two or three panels, and station employees did the voices, a role they enjoyed (Tom Craven, a studio director, was a particularly effective Richard Nixon). The punch line was on a sign carried by a small teddy bear in the last panel. Sandy's cartoons got under some skins, which is the nature of cartooning, and he struck a sensitive vein when he took on the venerable Portland Rose Festival.

The festival is a Portland tradition, more important in the seventies than later; to be a Royal Rosarian was an honor in business or civic ranks. Rosarians marched in the Rose Parade in an "ice cream suit" and straw boater. Richard Ross was a Rosarian, enormously proud of the distinction. Sandy drew a single-panel cartoon showing ranks of Rosarians parading in their fancy dress, looking properly aristocratic; the only sound was that of marching men. The camera then panned down to Sandy's teddy bear trailing the marchers— wielding a pooper-scooper! Nothing more was said. Ross was not amused and told Godfrey so.

A year later, Sandy did the exact same cartoon, and the newsroom wondered what would happen when Dick saw it. We didn't need to wait very long—Ross exploded, stormed into Godfrey's office, and refused to read the five o'clock news. The cartoon ran, but it wasn't long before Sandy's contract was not renewed, aborting our grand experiment in political cartooning.

We had the freedom to experiment and no one did that as well as Jon Tuttle. He was a storyteller and understood scripting for film better than anyone I ever worked with. He and cameraman Milt Ritter, who had a degree in music, choreographed a musical score from the unique pitches of cars and trucks driving on the metal surface of the Bridge of the Gods near Hood River. They blended the sound into a musical score; the piece ran on *NBC News* as well as our local newscast.

When I arrived at KGW, nearly all the stories were shot and edited on film. Film made for a madhouse editing process. The film was developed in our basement laboratory, then cut and spliced together on editing benches, with reporters hovering over the photographers as they put together a story. The edited stories were then spliced together and delivered on a large reel to master control, to be projected into the station's system. Stories on deadline were always hectic. Reporters and editors would shout at each other, film would break, and as five o'clock neared an editor would literally run the show down to master control. "Welcome to the longshoreman's picnic," was the cry of editor and later photographer Patricia Joy, the only woman in the film room when I arrived, one who gave as good as she took in the maelstrom.

The vagaries of film were actually a factor in the creation of a news format that began in television's early days and continues today in local newscasts. It was necessary to develop a format that could be immediately expanded or contracted to deal with sudden emergencies, particularly a film break or projector malfunction. This demanded a glib anchor not easily rattled in an emergency, a sports segment that could be shortened or expanded quickly, and a weather segment that could be cut to just local weather or expanded to cover the entire country. It didn't take long for audiences to develop loyalties, and this made it hard to change the format later when film was replaced by foolproof videotape. I wondered why, on a perfectly ordinary rainy Oregon day, we still ran a full weather segment. I got my answer when a late-breaking story actually did cause us to cut a few minutes from the weather segment. Viewers clogged the switchboard with complaints—"What are you doing, cutting Jack Capell off?" "We want to know if it snowed in Buffalo." Much the same reaction resulted from failure to list all the football scores. We were trapped in the body of our own history.

I had a natural bond with Forest Amsden, as both of us cut our teeth in newspapers and both loved politics. Amsden had the tough jobs of following Tom McCall as news analyst and later Ancil Payne as station manager. Forest realized that I was struggling with on-air presentations, and in my first year he did editorials a couple times a month. They were strong, calling for action, and I think we had a role in some positive developments, although none as powerful as Ancil's role in the Beach Bill.

We chipped away for years at Tri-Met's payroll tax exemption for banks and financial institutions (I had actually begun the crusade in

1969, in my *Statesman* columns). Rationale for the loophole was thin but bank lobbyists kept it alive. In 1974, I stood in front of the First National Bank tower and read my critique as the camera panned from the building's top to street-level. A bank executive called on Forest but we stayed on the chase and the following year the exemption was repealed as Portland legislators began to assert themselves in Salem.

It took some time to become comfortable with television's toll on personal life. Late dinners and long days were routine from my newspaper days; what was not routine was becoming "recognized" in public. I was never a television celebrity in the manner of anchors and, of course, Tom McCall. But dining out—a relatively rare experience with our young family—was often interrupted by a viewer with a comment, or simply the feeling of being observed and commented upon. People were invariably pleasant, however.

I had grown up in the "fly on the wall" concept of reporting: a reporter should be unobtrusive, watching and recording, not calling attention to himself. I was by nature a bit shy, and this style worked for me. Television, with its bulky cameras and bright lights, put both photographer and reporter on stage—clunking around, standing in front of people, every motion observed and often commented on by others in the audience—and I never did get comfortable with it, although it became instinctive to me over the years. I loved the ability to tell a story with visuals, and documentaries were a treat for me, with their need for research and in-depth reporting, where I was not constantly part of the show.

A return to print journalism was always tempting, but the *Oregonian* in that era was conservative to the point of stodgy and they owned the franchise in Portland. In 1974, I was approached by Ron Buel, Mayor Neil Goldschmidt's top aide and a former reporter for the *Wall Street Journal*. Ron was a good source and we shared common interests. He was planning a weekly alternative paper he would call *Willamette Week*. Would I be interested in becoming an investor in the new venture? We didn't have any excess capital or access to it, but I agreed to write a monthly political column, which

I did for four years. Ron's bent for hard news made an impact in Portland before the *Week*—like local television—fell under the spell of entertainment and social fads. In 1974 it was a tempting offer, but it was a wise decision to persevere and grow. My *Willamette Week* column gave me an outlet for longer-form writing, which the *Week* specialized in during that time.

I began to concentrate more on documentaries and in-depth news features, buoyed by my success with the massive *Timber Farmers* project of 1976, which won the nation's top broadcast news honor, the DuPont-Columbia Broadcast Award. Doug Vernon, my young photographer, was an unbelievable workhorse—he was hoisted to the top of a towering Douglas fir for one sequence—and we logged miles in our hiking boots. The hour-long documentary was accompanied by a fifteen-part series on the news hour. The effort was well received and King ran the documentary on all four stations. My best documentary work came after the *Timber Farmers* breakthrough, although the others were of the half-hour variety.

By 1978, I began to realize that the progressive political era in Oregon was nearing an end and we were in for a conservative run. The previous legislature had been tied in knots by a small band of rebellious Democrats in the House, and conservative initiatives were piling up. It was "Time for Atiyeh," the prescient ballot slogan that returned a more conservative Republican to the governor's office that year and slowed down the activism of the Tom and Bob years. California's Proposition 13 passed in 1978 and property-tax limits were on the move in Oregon.

I found myself in Salem less and less; we had good legislative reporters and Portland was becoming an exciting place to be a reporter, under the leadership of Mayor Goldschmidt. Sometimes in partnership with reporters such as Jon Tuttle and Don Porter, I was able to travel in and outside the region, including trips to Washington, DC, and to the Middle East for a 1982 documentary on Israeli-Palestinian tensions.

Ancil Payne came down to Portland one day, and over dinner in the London Grill asked me if I would like to go to Beirut and interview Yasser Arafat. King Broadcasting was concerned about what the owners felt was a one-sided network view of the Israeli-Palestinian conflict and wanted an unbiased view from the ground. I had no opinions on the conflict and immediately began gathering background information.

Photographer Mike McLeod and I accompanied a delegation of Seattle ministers to Beirut, where they were invited to meet Palestine Liberation Organization (PLO) leaders; it was a PLO public relations effort of the day. We interviewed Arafat and others and then independently moved on to Jordan, the occupied West Bank, and Israel. "Holy Land, Bloody Ground: The West Bank," aired on the eve of Israel's invasion of Lebanon. It was, as expected, controversial, but King stood by the product and never interfered. We visited the emerging Israeli settlements in the West Bank, and my conclusion that expansion of the settlements would prevent peace proved to be prescient.

I was having a lot of fun, but I knew time was running out on my approach to journalism. The handwriting was already on the wall. Technology began to dominate traditional newsgathering in the 1980s. Mobile satellite trucks allowed us to broadcast live feeds from almost anywhere—"Live!" became a nightly ritual, although often the only "news" was in the technology itself. We once took our entire news program on the road, setting up in small Oregon cities just to show what we could do.

Helicopters simply upped the ante; they cost a lot to lease and fly, so every night we had to discover something that could be covered from the air. In many cases the story could have been better covered from the ground. The big exception was when Mount St. Helens blew its top in 1980—that really was a job for helicopters and my colleagues did a superb job of covering a real news story.

Satellites affected us in many ways. The decline of meaningful local television news—even at KGW, one of the last holdouts—was partially due to the easy access satellites provided to national news and public relations feeds from politicians and advocacy groups. Producers religiously monitored the satellite, looking for action from someplace in the world. It was easy to find, and a riot in Rio could supplant a dull story from city hall or a feature on public education.

In search of a wider audience, we were dumbing down our content with visual tricks and an increased emphasis on special segments such as gardening and traffic problems. We began losing our serious viewers and never regained most of them. Those of us who refused to talk down to our audience were being voted off the island all across the nation as President Ronald Reagan's "Morning in America" cheerfulness permeated news as well as entertainment programming.

"Television news has abandoned any pretext of a community leadership role . . . and has become a deregulated tower of babble," I told an interviewer two decades later. The trend was already well underway when I left the station in 1986. We had begun to resemble all the others. I described a cross-country trip where I "tuned in to local news programs and could not find any regional differences; the same blonde twit, deep-voiced slightly older man, wisecracking sports guy, and bouncy weatherman with his electronic wizardry greeted me all the way from Washington, DC, to Portland."[2]

It is difficult to describe to a twenty-first century viewer the idea of a local television station with a community mission, but all Portland stations had talented people whose jobs were to promote community events. At KGW it was Neighbor Fair, a huge summer celebration at Tom McCall Waterfront Park, orchestrated by Joan Biggs. Television pre-Reagan was still regulated by the Federal Communications Commission (FCC), and stations were required to do public service. KGW was never in any danger of having its license seriously challenged, but we plunged into community events as if it mattered—and it did for us, because it was fun and attracted an audience.

We also did it because we could—from 1960 to 1990, owning a television company was "a license to print money," in the words of Ancil Payne. King Broadcasting chose to invest a great deal of

Governor Bob Straub steps up to acknowledge a crowd at KGW's annual
Neighbor Fair, one of the station's major public-service events in the 1970s.
(KGW-TV)

its profit back into the communities it served. Other companies
also made money, but none did community service as well as King.
Deregulation of broadcast under the Reagan administration gave stations an excuse to drop public-service programming, and most did.
We stayed with it as long as the Bullitts owned King, but technology
was beginning to change the playing field, and not in a positive way.

Cable television began as a way to reach remote communities that
couldn't get a signal with antennas or transmission relays. The combination of deregulation and new technology produced a rash of
cable outlets, some specializing in news and politics. Others brought
popular sports programming, consumer and food programs, and
so-called reality shows. The pioneers were squeezed and forced to
change their priorities and programs to compete with cable.

Cable brought with it the technology that I have often cited as the single biggest contributor to the decline of local television news: the innocuous remote-control clicker, which allowed viewers to surf endlessly through channels without leaving the sofa. A serious local news story (let alone commentary) could easily bring the sound of massed clicks as restive viewers searched for something that made noise or involved violence or sex.

Gone were the days when the three major networks and their local affiliates determined to a large degree the nation's agenda, and Walter Cronkite and his peers really were the most trusted people in America. After the Reagan deregulation, a new term emerged for television news—"free media"—as opposed to advertising or "paid media." Soon politicians could get "free media" by becoming celebrities. The dull work of legislating was relegated to print, and then the same troubles invaded print as well. Cable talking heads joined their radio counterparts in appealing to polarized audiences with a particular mindset.

I understand the argument that more voices and choices are better, and in buying soap and breakfast food that's true. But we have lost any semblance of a national consensus on anything, and the average busy and stressed American has no idea where to find reliable information in a sea of talking heads and recycled celebrities. Media has also lost most of its local owners, certainly in the Northwest. It was my particular good fortune to have worked at three family-owned media outlets during my twenty-nine-year career in Oregon journalism, and it was with great sadness that I witnessed, after my departure, degradation in the content and the soul of all three.

The *Springfield News,* where I began in 1958, was a scrappy, ambitious defender of its blue-collar city and arguably the best twice-weekly paper in Oregon. A few years after my 1960 departure it was sold to a chain and was finally shuttered in 2006. The *Oregon Statesman,* Oregon's second-oldest daily, continues as the *Statesman-Journal,* a pale shadow of the publication where I toiled from 1960 to 1970. Charles A. Sprague's heirs sold the paper in

1973 to the giant Gannett newspaper chain. It was an irreplaceable loss for readers and the community.

When Ancil Payne told me he would retire in 1987, I decided to look for other options. The opportunity came when Neil Goldschmidt was elected governor in November 1986 and asked me to come to the capitol with him. On December 19, I signed off the air, another Channel 8 commentator off to the governor's office.

Dorothy Bullitt died in 1989 and her heirs sold King Broadcasting to the Providence Journal Company, the first of three national media corporations to assume ownership of Northwest broadcasting's crown jewel. I left a company that still believed in something beyond profits, cared for its communities, and supported journalism and journalists. The retirement of Ancil Payne and death of Dorothy Bullitt changed the fate of King Broadcasting and another door shut behind my departure.

My old newsrooms are gone or diminished and the survivors take their orders from out-of-state corporations. Communities are deprived of leadership that helped forge an Oregon Story and helped defeat shortsighted faux-populist politics. We have lost more than an era.

SIX

Red Hat to Vortex:
The Reinvention of Tom McCall

Conventional wisdom holds that the state-sponsored Vortex rock festival and drug free-for-all in August 1970 was the turning point for governor Tom McCall and his legacy, which we came to call the Oregon Story, and I have contributed my bit. Vortex, however, was only the most *dramatic* event in a 1970 election that actually could have ended Tom's career after a single term as governor.

Tom had even pondered publicly—a typical tactic—about not running for a second term, in a long interview I did for the *Statesman* on January 13, 1969, on the eve of his second legislative session. He was still smarting from complete rejection of an ambitious tax package he sent to the 1967 legislature, based on an income-tax increase; Republican leaders in the House killed the bill without a hearing. Tom feared animosity from Speaker Bob Smith, who had been an obstacle in passage of the Beach Bill in 1967. He was unsure of the ground ahead, but obviously looking to run: "The kind of things we're doing really require more than four years of attention; they need watering and cultivating to bring to fruition. I hate to stop my work and campaign my head off, but I would be inclined now to think about doing it."

Would the 1969 legislature determine his course, I asked. "It might . . . it's the tone of voice in which they turn me down—if I am turned down . . . if they do it on a basis of just getting caught in some kind of partisan fight, and if very essential programs are victims of nothing but arrogant partisanship, then it would really be upsetting."

For Republican governor McCall, partisan trouble meant his own political party; House Republicans had been his major obstacle in the 1967 session. It was neither the first nor the last time that Tom was out of step with his own party—or the party was out of step with Tom. He was the governor and he did have Republican legislatures most of his two terms, but he was already aware that in order to take many of the bolder steps he hoped to take, he would need Democratic partners.

One of those partners was State Treasurer Bob Straub. In areas dealing with Oregon's environment and natural resources, the two men were ready and willing partners. Straub had a good 1967 session: he gained approval of a far-reaching law to allow the office to expand its investment practices, which would become his lasting legacy. Tom and Bob joined to secure a down payment on the Willamette Greenway with a modest $800,000 to purchase land.

Much of the acrimony of the 1967 regular session took place between parties, and Tom avoided the crossfire. At the close of the regular session, I wrote that the governor "survived the arduous and lengthy session with the respect and friendship of members of both houses and parties." His appointment of former legislators Ed Branchfield and John Mosser to key jobs in his administration helped. "But, mostly, it was the informal, frank-speaking manner of the governor himself, as he made himself available at all times to legislators of both parties and both houses." After eight years of a governor who set a rigid wall between executive and legislative branches, the McCall style impressed even when some of his proposals failed.

Republicans finally passed a sales tax in 1969, with a tepid endorsement from Tom. On June 3 voters delivered an eight-to-one trouncing to the proposal, which was heavily backed by the state's major industries and businesses. It was the sixth defeat for the sales tax since 1933 and the heaviest margin of loss. Sales taxes never got more than 29 percent of an Oregon vote, and that was in 1934. After the 1969 debacle, Tom chastised himself for backing a tax that he didn't favor and didn't expect to pass. His eyes were on other issues and I noted his increased use of the term "livability" to describe Oregon's most precious assets. He was on solid turf here, confident of public support, knowing that he would not encounter serious partisan opposition from Bob Straub or many other Democrats.

Governor McCall was caught in the middle several times as he approached the 1970 campaign, and he looked weak and indecisive as a result. He had supported the powerful State Highway Commission as it attempted to run a section of Highway 101 over beaches at Pacific City. Bob Straub's persistent opposition ultimately forced Tom to reverse field. In 1968, the governor again reversed field on Straub's Measure 6 initiative to increase highway taxes to purchase beach land, but by the time he came out for it, Big Oil had bought the election. Tom was caught unawares and out of town (in New York, plotting presidential strategy with Nelson Rockefeller) when the Oregon State Prison erupted in riots and fires in March 1968. He supported the Vietnam War as his constituents were turning against it.

McCall countered those negatives with his well-publicized leadership to pass a strong Beach Bill to protect the sands that Oregonians had always thought belonged to them. His bold Sanitary Authority move, described in Chapter Two, was a precursor of the more audacious McCall we were to see in future years. I was beginning to use the term "livability" in my weekly *Statesman* columns and assumed that would be the focus of a rematch between McCall and Straub.

My last piece of major reporting for the *Statesman* marked a turning point for Tom McCall, the first of two major developments in 1970 that allowed him to erase a shaky first term in office and emerge from the election as a courageous and popular leader. Tom's critical turning point would be the Vortex Rock Festival in August, but a secondary award should go to his dogged opposition earlier in the year to a Pentagon plan to ship huge quantities of nerve gas to the Umatilla Army Depot near Hermiston in northeastern Oregon.

The Pentagon inexplicably called it Operation Red Hat; Red Flag might have been a better label.

The governor was briefed by the US Army on December 1, 1969: nerve gas would be moved from storage on Okinawa—at the insistence of the Japanese government—to the Umatilla Army Depot, which already handled a variety of nasty chemicals. Tom at first accepted that the decision was really a federal one, but after an emotional appeal from his aide Ron Schmidt—who threatened to resign if the governor supported the plan—Tom came out in opposition.

I spent some time in Hermiston, for a four-part *Statesman* series in January. Hermiston mayor Joseph E. Burns—also the town's mortician—was sanguine about the lethal chemicals; his neighbors had lived with the threat for years, and the Depot's eight hundred good jobs in a town of fifty-three hundred made it an easy and patriotic decision to support the shipments. High school senior Mike Davidson conducted a telephone poll of the community and found 840 people supporting the shipments and only 218 opposing. "It doesn't matter how you are killed," he shrugged, "with a bullet, by being beaten to death, with an atom bomb or nerve gas." Even Stafford Hansell, a strong supporter of McCall on many fronts, declined to confront the US Army. I wrote, in an article for the *Seattle Times*:

> Stafford Hansell is a blunt and respected state legislator with a degree in economics. His computerized hog ranch is across the interstate freeway from the ammunition igloos. When the Army's plan was announced, he called his hands together and told them he had lived with the weapons of mass destruction for two decades and wasn't worried about a little more nerve gas. The workers agreed. "This is not a college community," Hansell observed. "We haven't argued the morality of the thing."

R. P. "Joe" Smith did argue the morality, from an unlikely position as district attorney of Umatilla County. Smith, a lean and articulate descendent of the Joseph Smith who founded the Mormon Church, was a bit of an anomaly in the rural county—a liberal Democrat, he had lived there only two years. He became the local lightning rod for the debate. "What you have down there (Hermiston) is a mini military-industrial complex," he told me, referring to chemicals stored at the depot as "genocidal weapons."

It was a precursor, I later realized, of any number of situations in which a small community would opt for good jobs despite an environmental or livability threat, while urbanites with more diverse economic opportunities would see a larger picture. Logging, coastal development, nuclear power, and field burning were some of the big-picture issues that looked quite different in Hermiston or Halsey than they did in Portland or Eugene.

As the Vietnam War generated anger and even violence nationwide, the nerve gas standoff brought into focus states' rights, and an increasingly unpopular war machine; ultimately it also brought national attention to Oregon's governor and the state's reputation for independence. Governor McCall wrote to President Nixon and Vice President Agnew to no avail. He lined up all but one of the Oregon-Washington congressional delegation to oppose the shipment. The holdout was critical, however; the hawkish Washington Democratic senator Henry "Scoop" Jackson had enormous influence with Nixon. When Jackson finally turned against the shipments in May 1970 they were abandoned. Jackson was credited for the victory, but McCall had kept the battle alive.

It took six months for the battle to play out, during which Tom emerged as a stronger and stronger advocate of Oregon citizens. In the midst of the battle, I moved to the unfamiliar world of television news, my home for the next seventeen years. My very first commentary, on April 13, 1970, was on the nerve gas issue. It was a somewhat convoluted argument—too complex for television, as I would learn—and it was based on the low-profile Third Amendment to the US Constitution (you know, the one prohibiting the quartering of soldiers in civilian homes). I argued:

> The Founding Fathers had no crystal ball to tell them that two centuries later the Army would try to move trainloads of lethal nerve gas through

the Pacific Northwest in the name of national security. Yet the circumstances that led to the Third Amendment are similar to today's gas controversy. The basic issue is the same. It is the matter of civilian control of the military . . . We are not being asked to quarter soldiers in our homes. But somehow the difference between that and having trainloads of lethal gas shipped through our backyard is a nicety that escapes us.

My new employers were probably holding their heads in dismay as I used my introductory commentary to declaim on an obtuse legal theory!

We saw in the nerve-gas campaign a governor beginning to feel the power of personal leadership. During his first term, Tom's efforts were largely environmental and successful. But he had failed to impose his will on the legislature and he had muffed the ball on taxes, beach highways, the prison riot, and several other happenings. He remained popular, but politicians and reporters who watched state government did not see a strong governor.

Despite his courage on the stump and in speeches, Tom was extraordinarily cautious when his own political future might be at stake. He disliked confrontation and did not take criticism well. The net result was a reluctance to push hard for his initiatives, and during his first term a great deal of the hardball politics was left to his executive assistant, Ed Westerdahl, who had no qualms about a good political fight.

The Operation Red Hat battle was the beginning of a new image for Tom as one who would stand up to the White House, the Pentagon, and anyone else who threatened the livability of Oregon. At one point, he emotionally declared that he would stand on the railroad tracks to stop a train delivering the nerve gas. The issue went beyond environmentalism, and it stiffened his spine for the campaign ahead. But for the idealism and courage of Ron Schmidt, it might not have happened.

The nerve gas affair ultimately would prove to be one bookend for a 1970 campaign that began much closer than was generally assumed. An April 12 poll published in the *Oregonian*—during the heat of the nerve-gas debate—showed a dead heat: among registered

Governor Tom McCall and his wife, Audrey, with their troubled son, Sam, whose issues with substance abuse caused trauma for the entire family. (Gerry Lewin Photo)

voters, Bob Straub had a 43–42 lead and among prospective voters Tom McCall had a 41–40 edge.

A month later, the primary election pointed to Tom's Achilles' heel—his own Republican Party. He was always vulnerable to a strong challenge from conservatives within his party, but in 1970 as an incumbent running against two unknowns, he drew an unimpressive 74 percent of Republicans. His total of 183,298 votes was only 615 votes more than Bob Straub won against seven minor candidates. Even more than in 1966, Tom would need to fish in Democratic and Independent waters.

He was also facing a serious personal tragedy that was becoming public: the drug addiction of his younger son, Samuel Walker McCall III. Tom and Audrey had a heartbreaking time with Sam, whose serious drug habit had escalated into petty thievery. I sat with Tom one day in 1965 while he despaired at an early episode, alternately blaming himself and the medication his son had become addicted to after an illness and surgery. Tom's craggy face was wracked with grief and guilt, tears were near in reddened eyes, and his bulky frame slumped in his oversized leather chair. There was nothing I could say or do, so I listened to him grieve.

Sam McCall's illness took his life at an early age. We wrote stories in 1969 when we learned that state police had been pressed into special duty to search for Sam, but we didn't always know about other such errands, and we made no special effort to seek them out. In later days, there would have been reporters all over the story. During the 1970 campaign, Sam was involved in a serious incident at Dammasch State Hospital, where he was being treated; the governor's office was forced to go public with more details of Sam's troubles. That July, Tom and Sam agreed to do an interview with Sander Vanocur of NBC for the network's *First Tuesday* show; it was a quiet time for politics but things were heating up in Portland, leading to Vortex.

Father and son gained public sympathy for going public with their problem. The Straub campaign never used Tom's family agony in any way, although Sam showed up at the Straubs' house several times, as if to challenge his father. Bob Straub, who had children of a similar age, counseled the troubled youth as best he could. Reporters did not learn until much later that, as Sam's problems deepened, a fund was created by Glenn Jackson and several wealthy friends to pay for Sam's treatment at the Menninger Clinic in Topeka, Kansas. That would have raised legitimate political concerns, but it was a well-kept secret for years.[1]

The candidates differed very little on major issues, even on taxation, where it was generally known that the failed sales tax was never Tom's idea. The Vietnam War began to intrude, however, particularly after President Nixon ordered an expansion into Cambodia. Campus unrest threatened to explode into violence, and it was a field that invited demagoguery.

Students descended on the capitol and the governor walked out to meet them; he defused their anger but yielded no ground in his support for the war. He also toyed with various proposals to get tough with campus protesters; Portland State and the University of Oregon were seething and political pressure was building. I registered concern when a group calling itself Citizens Coalition for Social Responsibility announced it would be monitoring campus activities and names would be taken.

Greater danger was on the way, however, as Portland prepared to host the annual convention of the uber-patriotic American Legion, where President Nixon was to speak. War protesters swung into action, raising fears of Chicago 1968 re-dux. I'd been there, done that. On August 6 an incongruous consortium of the hip and the clean-shaven announced, with Ed Westerdahl speaking for the governor, that the state would sponsor a rock festival during the convention to divert the expected throngs of youth. I immediately endorsed the idea:

> Governor McCall and the Clackamas County officials who are cooperating . . . will be accused of pandering to hippies and dissenters. And if there is trouble at the rock festival, the criticism will double.

> Majority sentiment in the state probably runs against rock festivals in any form. Particularly against a free one backed by the state. So the easy political route is to do nothing about the upcoming convention and have lots of police and national guardsmen on hand. There's plenty of precedent for that approach. Mayor Daley used it in 1968 in Chicago. His standing with the voters improved as a result. But those who call for a strong hand and criticize the governor and others for backing the rock festival need to be reminded of the alternative. The alternative to planning to avoid chaos is often chaos itself.

Tom's decision to sponsor a rock festival at McIver Park in rural Clackamas County put his political career on the line. Serious violence at the park, a death from a drug overdose, or a deadly accident would have fallen on his shoulders only weeks before voting took place.

Throngs of young people descended on McIver Park in Clackamas County for Vortex, the nation's only state-sponsored rock festival. Lots of fun, some fueled by drugs, diverted protestors from the American Legion Convention in downtown Portland. (Gerry Lewin Photo)

Privately, I felt Tom had overreacted; I simply couldn't believe the so-called Peoples Army Jamboree could put together the fifty thousand insurgents the FBI was predicting. But I had no way of knowing who was correct; paranoia was beginning to manifest itself on all sides and I felt a decision to do nothing would lead only to disaster. On the eve of the convention, the governor made a powerful speech carried statewide by all broadcast media. We held our breath.

The overwhelming majority of the thousands of young people at Vortex took no notice of its political ramifications, for Tom or anyone else; they were there to have a good time. And they did; they certainly did. Drug laws were blatantly violated, as was the societal rejection of public nudity. Uniformed police were kept away, although a few undercover officers were on site to help calm things down if needed. It really wasn't. It wasn't my generation at McIver, and when I made the obligatory tour with several colleagues, I felt more voyeur than reporter, but I saw nothing that made me think Vortex was a mistake. Somewhere around thirty-five thousand revelers were at McIver at one point.[2]

Portland reporters and editors resisted the temptation to sensationalize the carryings-on at Vortex and, by and large, reporting was balanced and fair. No reader or viewer doubted that drugs were ingested and smoked and that nudity was widespread. Broadcast codes and common sense dictated that photos of nudity—at least that of the frontal variety—would not be shown to scandalize or titillate our viewers, although that didn't prevent a good crowd around our film-editing benches. Most of our younger photographers and reporters were not strangers to marijuana and older hands had long since learned to tolerate the practice. The fact that media were not scandalized went a long way toward calming the waters. The governor had lots of friends in Portland's newsrooms, and most of us gave him slack that another governor might not have been granted.

The threatened invasion of thousands of Yippies and violent anti-war protestors simply didn't happen. The legionnaires had a subdued parade; as many people clapped as booed, and downtown Portland emerged unscathed. Portland's establishment was relieved; its leadership had supported the Vortex gamble and felt vindicated.

We were all pragmatists with Vortex; we allowed the law and ordinary codes of public decency to be broken and the drug use and nudity to be flaunted as well. I thought the occasion would soon lead to legalization of marijuana, just as we had ended prohibition. In a post-Vortex commentary I noted the irony: "An individual caught with marijuana on his person can wind up in jail. But put twenty thousand individuals together and much more serious drug use is freely allowed. Not because society condones its use, but because society is all but powerless to enforce the law against a mass of violators." I predicted that legalization of marijuana was just around the corner; the corner took forty-four years!

The entire Vortex affair showed Tom McCall at his audacious best, and as the debris was cleaned up at McIver Park, the hopes of Bob Straub were effectively swept away as well. Straub had been skeptical of Vortex but kept his views very low-key, mildly criticizing the breaking of state law and doubting the need for such actions. Bob was a true "straight arrow" in terms of morality, and the concept of a state-run drug festival was beyond his ken. His views in any event were swallowed by the tide of favorable media reaction and the sense on the part of many ordinary citizens that Vortex said more about our governor than encouragement of loose behavior on the part of a lot of young people. Tom became a national celebrity.

Talk of an indecisive governor, a flip-flopper on big issues was now in the past and a newly energized chief executive emerged from the marijuana smoke. Bob Straub campaigned energetically and tried to switch the spotlight to economic issues, but he and his friends knew it was over. If nerve gas was one bookend for 1970, clearly Vortex was the other.

The governor had made the critical decision on Vortex—only he could involve the National Guard or commandeer a state park—but the work of key staffers, Ed Westerdahl in particular, made the gamble work. Vortex was the work of a good executive, a quality often overlooked in the attention given to Tom's messaging talents. He had learned from his experience as chief aide to Governor McKay, but he later had staff troubles as secretary of state. In the governor's office, however, Tom applied lessons from both previous positions, to his benefit. He had a very good staff and he used it; Tom was a real listener, not a person who simply kept quiet until he could make his point.

In the case of Vortex, he used Westerdahl to his fullest ability. Westerdahl was worn out after Vortex and a full term as Tom's right hand; he resigned and was replaced by Bob Davis, a moderate Republican from Medford who had served in the legislature. It was a superb choice; Davis had respect on both sides of the aisle and he knew legislative procedure and protocols. Tom's second term would be all about legislation; the Oregon Story was about to be fleshed out in the wake of the great rock festival.

The 1970 general election was my first on television and it went well, with kudos from colleagues. When I broke into journalism, election news was largely the work of newspapers and the Associated Press—member newspapers quickly fed the AP wire with local results, a very efficient cooperative system. KGW designed a special election night news set, with desks for reporters to read local election results. I was on the main desk with Dick Ross. My job was to analyze results, do an interview if a candidate dropped by, and declare an election victory. A live interview with a defeated candidate, particularly if he had been drinking, was dancing with a live grenade. I always kept it light, hoping they would respond in kind, but on a couple of occasions sore losers had to be herded away from the set. We eventually dropped the studio interviews when we could connect remotely to a candidate's celebration—or wake, as the case might be.

Live election coverage was an entirely new challenge for me, but I called on an old newspaper tactic to make it work. I set up a network of courthouse correspondents to call in returns and updates from key counties. I determined which counties to watch—how big a vote would a Democrat need in a downstate county to become a statewide winner and, conversely, was a Republican running well in Portland or Eugene? In 1970, it was quick and easy: Governor McCall was re-elected with 55 percent of the vote.

Calling a winner in the McCall-Straub contest came early in the evening and gave KGW a huge free promotion. *Oregonian* photographer David Falconer was staked out with Tom in his hotel room watching returns—on his old station, of course—and Tom was glued to the set as I declared his win. David got a great shot and the *Oregonian* played it at the top of a full-page election spread. I heard the next day that David and a desk editor caught all sorts of grief; at that time the *Oregonian* owned our closest rival, KOIN. Tom autographed a copy of David's photo, "To one star of General

Governor Tom McCall wins re-election and watches as KGW news analyst Floyd McKay calls the victory in 1970; McKay held the job originated by McCall at KGW. (David Falconer, *Oregonian*)

Election night from another; from McCall to McKay." After a very tense night following eight months of newcomer nerves, I felt finally that television might work out.

Ed Godfrey sent me a very gracious note, stating that he had "never seen a better, more professional presentation by any news department at the local level. We ended up with the edge on the overnight ratings and it was due to the efforts of all of you." Election coverage, where I had a strong background and knowledge of the players, was always a strong point during my television career, and the station actually called me back from retirement in academe to analyze the election of 1992.

I could have called Governor McCall's victory a week after Vortex, the impact was so strong, but Portland had four city council races and one—Tom Walsh's aggressive challenge to Commissioner Frank Ivancie—was very close. There was a sense of excitement about Portland's election; political newcomers Walsh and Neil Goldschmidt mobilized a small army of enthusiastic supporters with a promise of new ideas and new energy at city hall. Ivancie won a narrow victory and settled into a role as a lonely defender of the old Portland City Hall crowd. Newcomer Goldschmidt won big, as did Lloyd Anderson and Connie McCready, appointed earlier in the year to fill vacancies. Portland's leg of the Oregon Story, which I describe in Chapter 10, would soon be rolling, as Tom McCall prepared to use his second term to seal his legacy.

The election of 1970 kept Republicans in control of the legislature, although it was razor-thin in the Senate; it was the last gasp of the old coalition Senate. In the House, Republican speaker Bob Smith led thirty-four to twenty-six.

Governor McCall was heavily committed to a measure destined for the Oregon Pantheon: the Bottle Bill, introduced in 1969 but killed in committee, was revived and enacted in 1971. The Bottle Bill had less long-term significance than the Beach Bill and land-use legislation, but it was an easy headline, with great visuals and stereotypical heavies from industry, and anyone could relate to it. The Bottle Bill was a premier example of unusual alliances in Oregon in this period, as people were able to set aside past disagreements—sometimes very strong disagreements—and work together for a common purpose.

America was a throwaway society in the post–World War II era; gone were the frugal patriotic wartime days of recycling everything from paper and bottles to rubber bands and tinfoil. Post-war consumers ate and drank from throwaway packaging and threw away bottles and cans in particular. Going for a hike was a day at the junkyard. We took to collecting the trash in a backpack to get it off a trail or streamside. Richard Chambers, a Salem resident who had a beach cabin at Pacific City, had taken up that practice with beach litter. Working with his friend, Representative Paul Hanneman of

Cloverdale, he developed a measure to require a deposit on throw-away beer and soft drink cans, based on a British Columbia law that Chambers discovered in the newspaper.

In some ways, Republican Hanneman was an unlikely ally—he had opposed the Beach Bill just two years before. But his friend's enthusiasm was contagious and Paul promised to introduce Chambers' bill in the 1969 legislature. Paul Hanneman was a likeable man somewhat set in his conservative political views, but colleagues respected him even in opposition. He had trouble getting sponsors for Chambers' bill, however, and it drew opposition from Speaker Smith, who buried it in committee. The governor also opposed Chambers' plan; he set up his own organization, Stop Oregon Litter and Vandalism (SOLV), an advertising and public relations campaign favored by grocers and other opponents of the 1969 Bottle Bill.

But as his 1970 re-election campaign gathered momentum, McCall changed course and urged revival of the Bottle Bill in the 1971 legislature. The two-year delay allowed Chambers to rally the public, and the news media found it easy to show litter and garbage on beaches, streams, trails, and highways. The delay also allowed the container industry to prepare a counterattack, encouraged by the re-election of Speaker Smith, their ally in 1969. Smith wasn't helping the container industry in 1971, however, and the bill passed the House easily (54–6).

Industry dug in when the Bottle Bill hit the state senate and the capitol reeked of New York suits and nifty briefcases filled with legal opinions. But instead of intimidating the yokels from 'Oreegone," they built hostility with their heavy-handed tactics. Oregonians prided themselves on a lack of corruption in legislative matters. Senator Betty Roberts, whose committee handled the bill, and Senator Ted Hallock were incensed at what amounted to bribe offers. Then everyone was incensed and the bill passed, 22–8. As Tom signed the bill, he termed it the "innovative highlight of my ten years in elective office."

The Bottle Bill was emulated in several other states and became part of Oregon's growing national reputation. Tom used the bill as a calling card as he expanded his growing national image for environmental leadership. The Bottle Bill was easy for anyone to understand and it was common sense—somewhat like the talkative governor himself.

Don Stathos, a freshman Republican from Ashland and a great advocate of alternatives to automobiles, added a notch on Oregon's environmental belt without any help from the governor. Representative Stathos wrote a law setting aside 1 percent of state and local highway funds for bicycle paths and lanes; it fit the pattern of the Oregon Story (See a profile of Stathos in Chapter 8).

Oregon's economy was still strong, and budgets for new and existing environmental programs were increased, some by large amounts. Legislators also began work on other big ideas that would require future sessions to fund. One was Senate Bill 10, requiring counties to finish zoning plans; the modest little law later became a very big law, Oregon's groundbreaking statewide land-use planning system.

Tom had one more legislative session to complete his goal of Oregon as a national model of livability and sustainability, a place that protected its jewels and was selective about how it grew and prospered. The 1973 legislature would also be his first with Democrats in control of both House and Senate, and he rode into Salem that year with public acclaim and a growing national reputation. He would put this to the test in his final two years in office and, by the time he was finished, most of the Oregon Story would be written.

Profile THE ODD COUPLE: RON SCHMIDT AND ED WESTERDAHL

Tom McCall made some poor appointments, as every governor does, but his inner circle was very strong. His administrative assistant and spokesman, Ron Schmidt, and his executive assistant, Ed Westerdahl, had been with Tom since his 1964 campaign for secretary of state. After hearing a speech Tom gave to a Jaycees convention, Westerdahl and Schmidt signed up immediately and became the bulwark of Tom's campaign. Both were experienced in the public arena, Ed as an effective lobbyist for Portland General Electric (PGE) and Ron as public relations manager for the Lloyd Center, the first major shopping mall in the nation. They were an enormously effective pair despite—or perhaps because of—very different styles and roles.

Neither went to Salem with Tom in 1965; the secretary of state's office had no positions suited to their talents or interests. Schmidt began organizing for the 1966 gubernatorial campaign, but Westerdahl took no part until the campaign's final moments. Tom was in some trouble after poor performances in debates, and Schmidt feared a blow-up. He called Westerdahl and pleaded for help. The pair resurrected a tactic they had used in similar circumstances in 1964: they got Tom out of sight for the closing campaign days. Ed holed up with the candidate in a Portland hotel until the clock ran down. "It was just the two of us; no one came in and no one left," Ed later told Brent Walth. It had worked in 1964 and it worked again two years later. Reporters and the Straub campaign were kept ignorant with a variety of ruses until it made no difference.[3]

It was classic Ron and Ed; they were the yin and yang, the Click and Clack of a very successful operation. The pair in some ways worked similarly to the way Warne Nunn and Travis Cross worked with Governor Hatfield during his two terms. Cross played a critical role in press relations—Hatfield was not comfortable with informal encounters with reporters—but his boss seldom left him with messes to clean up, and Schmidt's boss often did. Nunn came out of the state bureaucracy and was comfortable with underlings; Westerdahl came from private business and could be very tough and sometimes brutal with subordinates. Both, however, spoke for the boss and everyone knew that.

Schmidt and Westerdahl were intensely loyal to Tom McCall, but they were quite different in personal style and interests. They traveled in different social circles but joined up as partners in a public relations and advertising business with John Pihas in 1980; it soon became one of the state's largest and most influential.

With his 1950s-style crew cut and crisp demeanor, Westerdahl played the role of enforcer and allowed Tom to be the softie in the office. He delivered the hard news to subordinates and Tom alike; he could appear to be a martinet and sometimes he was, but Tom needed a tough guy to shore up his own insecurities in his first term in office.

Ron Schmidt was—in a term of the day—a snappy dresser, and presented the image of someone who was hip and cool in contrast to the controlled Westerdahl; Ron wore sideburns and flamboyant neckties to Ed's crew cut and narrow ties. Schmidt was deeper than his flashy image, however; with his wife, Edie, he was a serious art collector and served nationally on the President's Commission on the Arts and the board of directors of the John F. Kennedy Center for the Performing Arts in Washington, DC.

Westerdahl, too, was a complex individual; he'd been an Army intelligence officer at age twenty. After his partnership with Schmidt and Pihas, he served as president of Metra Steel, which later became Schnitzer Steel Products, an industry giant. Later he owned a large equipment rental company and a small steel company. Shortly before his death in 2010, Ed sat down for a long interview with Oregon Public Broadcasting, for its program on Vortex. As was his wont, he was concise and to the point, obviously proud of what he, Ron, and Tom had pulled off but careful to control his emotions. Ron was gone by then, felled in 1992 at age fifty-six after a long battle with cancer of the esophagus. Together with their boss, governor Tom McCall, Schmidt and Westerdahl were lasting models for successors in the office.

SEVEN   People for . . . Friends of . . .

Americans—including normally well-mannered Oregonians—were in the streets in the 1960s and 1970s, two decades of turmoil that shook to the roots our faith in representative government. Oregon was fortunate in its leadership at this time, but we were not immune from the national trauma of the Vietnam War and the moral corruption of the Nixon White House.

Protests engendered by those traumatic events riveted our eyes on front-page photographs of grief and chaos, largely overshadowing a movement that would outlast these outpourings and produce—in our part of America—results that have lasted half a century and continue to define Oregon. We had our share of marches against the war, our reactions to the deaths of national figures, and our rallies on the state capitol steps. While this was taking place, a new generation of Oregonians was moving to the fore; sometimes it was their first exposure to politics and important issues.

The times sprouted a number of organizations that used the term "friends" in their name and their literature. "Friends of" became an alternate version of the "people for" campaigns that Bob Packwood pioneered in the 1960s. "People for" lawn signs were still heavily used by Republicans, but "friends of" were increasingly linked to Democratic or Progressive groups—1000 Friends of Oregon, Friends of the Columbia Gorge, and so forth. "People for" was candidate-oriented, but "friends of" was cause-oriented, which seemed to attract liberals. It was, perhaps, a more intimate term than "people."

Whether one called them "friends of" or "people for" or by a host of other names, these groups were at the root of the seventies renaissance in Portland. Activists, sometimes working with professional staff of elected officials, organized protests and letter campaigns, spoke articulately at endless public hearings and forums, and let political candidates know who they were.

Umbrella agencies also emerged to give small groups the larger clout of combined effort. Oregon Environmental Council, formed in 1969, spoke for several smaller environmental organizations and was an effective advocate for a host of environmental initiatives. Director Larry Williams understood the media and was a good source and later a close friend; he was a one-man show for years but OEC in 2015 has a sizeable staff and represents both organizations and individuals.

The Oregon Story proved to be a lure for young professionals seeking rewarding careers outside private business or government agencies. A small industry grew out of the fledgling efforts of the 1970s, and the emerging field of nonprofit organizations became a formidable force. Their causes and campaigns drew an interesting array of young people. Neighborhood volunteers worked for a better school or to stop a freeway or garbage dump; architects and planners added to their day jobs by helping activists promote livable urban spaces.

Much of the activism was of a traditional nature, hatched over coffee cups or wine glasses as homeowners, hikers, parents, or naturalists shared concerns about what was being done—or not done—in this special place. Many of the best organizers were women who were well educated but underemployed or choosing to stay home with young children; they were eager to find outlets for their intelligence and energy. They networked in the old-fashioned way before the advent of social media, with neighbors, friends from church or professional groups, parents with kids in the same school or soccer team, college classmates.

Environmentalism of one sort or another was an excellent arena for activists; in most cases it cut across party lines. Neighborhoods threatened by a freeway contained both Democrats and Republicans, and the noise and degradation of air quality affected people equally. Clean rivers and controls on suburban sprawl carried little partisan baggage. Schools, including the huge and powerful Portland Public Schools, were under attack by parents as well as the courts—not always for the same reasons.

Volunteers such as Janet McLennan, a powerful force in stopping the highway on Nestucca Spit; or Betty Merten and Elsa Coleman, who played a huge role in defeating the Mount Hood Freeway, happened to be Democrats. Richard Chambers, who pioneered the Bottle Bill, was apolitical. Hector Macpherson, who worried about urban sprawl and its impact on farmlands, was a Republican farmer. His Linn County constituent Liz VanLeeuwen, a Republican farmer who saw things from a different angle, organized her neighbors to oppose the Willamette Greenway. Columbia Gorge defender Nancy Russell was a Republican, OEC pioneer Larry Williams was a Democrat. Their issues and followers cut across party lines.

None of these issues involved deep-seated moral or religious questions. That came later, as the Republican Party coalesced around opposition to abortion and pushed for school prayer and other religious tenets. Democrats in turn sought greater racial and gender rights and a woman's choice in the abortion debate. Bipartisanship was more difficult to achieve in these areas, which were not easily negotiable, and the heat generated by social issues damaged the ability to coalesce around secular issues as well.

America in 1970 was beset with activism on all fronts—not the least of them the ongoing Vietnam War—and many people found respite in a national event that had profound consequences for the future. Earth Day was unveiled on April 22, 1970, during my first week at KGW. It inspired two commentaries and a *Viewpoint* program on which my guest was Denis Hayes, the national coordinator of Earth Day. Denis lived across the Columbia in Camas; Earth Day made him a national figure at age twenty-six. He eventually wound up in Seattle running the Bullitt Foundation, established by the King Broadcasting family.

I thought Earth Day was important as a means of bringing people together for goals we could all celebrate, and I particularly liked the way schools were participating in the celebration. As the week concluded, I observed:

> For some it was the realization that after years of battling for environmental quality, they were no longer alone. For others it marked a new awareness. Some were surprised to find they could question conventional wisdom and not sound like a heretic. Certainly it marked a shift in our national goals and our national heroes. For half a century we have worshipped at the shrine of the engineer and technologist. We have asked only if it could be done. Now we are asking if it must be done. The new heroes are the ecologists. They have replaced the automaker, the dam builder, the atomic scientist and even to some extent the space engineer. This is a significant shift. It has not been lost on political leaders . . . But if we are to make this shift more than a passing event, we must be prepared for the next Environmental day. That day is May 26 . . . Oregon's Primary Election. All the lofty ambitions of this week are lost if we don't translate them into action at the polls. We have asked tough questions of the scientists. Now we must ask them of the politicians.

Earth Day was a temporary respite from battles on many fronts and it allowed thousands of people to come together on common goals. The shift in power that I predicted was never complete—nor should it have been—but the scales were better balanced than in the earlier half of the century. Neither technology nor engineers were on the way out—quite the contrary in the coming four decades—but ecologists now had a seat at the table.

Oregon had two environmentalists at the top of the ballot that year: Republican governor Tom McCall and Democratic treasurer Bob Straub were a win-win choice. But many legislative races posed significant differences. Activists at the state and local levels were working on measures from the Bottle Bill to urban housing and mass transit, from the Willamette Greenway to field burning. Activists came in all shapes, sizes, and genders, but many were not Oregon-born. In the post-war era, many young couples looked for a new place to make a fresh start. Oregon's growing reputation as clean and green, independent and progressive, began luring these young people. Some came from cities deteriorating with crime and pollution, others from rural areas where the land and the job base were played out. Many were fresh out of college, with idealism and energy ripe for a cause. The trend that began in the wake of World War II produced many of the state's political leaders.

Bob Straub, Jim Redden, and Bob Duncan all moved from elsewhere to start careers in Oregon; so did Betty Roberts, Vera Katz, and Jason Boe. All were Democrats and they were critical in building and holding the party in power. The Republican roots in Oregon were deeper, and natives were more prominent in the GOP leadership, including Mark Hatfield, Bob Packwood, Vic Atiyeh, and Clay Myers.

Portland needed new blood; the city had not shared in Oregon's population growth. Portland had only 366,383 residents in the 1980 census, 7,245 less than in 1950. People were flowing into the suburbs; Portland during this thirty-year period was outflanked by mushrooming growth in unincorporated East Multnomah County, which lacked many building regulations of the city. Growth also took place in Clackamas and Washington counties and across the Columbia River in Clark County. But 1980 was the nadir for Portland; by 2000 Portland had grown to 529,121, up 42 percent from the 1980 low, breaking the half-million mark for the first time. Much of the city's growth was through annexation of areas needing sewers.

Immigrants to the city in the slow-growth 1960s and 1970s lacked numbers but were heavily involved in their new hometown. Something in this period seemed to attract activists; together they laid the groundwork to make Portland the magnet that it became in the 21st century. Activists could be roughly divided into three classifications: 1) the Lone Wolf, totally dedicated to the point of zealotry but often amazingly successful in the long run; 2) partisan but unofficial groups that often eclipsed official Republican or Democratic party organizations; and 3) volunteer groups focused on specific issues or projects.

Richard Chambers and Lloyd Marbet epitomized the Lone Wolf activist. Their crusades were, respectively, the Bottle Bill and efforts to shut down nuclear power in Oregon. Chambers won his battle and retired from the field. Marbet continued to work the progressive front lines for years after nuclear power was effectively ended in Oregon. Chambers never sought elective office; Marbet campaigned several times without success and was an inveterate sponsor of initiative measures.

A Lone Wolf has learned the system but is willing to go outside it if ignored. The wolfster finds multiple ways to be heard. Lloyd Marbet stood out but never built an organization. A traumatized Vietnam veteran who lived to fight battles of a different kind, his personal commitment and the power of his anger drove his activism. "Persistence powered our ultimate victory," Marbet told *Willamette Week* in 2005. "We just came back again, again and again at them."[1]

Marbet did not shut down nuclear power in Oregon alone; working at the same time but usually not in concert with Marbet, the Trojan Decommissioning Alliance (TDA) and Physicians for Social Responsibility, among others, passed Ballot Measure 7 in 1980, effectively barring any future nuclear plant. While Marbet was laboring—with support from attorney Greg Kafoury—in court and in front of public agencies, TDA occupied Trojan three times in 1977 and 1978; hundreds were arrested. Harassed by Marbet and by antinuke organizations, PGE finally was forced from the field and closed Trojan, which had become untenable to maintain and needed costly repairs.

Oregon's antinuclear image came without the blessing of the major players in the Oregon Story; none of the governors of this time supported a shutdown, nor did most of the media, including myself. For my part, I spoke often on nuclear issues but never really confronted the heart of nuclear energy.

In 1972, I deplored a plan by PGE to build a nuclear plant on the coast near Cape Kiwanda—which I was campaigning to place in public ownership. Ray Atkeson, whose photographs defined Oregon's image in the public eye, hiked the cape with me and a small group, including Norma Paulus, to call attention to the fact that it was for sale by its owner, McMinnville banker B. A. McPhillips.

Ray and I were concerned about the intrusion of a big nuke and its transmission lines on the cape's vistas. Those concerns were proper but missed the overall question of building more nuclear plants. McPhillips later gave the cape to the state and PGE dropped its plans as antinuke protests increased. Oregon's rejection of nuclear power could be placed in the Oregon Story category as a true example of citizen activism despite the indifference or opposition of political leaders—or media, for that matter.

Not until the Washington Public Power Supply System (WPPSS) collapsed in the 1980s did I truly understand the full impact of giant nuclear plants that were planned in the Northwest by public and private boosters. Driven by draconian predictions of massive power shortages as the region grew, the public utility boards that made up the consortium known as WPPSS committed bonding for five giant nuclear plants in Washington. When construction estimates hit $27 billion in 1982, the WPPSS governing body pulled the plug, the biggest municipal bond default in US history. Only one of the five plants was built; the bond default was in the courts for thirteen years.[2]

WPPSS ultimately forced a genuine Northwest commitment to replace costly nuclear energy with conservation and alternative sources. Those decisions were driven by economics, not safety or public health. The entire WPPSS affair, driven by the hubris of public officials who were sure they knew what was best for everyone else, perhaps defined the end of a post-war era of trust and good feelings about government in the Pacific Northwest—just as Vietnam and Watergate ended it nationwide.

I've never covered an issue as complex, although tax-reform initiatives came close. WPPSS defined the limit of television's ability to inform thousands of intelligent people who were committed to pay the bills for a system impossible for me at least to explain in a minute or two. I finally concentrated on the importance of shifting energy supply from costly nukes to conservation and alternative energy, which made sense to me and could be explained to our viewers. The region could take no victory lap for the results that emanated from WPPSS, but it was a turning point both politically and culturally.

The long struggle over nuclear power, conservation, and accountability did not engage traditional political powers and tended to draw a different set of citizen activists. Political activists tended to group around candidates and core issues—of which energy was peripheral at that time.

Both political parties were challenged by nontraditional groupings that overshadowed the regular state party organizations and often fought them as well. Typically, such groups form when traditional political parties are in trouble. Bob Packwood's Dorchester Conference, for example, opened in the wake of the Barry Goldwater meltdown in 1964. Dorchester had the effect of a splash of cold water on a reeling boxer. That helped the GOP in Oregon for a while, but it faded.

Dorchester remained a popular venue for big-name speakers and attracted news coverage. A memorable occasion was when Governor McCall in 1972 wound up a prosaic speech by advocating "death with dignity" as opposed to "death as a vegetable." His stark turn of a phrase was both shocking and sobering. The topic of assisted suicide for those with terminal illness was simply not aired in public in 1972. Tom said he had been thinking about it for some time and, in his typical style, he went public. Tom's Dorchester speech was light on details—he later said he was only calling for "living wills" that directed physicians to stop life-support—but the debate began, and the following year the Oregon legislature took up the topic, driven primarily by Senator Ted Hallock of Portland. The idea went nowhere, but two decades later, Oregon in 1994 became the first state to allow what Tom had called "death with dignity." Washington followed suit in 2008 and I wrote extensively on the controversy for the *Seattle Times* and *Crosscut*, citing Oregon's generally successful record with the 1994 law, which allowed a person with a certified terminal illness to take life-ending medication prescribed by a physician. Tom was gone by the time of the 1994 law, but I think he would have approved.

From the 1973 Dorchester I noted that participants were "preoccupied with youth—or the lack thereof in the Republican Party."

The Republican bench in Oregon was nearly empty. "The voting age is now eighteen," I commented, "and a young candidate may be anyone under age thirty-five." Yet, I could identify "only a handful (of Republicans) under age forty who have the equipment to go all the way to statewide or congressional office." By contrast, Democrats had developed a host of candidates under the age of thirty-five. The tide was about to turn.

Democrats, primarily from the Portland area, formed Demoforum in 1969 when Republicans controlled the legislature and most state offices as Democrats were reeling from Vietnam War discord. Demoforum operated until 1975, focused on issues and developing candidates. Writing in the *Statesman*, I described the first Demoforum participants as young, professional and urban, "many of whom had worked on campaigns but few of whom held political office." Elected politicians kept back, letting newbies try their wings.

By the time Demoforum disbanded in 1975, its early participants were in the wave that brought Democratic control of the legislature and statewide offices and revitalized Portland and Multnomah County politics. Others staffed important agencies or served on major boards and commissions. The Republican surge sparked by Dorchester in 1965 was echoed by the Democratic surge sparked by Demoforum in 1969.

Dorchester and Demoforum were not activist organizations as such—they were a venue for activists and a place to network, certainly in partisan politics but also in a host of public causes over the years. They pumped new blood into an old system. Specific issues drove many of the activists, particularly in urban areas. Citizen groups, some organized by veterans of political campaigns but others formed by people new to campaigning, grew up around freeways—in particular on the Oregon beaches and in Portland—and also around air and water quality in Portland, as well as the city's school system. The school activists were not your mother's PTA.

Portland schools were under siege in 1980, with a sharply divided school board and angry protests from the district's African American community and from parents upset about changes instituted by

Superintendent Robert Blanchard. In 1980 he marked his eleventh year at the helm, making him the nation's longest-serving big-city superintendent. He didn't last the year.

Nothing touches an activist nerve more than public schools, and Portland's school issues had been festering for years, as the school board and Blanchard tried to institute racial busing that they believed was required by law. The busing issue got caught up in a new middle-school program, controversial in itself. Parents marched on board meetings and elected new board members; in June the new board fired Blanchard in a 4–3 vote. It was personal and painful for all involved, and it split some long-term friendships; I had friends on both sides, as did many others.

My concerns dated to 1977 and what I thought was insensitive handling of Jefferson High School's predominantly African American parent-activists. After one agonizing public hearing, I vented against a procedure I had seen used before by school boards: wear the audience out with long reports and bureaucratic presentations before finally calling for comments after citizens are fed up with the long wait and worrying about babysitters. No wonder they sounded so irritated. "The tactic only serves to inflame the discussion. The human element of the Jefferson plan needs more examination, and that examination cannot take place in the present atmosphere," I commented.

As the situation became tenser, I ultimately sided with those calling for Blanchard's dismissal and, during a yearlong shuffle of seats due to resignations and election, pushed for an African American board member. I was moving into more of an activist role myself, abandoning my usual caution about overtly backing candidates for public office. I had been studying and commenting on Portland's renewal for a decade, however, and saw the board and particularly Superintendent Blanchard locked in an old Portland establishment style that was no longer stylish—or effective; the district lost several critical funding elections as the tug-of-war between rival factions continued.

The split vote that led to the firing of Blanchard on June 16, 1980, brought strong reactions, and each side circulated petitions to recall the opposing faction. I was particularly hard on a high-profile group defending Blanchard. The matter, I commented, was one of power, not education. Blanchard supporters played the race card, I accused, noting that Blanchard himself did not feel race had ended his job. "Portland schools are in no danger of being taken over by radical blacks," I commented. "They are threatened with months of disruption, however, by radicals masquerading as the civic leadership." Cooler heads finally prevailed and both sides withdrew their competing recall petitions. KGW had so many requests for my commentaries that we printed and sent on request a mini-collection of three focused on the firing.

The new board began working with its critics and in 1981 passed an operating levy for the first time in six years. I credited a "much broader citizen role in board decisions, including the budget." The African American community was brought into the conversation: "this board sold its budget in parts of the city that past boards avoided in previous elections. The message from all this is that bringing more people into the school system works."

Blacks of either radical or moderate stripe did not take over Portland schools in the wake of Blanchard's departure—but in 1982 the district hired an African American named Matthew Prophet as superintendent, certainly one of the best in the district's history. The process had been messy but necessary; I was glad when it was over but I felt vindicated by the outcome. Matt Prophet served for a decade, and glued humpty-dumpty back together again. Future superintendents became more parent-friendly than Blanchard, with his top-down management.

Conservatives were not immune from the activist bug, and in Oregon at least they clustered around the venerable initiative and referendum system, which had been dormant in the post-war period until tax reform jump-started the engine in the late 1970s. The use of initiatives surged between 1904 and 1912, when the system started in Oregon, then steadily declined to an all-time low (averaging less than two per election) between 1954 and 1974.

Was it a coincidence that the 1954 to 1974 period of low initiative activity also produced the Oregon Story and countless public policies that set the state apart? I don't think so; Oregonians in this era had confidence that their government would respond to their activism and that they didn't need to resort to petitions. Activism gave people an outlet for their concerns, from schools to beaches, from freeways to rivers. In a remarkable number of instances, their elected leaders responded. The rush and clamor of those years produced high expectations that could not always be met fully. Folks were getting restless again after two decades of feel-good politics, and the number of initiatives began to climb in the late 1970s.

The property-tax rebellion began around the kitchen tables of East Multnomah County. Retirees Ray Phillips and Al Guildemeister did a lot of the petition circulation themselves, helped by other fed-up homeowners with time on their hands. Their efforts created a lot of work for both the media and Oregon politicians. We explained and legislators reacted with one tax proposal after another in an attempt to stem the onslaught. It was a stalemate—people wanted property-tax relief but the initiative measures were too radical, and the legislative proposals were complex and faced growing distrust of government.

I've always supported the initiative and referendum as part of Oregon's commitment to citizen government, but complex taxation measures simply don't work as initiatives. Even people who spend their days figuring out complex issues are hard-pressed to decipher the jots and tittles of taxation; white-shoe lawyers get rich by figuring that stuff out. The common sense of Oregonians does not make a voter—or a newsman for that matter—capable of an informed decision on such complex issues. I got tax professionals to help me, but in presenting the data on television there was little to rely on beyond any credibility I might have acquired with a viewer. Never, ever, talk down to an audience was my mantra, but finding a line between "govspeak" and pabulum was difficult.

None of the tax-relief panaceas passed on my television watch but in 1990, Tom Denehy and Don Mcintire passed Measure 5 and governor-elect Barbara Roberts found her victory came with a terrible burden. Paid signature-gathering became common; instead of volunteers carrying petitions, the system was taken over by operators who found a way to make a buck by milking conservative donors for money to pay hired solicitors and, not so incidentally, rake off a percentage for themselves. It became very profitable to promote not only tax relief but also conservative social issues.

As early as 1974 the growing grassroots rebellion was a factor in the retirement of two Oregon members of Congress, rare examples of politicians at that level leaving on their own volition. Democrat Edith Green and Republican Wendell Wyatt were widely respected, but I noted that "a sense of frustration ran through (their) retirement speeches" on February 15, 1974. Wyatt was close to President Nixon, a difficult role in 1974. Green was seeing many of the Great Society programs she had supported weakened or crippled by their own ineptness. But there was more, I observed:

> Both find it almost impossible to give personal attention to the mail and contacts generated by citizen lobbies. This frustration is real. Few citizens realize how much we expect of our elected officials. Congress is an eighteenth-century institution, near collapse trying to cope with the politics and mass communications of the late twentieth century. But good public officials with roots in traditional politics sometimes misread the intent of people who join citizen lobbies. They don't expect personal replies or contacts. Most are well-educated folks who know they are not expert on the ins and outs of new law. But they want to be counted on general ideas.

> They are tired of waiting for the Gallup Poll to call, and they see the questionnaires of congressmen as mostly publicity. Most people in citizen lobbies don't really expect all that much. They want to be heard, and they take their role seriously. Their frustrations are as real as those who have a vote to cast.

Wyatt and Green represented Oregon well, Wyatt for eleven years and Green for nineteen years; they became friends despite party differences, and the Green-Wyatt federal building in Portland is an apt tribute. Green was a power in the field of higher education, a key player in creating Title IX with its gender-equality regulations, and also (with Wayne Morse), the groundbreaking higher education acts of 1963, 1965, and 1967. In later years she found herself to the right of the House Democratic center and she alienated Democratic liberals in 1972 by supporting Washington senator Henry (Scoop) Jackson for President. She was not treated well by colleagues at the Democratic National Convention that year, and I felt for her, considering the contributions she had made over many years when only a handful of women served in the Congress. By the time Edith Green left the Congress, she was no longer alone as a woman subcommittee chair, but it would be another three decades before Nancy Pelosi became the first female speaker. Much of Green's time had been lonely; in her early years she endured the sexism of "good old boys" who ran the House. She worked longer and harder to prevail, as did many women in politics.

Women activists in Oregon were encouraged by the strides made by female legislators during this period. My first legislative session in 1965 saw only six women members; it was the first session for Betty Roberts. By the time of my last session in 1985, Vera Katz was speaker—with Senate President John Kitzhaber it was Kitz and Katz—and women chaired committees in both houses. Nineteen women served that session, and a second-term Democrat from Parkrose looked like a future leader; Barbara Roberts served as House majority leader in 1983 and 1984.

The presence of more female legislators made profound differences in areas of particular concern to women. Issues such as women's health, funding contraception for welfare recipients, abortion, childcare, and consumer protection had support from an increasingly united bipartisan group of women. They organized in 1973 to pass the Equal Rights Amendment sent to the states by Congress. Senator Betty Roberts and Representative Norma Paulus headed a bipartisan effort that saw all eleven female members caucusing and working as a team for passage of the ERA. The bipartisanship continued on several other issues during the 1973 session, the first in several years under Democratic leadership in both houses.[3]

When the legislature passed the Equal Rights Amendment in 1973, I used the occasion to note that the time was approaching when another woman would join Senator Maurine Neuberger in holding a statewide office. Noting the rising influence of female legislators, I commented:

> Women in Oregon politics are emerging from the shadow of well-known husbands and also from the shadow of political errand running. It just could be that the state is ready for a woman or women in statewide office . . . We've had no other woman elected by the entire state and no female Supreme Court Justice. Last year, Senator Betty Browne and former Representative Beulah Hand made races for state office and failed. Others might succeed. Among the women in the legislature, Democratic senator Betty Roberts and Republican representative Norma Paulus appear to have the experience and campaign ability to make it work. . .

> But the important thing here is not that women will come into more political participation, but that they will come on their own terms. That's happening, and ease of passage of the Equal Rights Amendment is testimony to the ability of women in the legislature.

Many of the women serving in the legislature in this era began their politics as activists; the activism of the sixties and seventies prepared them to become excellent legislators, quickly moving beyond the traditional "women's committees" of education and health to the big-ticket committees, Ways and Means and Revenue.

Why did it take so long? My generation was raised by women who had stepped aside for men. As the Great Depression deepened, women whose husbands had jobs often lost theirs. My mother was a telephone operator ("central" for a small North Dakota town), but she lost the job when she married a farmer, losing some of her identity in the process. After World War II, women who held good jobs in wartime were laid off or voluntarily quit to give jobs to returning veterans. The *Statesman* newsroom where I worked had a female city editor during the war, and a capable one at that; she lost out to a returning GI. A grateful nation supported that practice, but it slowed the advancement of women by at least a decade.

Change took place a lot faster in politics than in business. The parade of political "firsts" was underway: Norma Paulus, first female secretary of state (1977); Betty Roberts, first female Supreme Court justice (1982); Vera Katz, first female Speaker of the House (1985); Barbara Roberts, first female governor (1991). There were no female Highway Commission members until 1987, eight years after Glenn Jackson left the commission, when governor Neil Goldschmidt appointed Cynthia Ford—Glenn Jackson's daughter.

In 1986, my last year at KGW, a survey of Oregon's top business leaders (ranked by salary) still showed no women among the top fifty. A 1985 survey of the hundred largest locally owned Oregon companies showed not a single female CEO. The world of Glenn Jackson and counterparts had no seats for women or minorities, but that world was beginning to change.[4]

Female legislators helped open opportunities for women; in part because so many of them came from activist backgrounds, they welcomed more ordinary citizens into the process and they were more sympathetic to their concerns. The legislature had its share of sleazy operators, but I cannot remember one who wore a skirt, which is not to say the women weren't tough in bargaining or selling a bill.

The legislature was changing, and the advent of strong women in both houses was part of the change. The Senate coalition of Republicans and conservative Democrats was gone in 1973 with Senator Jason Boe's first of four terms as president. Democrat Boe, elected without Republican support, was an ideal transition—an optometrist from Reedsport, he was born and raised in Los Angeles. Jason understood cities, but also the farmers and fishermen in his Douglas County district. He slowed the passage of some Oregon Story measures but skillfully maneuvered others to passage despite complaints from rural senators. Boe ended his Senate career in 1980; another Douglas County senator—John Kitzhaber—began his three-plus terms as president in 1985.

The two nearly clashed in 1978 when Boe was at the height of his power, and I found myself in the unusual role of helping head off the collision. Dixie and I were visiting our longtime friends, Ralph and Betsy Grenfell, in their North Umpqua River home when Betsy, a nurse, asked if I would like to meet her doctor, a young man named John Kitzhaber, who was pondering a political plunge. I was curious about Betsy's young doctor. John was keen to unseat Jason Boe, whom he (correctly) believed to be indifferent about some of the environmental issues dear to John's heart.

I was instantly impressed by Kitzhaber and knew he would be valuable on both medical and environmental issues. He was making a mistake, I cautioned him, to challenge Boe, who would attract money from interests hoping to influence the Senate president; Boe's election record was good and he bridged the gap between forest and coast in the spacious district. Be patient, I counseled, and take on a freshman Republican House member from Roseburg and get some experience under your belt. He did, and won the House seat handily. Two years later, Boe left the Senate to run for state treasurer, Kitzhaber won the Senate seat . . . the rest, as they say, is history.

Oregon passed the two-million population mark in 1970 and continued to grow. Inevitably, more people came to the capitol, particularly as the Oregon Story progressed—hearings on the Beach Bill or Bottle Bill drew throngs that had to be turned away from the cramped rooms. Constituents wound up in the halls, very unhappy after driving miles to testify or just listen. Activists drove the change by their very numbers, but also by changing the atmosphere of the old lobbyist-dominated process. Committees were forced to open all meetings, more television cameras were seen, and the smoking habits of legislators were doused by law. That alone cleared the air, so to speak; although I had contributed pipe smoke to the mix, I later realized that lots of people were seriously offended and even sickened as a cloud of smoke descended on a committee room. When the veteran dealmaker Tom Mahoney left the Senate in 1974, the last brass spittoon also left; neither was missed.

Legislators historically had no private offices and did much of their business right on the floor of Senate or House. Two-person desks allowed a secretary to sit with legislators—the secretary was often the member's wife (I don't recall a husband in such a role). It was nepotism of course, but all of us knew wives who were a lot brighter than the man who cast the vote. Nearly everyone who served before the Capitol Wings tends to wax nostalgic about those desks on the floors of House and Senate and all the camaraderie that resulted. But something had to be done about the capitol's cramped quarters. President Boe's persistence and vision produced a $12.5 million expansion, doubling the capitol's space in 1977. By the time of Kitz and Katz, the venerable capitol had a new set of offices and hearing rooms that we called "Jason's Wings." A decade later the Senate side of the expansion was officially named the Jason Boe Senate Wing.

Legislators were beginning to match the times—urban women joined farmers and small businessmen as dominant groupings; the average age plummeted and we saw as many teachers as lawyers. The changes benefitted the Oregon Story; in fact the Story would not have been accomplished in the days of the Old Boys Club.

The legend was emerging. Governor Tom McCall was energized by his success with the Vortex gamble and rushed to take advantage. In Portland, an entirely new crowd was in control at city hall and the highway-dominated model that drove Oregon's transportation planning for a century was forced to share the right-of-way with a train we called MAX. It was crunch time for the Oregon Story.

Profile VERA KATZ: FROM BROOKLYN WITH LOVE

Vera Katz was a poster woman for immigrants who were drawn to Oregon in this era. Vera Pistrak was born in Germany into a Menshevik Jewish family that fled to France and later Spain and Portugal to escape Hitler. She wound up in Brooklyn, where she earned bachelor and master's degrees from Brooklyn College. Vera married artist Mel Katz and in 1962 the couple chose Portland from a list of possible destinations that included Seattle and San Francisco.

Oregon's political climate, including the national reputation of Senator Wayne Morse, was a draw for Vera, who almost immediately began involving herself in activist causes in her new home. The Katzes had a son, Jesse, but later divorced. I encountered Vera at the first Demoforum at Mount Hood in 1969. You just couldn't miss Vera—then or later, as she served the city and state for three decades. Strikingly attractive and given to colorful and stylish dress, her sharp Brooklyn accent rang out as she promoted a cause or sold a bill on the floor of the Oregon Legislature. Vera didn't drive a car—she was a genuine city girl—but she seemed to be everywhere and she was a joy to be around. Like so many other immigrants who helped shape the Oregon Story, Vera was here by choice rather than by birth, and she knew why she was here and what was needed to keep Oregon special.

Vera had been active in the presidential campaign of Robert F. Kennedy; after Kennedy's assassination, she turned her energies to gun control and Cesar Chavez's campaign to boycott California grapes. She worked both issues at the first Demoforum and was among several immigrants to Oregon who stood out at that gathering.

By 1972, she was running for the legislature in a district that had been Republican for years but was transitioning Democrat. Her core support included a group of young mothers who were becoming active in promoting feminist causes. Dixie was drawn to the group by our friend MaryAnne Buchanan and wound up running lawn signs for Vera's successful campaign. The POW group (Politically Oriented Women) always held a special place in Vera's heart.

The 1973 Oregon House was full of newbies—twenty-eight of the sixty House members were freshmen—and women were taking prominent roles. Democrats controlled both legislative bodies for the first time since 1957, and they were feeling their new muscles.

Vera immediately gravitated to the power spots—she was the first woman co-chair of the powerful Ways and Means Committee and in 1985 she became the first woman Speaker of the House. She served three terms as speaker; strong but flexible, she worked

Speaker of the Oregon House Vera Katz, the first woman to hold the position, surveys her domain. A refugee as a child from Nazi Germany, she served 18 years in the House and 12 as mayor of Portland. (Gerry Lewin Photo)

well across party divides despite her liberal politics. With Senate President John Kitzhaber, the Kitz and Katz team dominated the legislature until Republicans took control of the House in 1991.

Speaker Katz enjoyed her job and she was fun to watch in action; she invited the widest range of chaplains to begin daily sessions that legislators had ever seen; jaws dropped when a red-clad Rajneeshee did the honors. Few Oregonians did as much for feminist causes as Vera Katz, in the legislature and as Portland's mayor from 1992 to 2004. She was a big-ideas dreamer with practical skills and a wonderful personal style; I'm truly sorry I missed her mayoralty, but her vision of the city was in the mode of the Oregon Story. The young Brooklyn export who chose Oregon made it an even better place.

EIGHT

Saving the Land

Mostly we came by land and we came to the valley of the Willamette, immigrants of 1840 through 1950, when the State of Oregon claimed 1.5 million inhabitants. When we arrived and crested one of the Cascade passes that looked to the west, there was . . . green! Towering green Douglas firs and rolling hills with green pastures for cattle and wintering crops. When summer warmed, as it did when the McKays of Bottineau, North Dakota, arrived one day in 1947, fruit was ripe in the orchards and we could reach up and sample a cherry or a peach.

Native Oregonians of those days were living in a paradise compared to the dust-blown prairies many immigrants had fled—or the freezing blizzards of the farm my family owned a dozen miles from the Canadian border. Oregon's population grew by nearly 40 percent in the war decade, and it seemed as if everyone wanted to live in the Willamette Valley in a single-story house with a spacious yard.

The state's only real city was not the destination of the newcomers; Portland grew by less than half the state rate in the forties and actually lost population from 1950 to 1980. Many of those who came to work in the shipyards and defense factories returned home or drifted on; this was particularly true of African Americans, many of whom migrated to Seattle, which they perceived as more friendly to people of color. Many of the war workers who stayed moved to the suburbs now emerging on all sides.

The end of the war meant a sense of restlessness as young men returned from war serious about settling down; families finally had a chance to upgrade their pre-war automobiles and take advantage of cheap gas for a trip west. Housing became a question and suburbs were the answer. A young veteran with a pickup truck and a set of tools could become a pillar of the community by hopscotching homes across a pasture. Our government was there to help with GI loans; Oregon had one of the best programs in the nation for veterans. Young Bob Straub in Springfield was one of those homebuilders.

Only eleven years after my arrival as a skinny preteen in 1947, I found myself chronicling one result of the land rush. The cub reporter for the *Springfield News* found himself traipsing through some very smelly land east of the booming city, where instant suburbs spurted from the ground . . . as did their effluent. Thrown up between the city and the new Weyerhaeuser mill where the men worked, the unplanned and unsewered jumble was in serious trouble; the county health officer was on the march and someone would have to pay the piper.

Springfield was a vibrant, progressive city and the young McKays loved the town and its hustling, activist culture. The city itself did well under really good leadership; Mayor Ed Harms and others tackled growth with energy and foresight. But the sprouting suburb east of Springfield was a no-man's land, unincorporated but in need of urban services. All over Oregon, similar dilemmas were arising.

Springfield's suburbs were not built on prime farmland, but many post-war developments were; farmers or their children sold the farm to pay for a well-earned retirement. Developers were only too happy to oblige them, and young families only too happy to settle into the rambling one-story houses. The land—that magic lure that drew people to the valley—was under siege and you could almost see the tracts marching into the next vetch field or filbert orchard. It was time to wake up and smell the barbecue, and Oregon was fortunate enough to have people who were willing to sound the alarm.

One of them was my energetic friend L. B. Day, in 1964 a freshman state representative. L. B.'s Teamsters union members needed a healthy farm economy for their cannery jobs, and row crops were often close to urban areas, easy targets for developers. As I grew up in the valley, I had picked those crops and later driven trucks and buses for pickers. L. B. and I talked about that and his hopes to grant to "prime agricultural lands" some type of farm-value tax assessment in exchange for continued farm use of the land. Senator Cornelius Bateson, who farmed east of Salem, was also active on this front, but farmland proposals died quietly while most reporters, including myself, were watching to see how new governor Tom McCall was doing.

Once elected as governor, Tom McCall jumped into the game and began working on measures to protect farmland. While Mark Hatfield was governor, central planning was under Economic Development; McCall placed it directly under the governor and brought Arnold Cogan from the Port of Portland to be Oregon's chief planner. In a later oral history interview, Arnold recalled working with L. B. Day to craft four land-use bills for the 1969 legislature; only Senate Bill 10 passed. Day was a trader at heart, Cogan recalled:

> I was working away on trying to lobby these four bills, and if those four bills had passed, we would have had land use planning in Oregon with an anniversary from 1969, not 1973. They contained practically everything that was in Senate Bill 100. Suddenly—and I was just a novice at lobbying then—before I knew it Senate Bills 11, 12, and 13 had been traded for stuff—I never found out what . . . So nothing came of it. All that we got was some speeches about how good land use planning is and all this stuff, but it didn't accomplish diddly really, except to set the scene later for Senate Bill 100. So we came very close, at least hoping that we might have had a land-use planning bill at that time. But it wasn't to be. It took another four years before all the stars were in the right constellation.[1]

Cogan was certainly correct in his assessment of Day; he might have been wrong, however, that the 1969 legislature would have passed the full land-use package. It was Bob Smith's first session as speaker and he was flexing his conservative chops; the Bottle Bill was one of the premier casualties. The legislature grappled with land-use and finally passed Senate Bill 10, an awkward beginning. Governor McCall tried to make it work while rallying the cavalry for a second charge.

Senate Bill 10 sounded better than it actually was. Local governments were told to zone by 1972 or the state would step in and do the job, but there was more bark than teeth to this puppy, and a small army of planners and conservationists immediately began work on a stronger law. The state was awash with agencies, committees with impressive-sounding titles—the Willamette Valley Environmental Protection and Development Planning Council was just one: WVEPDPC!—but most had little authority.

Developers and landowners, primarily on the coast and in eastern Oregon, tried to repeal Senate Bill 10 by initiative in 1970, correctly seeing that the puppy might grow into a mastiff, but they failed in a vote of 56–44 percent. Gubernatorial candidates Tom McCall and Bob Straub were joined in opposition to the repeal by a coalition that included environmental groups, Associated Oregon Industries, and a phalanx of business leaders, including Glenn Jackson. It was the first of many votes ahead on the controversial land-use front.

Governor McCall forced land use back onto the public agenda in 1971 in his second inaugural speech and the issue just kept growing. Tom was at his rhetorical best in promoting his land-use agenda; there was talk of a "buffalo-hunter mentality" and "grasping wastrels of the land" and "sagebrush subdivisions and coastal condomania." Before long the images morphed into one, and the image was getting legs. But nothing got legs more quickly than a short sound bite that Tom slipped into a national television interview on January 12, 1971, a day after his second inaugural: "Come visit us again and again. This is a state of excitement. But for heaven's sake, don't come here to live."

There it was: The Quote, captured on film by Terry Drinkwater of CBS. Tom and I had talked over the years about his feelings for Oregon and its fragile environment, and I would have given my left arm for that quote, but Tom knew exactly what he was doing

when he placed it on national television. His comment smacked of
the mythical James G. Blaine Society, created by author Stewart
Holbrook to keep visitors—let alone new residents—from his
Oregon home.

Holbrook, an unemployed logger from New England, arrived in
Portland in 1923 and until his death in 1964 ranked with Richard
L. Neuberger as Oregon's best-known author. The self-identified
lowbrow historian had friends and fans all over the country, but he
remained most at home with ex-loggers and characters sometimes
found on Portland's Skid Road (not "Skid Row," dammit, he complained to outsiders). Holbrook found a home and didn't want it to
become overcrowded; in 1962, he discovered James G. Blaine.[2]

Blaine was a peripatetic American politician from Maine, a senator and secretary of state; he was the Republican candidate for
president in 1884 and campaigned in all but one state—Oregon.
Holbrook liked Blaine's good judgment and formed the mysterious
James G. Blaine Society to discourage visitors. The cause was taken
up after Holbrook's death in 1964 by Ralph Friedman, also a noted
author and collector of characters.

Many of us played at being Blainesmen; the colorful report-
er-cum-lawyer Scott MacArthur founded the Monmouth Winter
Olympics. I suggested moving the capitol building to Shaniko, just
north of Antelope, in lieu of building the capitol wings (instead,
Antelope got the Bhagwan Shree Rajneesh). The society lives on, but
if you have a membership card, you aren't really a member.

Tom McCall would have known both Holbrook and Friedman,
and his famous quote for Terry Drinkwater was "Blaineism" at its
best. This was in contrast to what I once described as "McCallism"
after one of Tom's several verbal jousts with governor Ronald
Reagan, a frequent sparring partner at governors' conferences:

> No political dictionary is complete without a definition of "McCallism."
> A "McCallism" is a reflex action, brought about when confronted with
> an open microphone. This spontaneous and entirely uncontrollable out-
> burst is delivered in haste and sometimes repented in leisure . . . From

the public it invariably brings the response, "Oh, that's just old Tom!" Ronald Reagan shouldn't feel too badly about coming a cropper of a "McCallism." He travels in good company. McCall once accused Spiro Agnew of "carrying a knife in his shawl." A rather unlikely costume, although an intriguing idea.

Tom had welcomed Agnew's place on the Republican national ticket in 1968, trumpeting him as a Republican moderate in the McCall style. Agnew emerged as the White House heavy—shawl, knife and all—particularly nasty in his diatribes against the press.

The former allies met again in December 1971 at a conference of Republican governors , where Agnew was the main speaker. Agnew made an effort over drinks to reconcile with Tom, but when the vice president launched into an aggressive defense of his attack-style politics, it was too much for Tom. He stomped out of the room, quite naturally drawing a crowd of reporters. "There was the most unbelievable, incredible misunderstanding of the mood of America in that rotten, bigoted little speech," Tom intoned for the gathered microphones and notepads. As the conference continued the following day, Agnew confronted Tom at a closed-door session. "I can't believe you said this," he shouted. Tom, surely realizing he was distancing himself from his own party of years standing, replied, "I don't think I said 'little.'"

Tom enjoyed the trappings and socialization of the governors conferences, which were a bit like national political conventions in their ability to draw top political reporters despite the general lack of any real news. They came for the schmoozing, and McCall and Reagan competed to draw media attention. Both were powerful and charismatic, emblematic of politicians who "own the room," People gravitate to them, cock their ears to hear what they are saying to others, craving a personal greeting, maybe even a hug.

Tom McCall owned almost every room he entered, in part because of his size—he was a large man with an expressive face— but also because of his obvious readiness to engage people in conversation, laughter, even debate. To watch Tom McCall and Ronald

Two rivals who "owned the room" in political terms—Oregon Governor Tom McCall and California Governor Ronald Reagan—surveyed the field as Oregon and California battled in football. (Gerry Lewin Photo)

Reagan—another "room owner"—in the same room at the same time was a prized ticket to a unique production.

In my time, few other Oregonians "owned the room." Many powerful people don't have this characteristic. Glenn Jackson didn't and would have been embarrassed if he did. Bob Straub and Bob Packwood (except Packwood at Dorchester) blended into a crowd, as did Jason Boe, Betty Roberts, John Kitzhaber, and other prominent legislators. Mayor Neil Goldschmidt certainly did in his prime; he moved equally well among young activists and business executives. Speaker of the House Vera Katz had the chutzpah and charm to "own" legislative gatherings but also neighbors and activists, particularly women. Mark Hatfield didn't have the same "room-owning" qualities of Tom, Neil, and Vera, but his quiet, sincere interest in ordinary Oregonians—coupled with his remarkable memory for names and events—drew people to him wherever he went. That Oregon should have this collection of compelling personalities at the same time had something to do with the Oregon Story that emerged from the era.

Tom's confrontations with Agnew and Reagan were largely for publicity and to keep his ties with the media, but the Drinkwater interview on CBS was calculated to send a message that Oregon considered itself special. It served notice that Tom would not hesitate to ruffle a few feathers in corporate suites.

Tom McCall's speeches stressed "quality of life" and, in his first term, he grappled with beaches and dirty rivers, along with all the mundane tasks of governing a rapidly growing state in a time of national ferment. His staff struggled to make something of Senate Bill 10, to little avail. The job of building legislation with teeth fell to state senators Hector Macpherson, whose Linn County dairy was under siege from encroaching suburbs and malls, and Ted Hallock, an impatient and sometimes-volatile liberal from Portland. The vehicle was Senate Bill 100 (SB 100) in the 1973 session, Tom's last as governor.

McCall was often the odd man out in his own party, and much of his success in the legislature depended on Democratic votes. In 1973 both legislative houses were finally headed by Democratic majorities—the Senate Coalition had folded its tent. President Jason Boe of Reedsport and Speaker Dick Eymann of Marcola were veterans, but the legislature was full of inexperienced members.

Legislators in 1972 were elected in single-member legislative districts for the first time; under the previous system, some large districts had several legislators and a long ballot that favored familiar names. Those familiar names from large countywide districts were scythed down by challengers in 1972. The changes were so dramatic that I produced a special half-hour program to open the session, focusing on the new people and what they meant for Oregon's shifting political landscape.

Portland suburbs in Washington and Clackamas counties saw the biggest changes from the shift to single-member districts—only two of their seven House members from 1971 returned in 1973. The

House was young and inexperienced; forty-two of the sixty members were in their first or second sessions. Land-use legislation and the governor's tax-reform proposals would prove to be the big issues in the coming session, and Democrats would provide the votes the governor needed.

Senator Macpherson was appointed to the Senate Environment and Land Use Committee chaired by Hallock. An unlikelier pair could hardly be imagined. Macpherson was soft-spoken, diligent in his preparation, and a bit of a loner in the clubby Senate. Ted Hallock was a decorated World War II flier, a jazz drummer, and a Portland advertising man given to railing against a hostile witness, using language that Macpherson probably didn't use in his dairy barn. Ted was the equal of L. B. Day, and when things got really rough and SB 100 was under attack, he called on the "old labor goon" to break a few kneecaps.

Lobbyists for industries, homebuilders, and cities had formed an unlikely alliance to hammer at parts or the entirety of the measure that would become SB 100. Hallock could count only on Macpherson and Eugene Republican George Wingard in his seven-member committee; he desperately needed a fourth vote. Hallock had to at least neutralize opponents on all sides, and that required rewriting SB 100. He appointed Macpherson and L. B. Day—who in 1973 was lobbying for his union—to work with competing lobbyists to draft changes. L. B. called a small group of well-known lobbyists into a closed room and belabored them in a voice that nearly shook the doors; there would be compromises but there would be a bill, dammit with footnotes!

There was a bill. Hallock picked up the votes he needed and the Senate approved the amended SB 100 in an 18–10 vote. Hallock asked House Environment and Land Use Chair Nancie Fadeley to forego making amendments, to avoid a conference committee with the skittish Senate. It was Nancie's first committee chairmanship, and she was moving out of the large shadow of her husband, the bombastic and manipulative Senator Ed Fadeley. She wanted to leave a mark and show her independence, and she, like many liberals, worried that the bill had been weakened by compromise. But she swallowed hard and followed Hallock's counsel; SB 100 became the most important environmental legislation of the time.

None of us—not legislators or reporters, not the lobby, and not even environmentalists—could have predicted what an enormous impact SB 100 would have on the state and its reputation. It became a cornerstone of the Oregon Story, which Tom was beginning to work over in his mind, always seeking attractive phrases to call attention to his goals. Tom changed the state's quarterly economic-development publication from *Grow with Oregon* to *Oregon Quality* and later to *Oregon Progress*. He was a wordsmith and the title expressed his philosophy.[3]

Even Tom was worried that the bill might not do the job, but he promised to defend it to the last, which he did. He was also finding a growing national audience for Oregon's environmental leadership, riding primarily on three of his greatest achievements: the Beach Bill, the Bottle Bill, and now, land-use legislation. National reporters, who always loved McCall for his volubility, began to call more frequently. He was asked to testify in Congress as Senators Hatfield and Packwood tried (unsuccessfully) to pass a national Bottle Bill.

Tom's environmental legacy was impressive and he was feeling the love, but he overextended his reach in a failed attempt to pass the biggest tax-reform package since Oregon adopted the income tax half a century before. A Republican sales tax had been buried by Oregonians in 1969 by an eight-to-one margin, but Tom thought his growing popularity and an increase in Democratic voters gave him a chance at a goal many liberals had long supported: shifting the cost of public schools from the local property tax to an increased and more progressive state income tax. Business taxes would also shift from property to income. Low-income property owners and renters would get relief as well.

It was a breathtaking gamble, but Tom and colleagues told voters that 85 percent of Oregonians would pay lower taxes because of

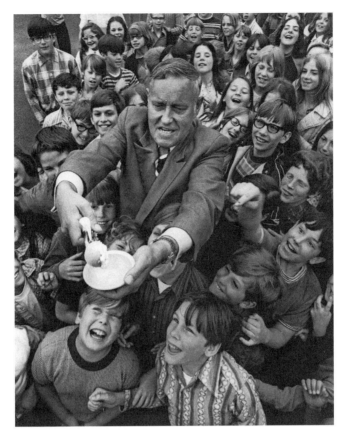

Tom McCall
with a bunch
of kids was a
treat for all.
Here he serves
ice cream
during a school
stop. (Gerry
Lewin Photo)

the shift to higher-income taxpayers. The plan was similar to the
McCall plan buried by the 1967 Republican legislature. This time,
a Democratic legislature approved the plan, voting close to party
lines. We pulled out the stops to inform our audience, with a five-
part series of analyses on the news prior to the May 3, 1973, special
election; other stations and newspapers also put special emphasis
on the proposal. Oregon was a progressive state and it was a very
progressive proposal, but it got only 41 percent, still the best of any
major tax proposal of the period.

"The board of directors has spoken and said I'm all wet," said
the chastened governor. He was devastated and threatened to

resign; Ron Schmidt and Clay Myers stayed up with him half the night, talking him down. Secretary of State Myers was next in line if Tom resigned, and Clay was already planning to campaign for the office in 1974, but he was foremost a McCall loyalist and close friend.

Every politician has a big ego, and Tom was certainly no exception; he had been reading and believing his press notices. Coming close counts only in horseshoes and hand grenades—there was no solace in the 41 percent who followed his flag. His legacy would be built on environmental gains; the Oregon Story would have no chapter on fiscal breakthroughs. Analyzing the defeat, I did not see it as a rejection of the governor, but perhaps, as a "defeat of the myth of the super-politician, who can even get a tax bill passed."

Legislators didn't see it coming when they adjourned on July 8, but a crisis was already heading down the road in the form of an energy crunch that would ultimately add a sidebar to Tom McCall's legacy.

During a quick 1973 tour of Israel, the governor characteristically drew headlines by musing that perhaps he would support the impeachment of President Nixon if Watergate disclosures continued to pile up. It would prompt "great discussions on the floor of the Senate and the floor of Congress about Watergate and it might be a healthy thing for the country—it might purge the country," Tom told reporters. It would also be one helluva big story, the old newsman must have thought.

Just when Tom was beginning to worry about what to do in retirement and how his taxation failure would affect his legacy, a bunch of Arab oil sheiks rescued him from perdition—or at least obscurity. Israel and an Arab alliance went to war five months after the governor's Israel trip. The Israelis overwhelmed Egyptian and Syrian forces in the Yom Kippur War, but the oil producers in Saudi Arabia and OPEC imposed an oil embargo on countries that helped Israel. American cars sat in lines to buy gas at four times its cost before the embargo. Other forms of energy were affected as well

During the "energy crisis" of 1973, KGW joined others in showing attention to an energy shortage—in this case, moving the noon news to the parking circle outside the studio. Ivan Smith is at the anchor desk, while Floyd McKay prepares to interview State Treasurer Jim Redden. Floor director Dick Lee is at left. (Courtesy of author)

and a mad scramble ensued for ways to cope. To add to the problem, 1973 was a very dry year in the Northwest, causing a shortage of hydroelectricity.

Oregon was a speed bump on the national energy scramble, but Tom managed to turn it into a glorious media event. As it happened, the Western Governors' Conference was slated for September at Salishan on the Oregon Coast. Ronald Reagan, the big-name governor, ducked the session, and Tom picked up the baton; he turned off the state's neon advertising signs and nighttime lighting of office buildings and other conspicuous power use. He was well past his legal authority, but few bucked his orders.

KGW scrambled to be supportive. For a few weeks we moved our noon news outside the studio to the turnaround in front of the building—saving the power from our studio lights! It was a gimmick, of course, but it was fun as well and part of the can-do image of the day. All of this on the threshold of the big governors' meeting.

The sessions themselves were sober, as governors heard from Ralph Nader and a passel of energy experts, all warning of doom unless the nation addressed its madcap consumption of energy. The White House sent Energy Director John Love and Interior Secretary Rogers Morton, but I commented that "they had nothing to say, and perhaps that was the most discouraging thing for the western governors. They realized they may have to try to solve this energy problem on a state-by-state or regional basis and that was a sobering thought."

As host of the gathering, Tom broke protocol. Governors were normally shielded from reporters at social events, but when Tom noticed some of us lingering in the hall to hear the music of the Harry James Big Band at a concluding dance, he swept aside the barriers and Dixie and I and colleagues with spouses danced with the governors until past midnight. It was so typical of Tom.

The energy crunch continued into 1974, and so did Oregon's growing reputation for innovation. A young man in Tom's energy office named Don Jarvi conjured the idea of cutting the long lines at gasoline pumps by telling motorists to buy gas on either an odd or even calendar date, based on their license-plate numbers. It was shockingly simple, and Tom blurted it to reporters first and then belatedly informed gas stations and others who would have to make it work. It did work, and it generated more national media attention.

To a certain degree, Tom was working in a political vacuum: the Nixon administration was under siege, the national economy was plummeting due to the energy crunch, Vice President Spiro Agnew resigned in disgrace to avoid criminal charges, and there were few stars on either Republican or Democratic benches. When the Dorchester Conference searched for a speaker for their March

1974 meeting, they wound up inviting Nelson Rockefeller, who had always been popular with Oregon Republicans but was seriously shopworn. I quipped that "one of the conference organizers jokes that Rockefeller was a natural choice because he could afford to pay his own way." When that invitation was accepted in December 1973 neither Dorchester leaders nor Rockefeller had any clue that less than a year later he would be President Gerald Ford's vice president.

In the wake of Watergate, pundits and political managers were beginning to talk of a fresh face for the 1976 presidential race. Eugene McCarthy—he of the 1968 youth insurgency—informally approached Tom about running together (without suggesting which of them would head the ticket). Other scenarios were being hatched as the nation imploded.

I was writing some long pieces in hopes of national magazine placement, and Tom did a couple of rambling interviews musing on life on the national political stage. "If I get in there and my stamina is good, then maybe I'm ready to put on my running shoes," he projected, but we both knew it wouldn't happen. Tom had undergone prostate surgery a few months before we spoke, and the rigors of a major campaign would be very taxing on his tired body. The governor of Oregon wasn't wearing his running shoes that day; he was wearing carpet slippers, rummaging around his office in an old gray sweater, thinking aloud, and brainstorming ideas for his bully pulpit.

The opportunity was there; a 1974 Gallup poll showed 34 percent of respondents wanted an Independent rather than a Republican or Democrat, and Tom chose his words carefully as he surveyed the field in our talk. He used "catalyst" rather than "candidate" and "force" rather than "party." There remained an element of fantasy in all of this. At some point, Tom said as much: "Other candidates build bandwagons; I'm building a pink cloud."

A national campaign would have been a serious mistake, and it was not the first campaign temptation he wisely rejected. Tom had actively considered a race against Senator Hatfield in 1972, based in part on his dislike of the senator. He was a *Viewpoint* guest in mid-1971 and I pointedly asked him whether he thought Senator Hatfield was doing a good job. "He just hasn't done a very good job," Tom replied, "and it might be provident for the State of Oregon to replace him." It was provident for Tom to avoid that race—Hatfield would have pounded him into a funk and curtailed what was becoming the Oregon Story, ultimately Tom's legacy.

More promising was a challenge against Senator Packwood in 1974, and Tom was on-again and off-again for months despite an earlier promise to Bob that he would not seek the position. The senator and his putative challenger had an explosive confrontation at Packwood's home in March 1974, but after a couple of weeks' agonizing, Tom withdrew to avoid what he believed would be a nasty campaign. It was the last of his national ambitions but not the end of the Oregon Story; he was in demand as a speaker nationwide and took several victory laps upon retirement.[4]

Meanwhile, Tom McCall's successors were charged with making his ideas work in practice, while they faced new challenges in social policy, taxation, and the expanding population and influence of Portland and the lower Willamette Valley. Some of their challenges would be less clearcut than saving beaches and would not as easily attract bipartisanship. There would be more and better-organized attacks on state land-use planning, as developers found out that the program had teeth and was making the conversion of farmland to subdivisions very difficult. Tom would make a last stand to defend his legacy and single-handedly defeat the forces that were bent on turning back the clock. I describe that episode in the next chapter.

When Tom McCall left office, the Oregon Story still had miles to go and others would provide the leadership. Portland was already emerging as a reinvented city and organizers were preparing to protect the breathtaking beauty of the Columbia River Gorge. But most of the pillars of the Oregon Story were in place: public beaches and the end of highways on the beach, the Bottle Bill, Vortex, statewide land-use planning, Willamette River cleanup, and the Greenway.

Some would also include state bike paths and trails and scenic rivers. It was truly a pantheon, put in place by others as well as the outgoing governor, most notably his rival and now his successor, Bob Straub.

Life was never the same for Tom, sixty-three years old when he left office after a rousing and laughter-filled final celebration roast that we broadcasted live. Tom loved the warmth and good fellowship and his response was upbeat. The evening of good feelings could not last, of course. Tom had to make a living and his successors had to find a way to govern while his shadow still lingered. He closed soberly: "He tried, oh Lord, he tried. There was no final victory. But did he not point the way?"

Oregonians did not always treat the heroes of the Oregon Story with appreciation. In 1972, voters overwhelmingly rejected a very modest pension plan for governors who served two terms, which would have given Tom some financial latitude in retirement. In 1974 one of the heroes of land-use planning, Senator Hector Macpherson, was unseated by a pleasant but undistinguished Democrat riding the tailwind of conservative opposition to state land-use regulation.

The Oregon Story had to be defended in Tom McCall's absence from the governor's office, but no one was a stauncher defender than his successor, Governor Bob Straub. My shift as chronicler of the Story had a decade to run. There were chapters still to be written.

Profile THE REMARKABLE L. B. DAY

When L. B. Day was hired to head the Department of Environmental Quality (DEQ) in 1972, I began a commentary: "An editor in this town has a prayer of sorts on his typewriter. 'Lord, send me an SOB with talent.' L. B. Day may have been the answer to a similar prayer by governor Tom McCall." To say that L. B. was an original would be an understatement. He was a force of nature who could fix his withering stare and thundering voice on a detractor, peel the very skin from his frame, and a minute later envelop him in a hug and one of his unique snorts of relief and seek an area of negotiation.

Nothing I could say, however, could rival Brent Walth's description: "When he walked, he hunched and cocked a wild look, as if he was on the verge of an outburst. Often, he was. In committee hearings, he berated witnesses, seemingly at random."[5] The hunch favored a bad back, which plagued him most of his life. But the look was purposeful and usually it was directed against someone trying to slip something by him. L. B. has been described by some critics and colleagues alike as a bully, and there is some truth to that, but it was not his nature to beat up on the defenseless, my definition of a true bully.

He sometimes referred to himself as a "labor goon," but L. B. Day did not grow up on the shop floor; a graduate of Willamette University, he bargained for workers in the canneries of the mid-Willamette Valley. L. B. was a Democrat who helped break Marion County's Republican lock in 1964 but switched four years later to Republican;

it didn't matter, he was still the quintessential L. B., and whether you loved or hated him (plenty on both sides) he was a man who saw the big picture and forged ahead.

L. B. Day, bombastic and colorful, was a moving force in the drive for land-use regulation in Oregon and left his mark as a legislator and state official. (Gerry Lewin Photo)

At DEQ, L. B. was a magnet for controversy. The big Boise Cascade paper mill, adjacent to downtown Salem, was dumping raw waste into the Willamette in blatant disregard of DEQ orders. L. B. determined to shut the mill down, putting 650 workers out of a job; their union organized a march on the capitol and L. B. and Governor McCall faced them on the capitol steps. Boise Cascade tried to pin the blame on the governor, turning the workers against him, but McCall and Day led the workers back to the paper mill and confronted management. The company backed down; ultimately, the mill was closed.

Tom and L. B. relished political theater, and the Boise Cascade showdown was in the political image of Teddy Roosevelt, who set the standard in this field. As a young New York City police commissioner, TR shut down the city's saloons on Sunday, prompting near-riots and a massive protest parade—which Roosevelt joined, saluting protestors along the way with his trademark toothy grin.[6] Seventy-five years later, there was Tom McCall, his trademark lantern jaw thrust forward and L. B. Day, with his trademark scrunched-up walk, emulating TR on State Street as they headed toward the embattled paper mill. It was classic.

When he died in 1986 of a massive heart attack at age fifty-four, the big new amphitheater at the Oregon State Fair was named for L. B. Day. It was wonderfully appropriate; the man never failed to entertain, even as he did the public's work.

Profile FRESHMAN CHUTZPAH: DON STATHOS AND WALT BROWN

Chutzpah might apply to Don Stathos and Walt Brown, two very different folks, neither of the Jewish persuasion, who simply could not wait in line to help write the Oregon Story. In their freshman year in the Oregon legislature, before the old-timers knew their names and while the veteran lobbyists were snoozing in the balcony, Stathos and Brown struck quickly and added to the Oregon Story.

Stathos was a Republican businessman from Jacksonville, an avid cyclist long before Oregonians discovered European cycling togs with advertising logos. He was forced off the road one day while riding tandem with his daughter, and he determined to do something about safety of bicycles on public roads. Don was a likeable man and a successful insurance salesman; in 1971, going from desk to desk in a legislature containing few cyclists, the freshman representative sold the idea of setting aside 1 percent of state and local highway taxes for bicycles. He won approval in committee by a single vote and on the House and Senate floors by a single vote.

One percent might not seem a lot, but state highway funds are enormous, and in 2014 the bill produced $5 million for bike trails and lanes. The influential highway lobby—contractors, equipment suppliers, auto clubs, and local governments—woke up too late to head Stathos off. Governor McCall originally opposed the bill but ducked when he saw the head of steam Don was building and became a supporter. He signed the bill on the seat of Don's bicycle and the ensuing state program became an Oregon Story chapter.[7]

Senator Walt Brown was surely the only Socialist ever elected to represent wealthy Lake Oswego in the legislature—he held the seat from 1975 to 1987 as a Democrat, and in his first session he introduced and pushed through the nation's first ban on the sale of aerosol sprays. Colleagues sometimes rolled their eyes when he began talking about the danger of aerosol sprays; here was this freshman who had yet to establish himself in the tradition-heavy Oregon Senate, and he was brandishing charts and scientific jargon about chlorofluorocarbons, for god's sake, and how they would destroy the ozone layer. Who knew?

Walt Brown knew and was not deterred. Long before most of us worried about the ozone layer and climate change, Brown sold his Senate colleagues by a single vote to ban the sale of chlorofluorocarbons; then he convinced the House and Governor Straub. Most of us knew the aerosol spray as Freon, a DuPont product, and the giant chemical company was taken by surprise. DuPont lobbyists hit the floor running—too late, it turned out; Brown was on the march. His measure drew additional national attention to Oregon a full year before the National Academy of Science issued the first warning about the dangers of the aerosols.

Brown was a career military lawyer with the mien of a college lecturer, which he was at Lewis and Clark Law School. He made no bones about his socialist faith—he knew and campaigned for Norman Thomas in 1948—and in his post-legislative life he ran for many offices as a Socialist or Green Party candidate; in 2004 he was the presidential candidate of the Socialist Party USA. None of those efforts succeeded, but he was a happy warrior all his life and a self-described "hardcore conservationist." Walt always had a mission, and in 1975 the freshman senator wrote his own chapter of the Oregon Story.

NINE   Holding on in Changing Times

A Mrs. Powel of Philadelphia asked Benjamin Franklin, as the Constitutional Convention adjourned in 1787, "Well, Doctor, what have we got, a republic or a monarchy?" With no hesitation whatsoever, Franklin responded, "A republic, if you can keep it."

For the thousands of Oregonians who in one way or another helped Tom McCall write the Oregon Story, the sight of the tall, stooped governor leaving the platform after his successor and friend Bob Straub was sworn into office in January 1975 was sobering. He had given us a legacy . . . if we could keep it.

The problem was never willingness; much of the legacy had long since shed shackles of partisanship or regional rivalry. Who could be against clean rivers and beaches? The way ahead would be rockier, however, for statewide land-use regulations, and there was a question as to how far the emerging new leaders in Portland could push their urban agenda.

Many ideas of the previous decade did not originate with Tom; Bob Straub played a huge role, as did key legislators and private citizens. But Tom had quickly—and characteristically—taken the lead, with his amazing ability to coin phrases and orchestrate events that took the wind from the sails of opponents. There was no other showman to match Tom, although some were beginning to think Portland's young mayor might be up to the job.

No one doubted the intentions of incoming governor Bob Straub. His hands were all over chapters of the Oregon Story. He was no showman, however, and was clearly identified as a Democrat in a way Tom McCall was never associated with the Republican Party.

The incoming governor had been through a difficult but civil election campaign both in the Democratic primary and the general election, where he had defeated Vic Atiyeh with 57 percent of the vote.

No fewer than fifteen candidates got enough votes to be listed in the 1974 official primary election summary; Tom McCall left a huge hole, but there were plenty eager to jump right in. The two leading Republicans were seasoned and well financed; secretary of state Clay Myers represented the McCall wing of the party and state senator Vic Atiyeh the more conservative Republicans. Democrats had a trio of strong candidates; this time Bob Straub faced two rising Democratic stars, treasurer Jim Redden and state senator Betty Roberts, who was hoping to become the state's first female governor.

Tom McCall's banner—the Oregon Story—was most clearly identified with Clay Myers and Bob Straub. The results of the election told us much about what was ahead in Oregon politics. In the May Republican primary, Atiyeh walloped Myers by a two-to-one margin. Tom had appointed Clay secretary of state in 1966, and Clay won decisive election to the seat two years later, and re-election in 1972; the McCall faction of the Republican Party hoped he was the heir apparent.

He was not; instead of Tom's mantle of popular support, Clay inherited Tom's Achilles' heel: the Republican Party. Tom was well to the left of his party in most regards, and Clay supported Tom's policies. Both paid the price of their apostasy, and both paid it at the hands of Vic Atiyeh, Clay in 1974 and Tom four years later. Vic's overwhelming 1974 primary victory foretold a challenge to the Oregon Story as written by Tom McCall; Atiyeh had voted for beach and bottle bills and the iconic land-use bill but had opposed the Willamette Greenway. He was a highway booster who backed the Mount Hood Freeway and gave mostly lip service to mass transit. He certainly was no enemy of progress in environmental matters, but he had never been a leader and no one expected that from him.

Taxation was his forte in the legislature and I found him a good source, always well informed and candid. Vic was a businessman, and with his brothers ran the Atiyeh Bros. carpet business in

Portland, founded in 1900 by their parents, who immigrated from Syria. The future governor was active in the business until his 1978 election as governor. He supported business legislation and business supported his political campaigns. He was as loyal to his political party as McCall and Myers were independent.

Vic was an Eagle Scout and reflected the best attributes of that honor; he was doggedly square in the age of cool. His parents prevailed by hard work, and he followed their example. In the rare instances where he dipped into political maneuvering, he often appeared uneasy. Of the five headline candidates for governor in 1974, Vic posed the only danger of reversing Oregon Story successes or—more likely—letting them atrophy through lack of funding or by appointing poor stewards to important positions.

Clay touted himself as a liberal Republican and he didn't back down in the 1974 campaign. He supported Measure 2, which would allow state highway funds for mass transit; Vic opposed the idea and so did two-thirds of Oregon voters. Clay backed the eighteen-year-old vote, which Vic opposed. Republicans had a clear choice and they spoke.

Matters were less clear on the Democratic ticket. Ideologically there was little space between Bob Straub, Betty Roberts, and Jim Redden. Business leaders preferred Straub, somewhat of a new experience for him. In terms of the Oregon Story, Redden had helped salvage the Beach Bill in 1969 and Roberts defended the Bottle Bill from industry lobbyists in 1971. Democrats could not go wrong among this trio; the party had been out of the governor's office since 1958, and partisans sensed an opportunity to return.

Bob Straub had been relatively quiet after leaving office in 1973, but we had spent time with him and Pat at the farmhouse. Along with other friends of the family, we were devastated when their teenage son, Bill, was killed in an auto accident in November 1973. Bob was despondent and turned to prescription drugs for depression—something no one outside the immediate family knew at the time.[1]

One of my concerns about Bob Straub was the inevitability that he would be compared with Tom McCall—and would fail the test.

They had worked so closely together on important causes and campaigned against each other twice; the Tom and Bob Show was a frequent phrase in everyday conversation. So often, I had seen good people fail when they followed a strong leader; nothing they could do would save them.

Jim Redden was an outstanding legislator and public servant; he would have made a good governor. Betty Roberts most intrigued me, however, beyond the fact she would have been a notable "first" in Oregon. Roberts had a mental toughness that stood out in the legislature, and the previous year I had singled her out along with Republican Norma Paulus as the most likely to break the glass ceiling on statewide offices. She was also physically tough; for the final six months of her campaign she ignored her doctor's order for a hysterectomy. She finally had the surgery a few days after the primary, in which she finished second with 31 percent of the votes to Bob Straub's 34 percent. Two months after the surgery she was back on the campaign trail, selected by Democrats as their candidate for US Senate when Wayne Morse died in Portland in the midst of his attempt to reclaim the Senate seat he still felt was occupied by an imposter.

She gave Senator Bob Packwood a run for his money (he had plenty) but lost in the final week when he unleashed a barrage of negative advertising. I have always thought that if Betty, rather than the fading Morse, had been the candidate against Packwood from the start, she would have won. One of Bob's core constituencies was feminists, but he would have lost many female voters to Roberts, who was an acknowledged feminist leader. Wayne Morse knew he was mortally ill—he was secretly taking blood transfusions just to stay alive—but his giant ego would not allow him to step aside; that decision may have cost Democrats a seat in the US Senate.[2]

Oregonians were not through with the Oregon Story. Bob Straub's 1974 gubernatorial campaign was greatly improved from his previous two, and the civilized and friendly Democratic primary played a role. Betty's young campaign manager Len Bergstein was quickly hired by the Straub campaign to work with a steering committee headed by former Republican legislator John Mosser. The talented Mosser was a favorite of mine, possibly the smartest guy in the legislature and certainly the most innovative—there always seemed to be a "Mosser Plan" on the table or in the works. John could be a bit devious and wouldn't always tell you what he was up to, but he could not be ignored, and he was frequently right.

In a column for *Willamette Week* shortly after the November election, which was headlined "This time Straub listened," I pointed to the Mosser-Bergstein team as critical to the outcome:

> Out of these circumstances (the close Primary) came the unlikely combination of Mosser-Bergstein, a pair of city-bred Ivy League lawyers trying to steer a headstrong candidate who hated hotel rooms, small talk and small airplanes, and most of all, details. Mosser's steering committee and Bergstein's staff convinced the impatient Straub to turn his calendar over to them and wait for research before hip-shooting on the issues. It didn't always work—but it worked most of the time, and Oregon will have a Democratic governor in January.

Bob benefitted from the help of the outgoing governor; Tom gave him an outright endorsement against the candidate of his own party. When the voters endorsed Bob 57–43 percent in the general election, there was joy in the Tom and Bob camp.

I played my Tom and Bob cards, built up over a decade of covering the two men, and they agreed to let us bring cameras to a transition session of old and new gubernatorial staffs at Salishan shortly after the election. The staffers were well acquainted and some had become friends over the years; the feelings were good as Mosser, Bob Davis, and Ron Schmidt, among others, warned of pitfalls and suggested ideas, knowing full well that the two governors had differing styles to go with their common ideals. The weather at the beach was glorious, and we filmed Bob and Tom during a long beach walk. The nation's political system was imploding in 1974, but all was well on the Oregon Coast; we walked freely on public beaches without a car in sight.

As governor-elect Straub entered office, I used the film in a half-hour documentary, *Bob Straub: At Home in Oregon*, a personal look at a man who had labored in the shadows of his predecessor and wasn't well known on a personal basis by most Oregonians. Steve Smith and I were filming only two days after the election, as Bob visited his eastern Oregon ranch. Later, at the West Salem farmhouse, Pat Straub's reflections on their life together exposed most of our audience to this remarkable woman for the first time. Making the documentary was special fun for me, because it also took me back to Springfield, where both Bob and I began our professional careers in the 1950s. I interviewed Bob's first boss, Charlie

Governor Bob Straub and his wife Pat were most at home in their remodeled farmhouse in the rolling hills northwest of Salem. The house, still in the family, looked out on orchards and farmland. (Robert W. Straub Collection, MSS 1, Western Oregon University Archives)

Preppernau, who had also been the landlord of the tiny house Dixie and I rented in the alley behind the Preppernau house.

Governor Straub's inaugural message was dominated by proposals to combat economic problems that were rolling across the nation and the state. A period of economic stagnation was upon us, making it doubly difficult to advance environmental and human-resources programs as the state budget took a hit from declining income taxes. Little mention was made of Oregon Story achievements, beyond recognition in his opening comments: "We have been granted a rare privilege, the privilege of writing the next chapters in 'The Oregon

Story.' And I need not remind you that the words, the phrases and the themes we choose eventually must bear the scrutiny of more than two million bosses." Bob asked for a major increase in the budget of the Land Conservation and Development Commission (LCDC), the state agency charged with managing the new land-use law.

Land use was easily the most contentious of the Oregon Story pillars. The law set up a spaghetti-like web of intergovernmental cooperation while, at the same time, staff was charged with a state-wide lands inventory, among other tasks. Governor McCall named L. B. Day as chair and Portland attorney Steve Schell as vice-chair of the first LCDC board; both were strong and forceful advocates of land-use planning.

During the buildup to SB 100 and also after the law was passed, an extraordinary citizen-involvement process resulted in literally hundreds of public meetings across Oregon, during which thousands of people shared what they wanted in their land-use goals. Citizen involvement became part of the Oregon Story, and it was transformed into rules and regulations. People had faith in the leaders' promise to listen and respond, a characteristic of this remarkable era. The outreach efforts were perhaps the most intensive sampling of public opinion in the state's history.[3]

It was the age of planners and several became friends and sources. In my more leisurely newspaper days a reporter could sit and talk with people in public positions, without worrying about looking for visuals and going through a "spokesperson" or gatekeeper. Some of the core group around Portland State University's pioneering urban studies and planning program were great sources of information, and they loved to talk about their work. Portland State had only achieved university status in 1969 and was still the newbie on the block; generations of old grads from the state's two established universities dominated politics and media and got most of the money and headlines. Neither the University of Oregon nor Oregon State was in a big city, however, and urban studies was a void that ambitious PSU president Greg Wolfe exploited.

It soon became apparent that the new land-use laws were complex and opponents would hire good lawyers to find its vulnerabilities. The LCDC had only limited assistance from the attorney general, who had few attorneys well versed in land use. Oregon was truly breaking new ground in this field, and it needed some bright young lawyers along with its bright young planners.

Necessity fills a void. Before he left office, Tom McCall took part in forming a citizen body to serve as a watchdog on state land-use planning. The organization that would do that, 1000 Friends of Oregon, was the brainchild of Henry Richmond, a young attorney with the Oregon Student Public Interest Group (OSPIRG), and Allen Bateman, a liberal California immigrant living in conservative Klamath County.[4] Several environmental groups were already active in Oregon and interested in land use, but none had a staff of attorneys and sufficient funding to pursue challenges in the courts. Richmond and Bateman wrote Governor McCall of their intent: "We are convinced that Oregon needs a statewide, full-time professionally staffed citizen organization whose sole purpose is to urge state and local bodies of government to make good land use planning decisions. The organization would also be capable of seeking judicial review of issues dealing with the proper administration of land use laws."

The governor agreed to help, and Richmond and Bateman used his name to line up an impressive list of supporters, including high-profile businesspeople, including Glenn Jackson and John Gray, developer of Salishan. If a thousand people would contribute $100 a year, Richmond reasoned, the organization could fund a small staff of attorneys and support workers. It was amazingly successful. In 1979, on the fourth anniversary of the founding of 1000 Friends, I commented:

> In its four years, 1000 Friends has played as large a role in setting state land use policy as the state itself. Because it is a private group, it could plunge in where political bodies feared to tread. Much of the case law on land use originated in briefs filed by lawyers for 1000 Friends. When

the state was under fire from developers, officials could always point to the threat of law suits from 1000 Friends. As Henry Kissinger might say, there's something to be said for having a credible threat.

One reason the group succeeded is that it escaped early predictions that it would be another no-growth organization. It has opposed development of farmlands and natural areas. But it has also pressed for housing and economic development . . . it even defended mobile homes.

Most of the big battles in the land use war have gone to those who want controlled growth, including 1000 Friends. The public has a short attention span and it's easy to believe the war is over. It isn't. The state has grown accustomed to having 1000 Friends as part of its land use process. We have all become accustomed to this private group doing a great deal of the public's work.

Henry Richmond recruited bright young lawyers with pedigreed undergraduate degrees for 1000 Friends; several had already done a stint at OSPIRG. Steve McCarthy, whom I met when he interned in Tom McCall's office in 1965, was OSPIRG's first executive director, and I was intrigued by the way the new group—the first in what rapidly became a national movement— channeled the concerns and energies of young student activists. When Richmond left OSPIRG to found 1000 Friends he brought Robert Stacey and Richard Benner with him. In later years both Stacey and Benner headed 1000 Friends.

Richmond, a slight, soft-spoken man, not a shouter or finger-pointer, somehow was able to work with a rancher as easily as a corporate lawyer. Several other states emulated 1000 Friends' model. Like much else in the Oregon Story, 1000 Friends began as the brainstorm of citizens—in this case Richmond and Bateman— and was then promoted by Tom McCall and soon grew into a national model.

Governor Straub in 1975 had a Democratic legislature, and he gained approval for an increased LCDC budget and creation of a new Department of Energy to confront the energy crisis that had begun the previous year. He was thwarted when he tried to advance his cherished Willamette Greenway, but his term was marked by an important turnaround in transportation. Combining forces with Portland mayor Neil Goldschmidt and others, Straub killed the Mount Hood Freeway, turning federal highway money into Portland's regional mass transit system, Tri-Met (see Chapter 10).

I commented that the 1975 legislature was the first to prioritize urban issues: mass transit and low-income housing, among others. All had the governor's support; Bob Straub had always shunned big cities and headed for the hills; to emerge as a champion of urban priorities was quite a step. I thought back to our conversation with Eric Hoffer—who would have known?

Portland had some effective advocates, and the House was now leading the way in Salem, the Senate struggling to keep pace. The 1975 House was shifting the playing field, I noted upon adjournment: "Some will criticize the Legislature for this shift of emphasis. But the Legislature reflects reality. Oregon itself is changing—perhaps even faster than the Legislature."

At year's end, in my *Willamette Week* column I compared Straub's first year with that of his predecessor and scored it as "easier" than McCall's first year, which had featured conflict with Tom's Republican counterparts in the legislature and a disastrous experience with the sales tax. Tom was emotionally spent by his first year on the job; Bob was relaxed and getting comfortable with the job he had sought for so long. But Tom had achieved the Beach Bill in his first term; Bob had no similar bragging right.

The two were getting along well, and Tom was willing to help when major issues came along. After dipping his toe into a host of speaking and organizational offers and teaching a class at Oregon State under a special professorship financed by Glenn Jackson and other worthies, Tom McCall went back to his old profession—and in the process nearly ruined our vacation.

Dixie and I were finally able to take a travel vacation with our kids. We started in 1973 with a whirlwind tour of the British Isles, thanks in a roundabout way to Bob Straub. Shortly before Bob left treasury that year, his longtime aide, Ken Johnson, resigned and the Johnson family took a yearlong vacation, headquartering in a rental house in a London suburb. They offhandedly volunteered that we were welcome to sleep on their floor. Coincidentally, old college friends Gil and Roma Stewart also bagged their jobs to spend a year in nearby Winchester; they made a similar offer.

For someone of Scottish descent, the offers had a double bene-fit—a chance to see the land of my heritage and to do it on the cheap. We jumped at the offers and spent a month in England, Ireland, and Scotland in 1973. We enjoyed it so much we returned in 1975, this time spending more time in the Scottish Highlands, home of the Clan Mackay and the most welcoming place on earth. We took a stress break—it had been a hectic five years for all four McKays. We were house-sitting for our friend Susan Bjork's parents near Oxford, en route to Scotland, when I got a letter from my KGW boss, Forest Amsden. This can't be good, I thought as I opened the envelope. I was correct; Forest wrote:

> Channel 2 has hired McCall as news analyst. I do not know under what conditions. They will have their hands full handling him and his campaign for governor against Straub several years hence. I don't know whether he is going to be fulltime or part-time or whenever he can make it or what. But he is highly promotable and top news and program executives here are a bit panicked. Hope you are having a good time and getting the batteries charged up.

They were panicked? For me, the only worse scenario would have been KGW offering Tom his old job, which was now *my* job. I don't know if Tom talked to Forest or Ancil, but I doubt it. Channel 2 Station Manager Tom Dargan was an old buddy from Tom's days at KGW, and Dick Ross had also made the move from our station to KATU.

Great. I would be competing with the old master with his fat Rolodex of contacts. The open spaces of the Scottish Highlands did a lot for my stress level, but a cloud hung over the remainder of our trip; perhaps a wee dram would help! I didn't know it at the time but Tom was getting $37,000 a year, well above the $21,000 I was earning in his old job.

Tom's decision should not have been a surprise, however. In 1969, as he prepared for a new legislature, I had sat down with him to review the first two years of his governorship. Having no idea that I would be sitting in his old KGW-TV chair in just over a year, I asked him, "Have you made your mark as a politician, instead of as a political commentator . . . do most people see you as a politician?" He thought about that a minute, then replied:

> I don't know . . . I think they still see me as a commentator. I still see myself as a commentator, in this new conversation, this role of trying to report everything that I know, trying to take them into my confidence and tell them what I'm thinking . . . Maybe it's too much of a spontaneous process to have in government. I don't see myself as a politician—I wouldn't be doing some of the things I'm doing; some are absolutely suicidal . . . supporting the sales tax, governmental reorganization . . .

Now he was back on the air; but was he commentator or politician? The new job cramped Tom's style; he hadn't written on deadline for years, and when he showed up on a story, he sometimes became the story. For eight years someone else had done his research, and his calls were always returned; he could be late, and others would wait for him. But now, when the camera light blinked red, there was no way out, and television formatting and scripting had become much more complex since he left the business in 1964. To add to the problem, Tom had a very thin skin, and actions by Governor Straub or others that appeared to be critical of his legacy brought an immediate on-air response, sometimes rather embarrassing.

We saw each other often, but not socially, and I sensed Tom's journalistic juices were drying up and he was getting restless again. I relaxed and stopped worrying about him as a competitor, figuring it wouldn't last very long. But it was a strange experience while it lasted.

The 1977 legislature was a dysfunctional, feuding group hijacked by a so-called "Six Pack" of House opportunists, but when it broke camp in July, I scored Straub with major victories, including a gutsy veto of a bill that would have advanced field burning in the Willamette Valley. He prevailed across the board—energy, school finance, corrections, economic development, aid to the elderly poor—and he turned back attempts to damage land-use planning and the Willamette Greenway.

It was really his first session outside the long shadow of Tom McCall. "The entire performance establishes Bob Straub as a strong governor, certainly as his own man in office," I commented, "That was the challenge he faced as this session opened—a challenge faced and conquered." Yet the breadth of his accomplishments left no single area that he could tout as Tom touted the Beach Bill and the Bottle Bill. Straub showed promise as an accomplished governor, but not as the political rock star his predecessor had been, and perhaps not what Oregon voters were looking for in 1978.

Tom McCall was also sensing his old friend's vulnerability, but we read a different set of tea leaves. Both of us feared the state was turning its collective back on the Oregon Story and moving to the right. But Tom foresaw a revival of his Oregon Mystique, where I foresaw a state hunkering down just to defend gains of the past decade. In early 1978, Tom announced he would seek his old office again, joining Senator Vic Atiyeh and Representative Roger Martin in the Republican primary.

In the 1976 election Tom had played a very active role in defeating Measure 10, which would have repealed LCDC, and he had been campaigning nationwide for other states to adopt a Bottle Bill. He was still a political force, but Oregon was changing. He should have paid more attention to his friend Clay Myers' defeat in the 1974 Republican primary. In previous statewide elections Tom didn't need to worry about conservative Republicans, because he faced no serious primary challenger; now he faced two, and both were younger and hungrier.

No one asked me if Tom should have entered the race, but I would have sided with those closest to him, including Ed Westerdahl and Ron Schmidt, who told Tom they would not campaign for him this time. Tom's brain was swallowed by his ego and sense of inevitability, and he paid no mind. I feared that a changing electorate would not welcome him again and, if he won, he would not have the energy to do the job. Second chances sometimes should be resisted, and I was sorry he did not resist the lure of another bully pulpit.

Smiling pleasantly at one of their joint appearances in 1978, Republicans Tom McCall, Roger Martin, and Victor Atiyeh were soon exchanging barbs in their hotly contested Republican primary for the right to face Governor Bob Straub in November. (David Falconer, *Oregonian*)

It was painful to see Tom campaign; he was an exhausted man, his long face haggard and his eyes dull. In three debates, he was bested by both opponents; there was no quick wit or comeback to cover his lack of preparation. He entered the race knowing he could not lose; by early May it was apparent he could not win.

Atiyeh won 46 percent of the Republican vote and carried every county. It was a race too far for Tom, and I was reminded of Wayne Morse. In commentary following the primary, I made that comparison:

> Politics is always a delicate balance between belief in the impossible and acceptance of reality. The ego is a mighty thing, capable of tipping this balance. Tom McCall was captured by his own press clippings, swallowed by the image we all created for him. Neither the first nor the last victim of this particular political disease.
>
> Wayne Morse fell before the obsession that his seat in the Senate was held by an imposter. He never left the Senate in his own mind, and he died knowing he would return.

Tom McCall believed that his own fate and that of the state were one and the same. The Oregon Story was the McCall Story, and vice-versa . . .

Many who watched at closer quarters could see the man we knew and enjoyed disappear—replaced by almost an institutional image. Less politician or journalist than spokesman—and increasingly a spokesman who seemed to confuse self and state. As Wayne Morse stayed Senator in his own mind, Tom McCall never ceased to be Oregon's Spokesman. Until finally no one was really listening any more.

Yet when the histories of Oregon are written, the chapters on Morse and McCall will treat their defeats as footnotes to how truly magnificent they were in their prime . . . For before we wrapped (Tom McCall) in an image he could not escape, there was the man. And a damn good one at that.

When Straub and Atiyeh squared off for the second time, Oregonians told pollsters they were primarily concerned about the economy—unemployment topped 12 percent—and environmental issues were well down their list. Tom's defeat in the primary was a further message that priorities were changing. It was "Time for Atiyeh," one of the more telling campaign slogans of the time.

Oregonians were not turning against the Oregon Story; they had read that story and liked it, but it was on the bookshelf now, and they were tired of the fuss and bother. Vic was ideal for the new climate; moderate in public and personal life, seldom flummoxed by events, he fit the image of quiet competence that voters wanted.

Atiyeh also elected to ride the tax-relief horse, released from the starting gate earlier in the year when California voted for Proposition 13, the historic property-tax limitation. Ray Phillips' Oregon Homeowners Association immediately put a clone of Prop 13 on the ballot and it picked up steam. Governor Straub opposed it strongly and, although Measure 6 lost narrowly in November, Atiyeh's image of fiscal conservatism was enhanced.

Vic knew more about taxes than almost anyone else in the legislature and had traditionally been a cool head on the topic. I felt his embrace of Measure 6 was irresponsible. I had done a lot of research on the measure and analyzed its complexities and its politics. My strongest commentary came on September 14, after Vic outlined another rationale for supporting the measure:

> There is a familiar cartoon of a man chasing a mob, running full tilt to catch it and become its leader. Not a very dignified posture, certainly not in keeping with Vic Atiyeh's record of service in the Legislature. I've watched Atiyeh in most of his 20 years and seen him support a lot of tax plans. None even remotely resembling Measure 6.
>
> Nor did he support it before it was apparent that 200,000 people had signed petitions (to place it on the ballot). Atiyeh has allowed raw numbers to replace the judgment he prided himself on in his long legislative career. Few people have served as many years on legislative tax committees as Senator Atiyeh. His zig-zag pursuit of a position on Six cannot be due to ignorance. It can only be explained by mathematics. The Senator counted to 200,000. And at that point forgot everything he had learned in 20 years as a legislator.

Combined with the momentum from his upset win over Tom McCall in May, Vic's support of Measure 6 carried him to a 54–46 percent victory in November 1978, reversing the results of 1974. He got the best of both worlds: he won and Measure 6 lost, leaving him with one less challenge as he took office.

The day after the election, I summed up Bob Straub as a politician and a private person who "could never bare his personal life to the curious," a man whose record "in general was marred by impatience. He wanted to get at it—whatever it was. Bob Straub had no patience for small talk or small minds." I concluded:

> Bob Straub followed a governor who provided entertainment for the press and public, and Straub was no entertainer. He found a public ready to slow down, to consolidate its gains and serve itself first. But he was too impatient to get on with it, so he never slowed down to catch the changing winds. That cost him the election, but he went down fighting for the things he had always fought for: Equity in taxes, a quality environment and social justice. Bob Straub left his mark—writ large—on his adopted state.

I felt as if I had written the political obituary of the Oregon Story in the defeat of its two prime architects. The scene was changing at the capitol and my interests had shifted to a renaissance of sorts in Portland. I was also picking up expertise and interest in national and even international politics and events that would play out for me in my final years at KGW.

Tom was fuming on the sidelines, still struggling to maintain his broadcasts but looking haggard and unfocused. He still got national speaking invitations, but his image began to fade. Much of his time was spent defending his "visit but don't stay" remark from the Atiyeh administration's obsession that it hurt business. Tom insisted that was not the case, but the remark continued to bug Atiyeh, and in July 1982 he made the mistake of inviting Tom to a strange ceremony on the California border to remove the "We hope you enjoy your visit" language from a "Welcome to Oregon" billboard. Vic originally wanted to dynamite the sign, but cooler heads prevailed; they failed to convince the governor, however, that inviting Tom was not a good idea.

Tom stood quietly through the ceremony, and then faced the television cameras to defend his original statement. It brought forth some of his colorful rhetoric that had almost been lost: "I am simply saying that Oregon is demure and lovely, and it ought to play a little hard to get. And I think you'll all be just as sick as I am if you find it is nothing but a hungry hussy, throwing herself at every stinking smokestack that's offered."

Only days later, doctors detected a rampant cancer that was savaging his entire body. We reported the cancer but not the fact that it was terminal, leaving that up to Tom. His time was quickly approaching, but he was still in the arena.

Oregon's economy had gone sour and created a sour electorate; opponents of LCDC and state land-use planning seized the opportunity. A coalition of developers, timber companies, and contractors bankrolled a campaign to put a repeal on the 1982 ballot. Polls showed this new Measure 6 passing by as much as 2–1. One poll also showed that only Tom McCall could convince voters to change their minds.

Reporters were tipped to attend a small dinner for opponents of Measure 6 on October 7. Tom would be there, and he had something to say. We knew he was fading, and our camera rolled when he began speaking. At first he was defensive of his legacy, the "scape-goating of the McCall years as somehow to blame eight years later." Then he moved closer to the microphones and shifted his position, obviously in great pain:

> If you really want to signal to one and all that Oregon is down—that we can't even agree on what we are doing, that we are ready to quit— just pass Measure 6 and totally repudiate the Oregon Mystique. You all know I have terminal cancer—and I have a lot of it. But what you may not know is that stress induces the spread and induces its activity. Stress may even bring it on. Yet stress is the fuel of the activist. This activist loves Oregon more than he loves life. I know I can't have both very long. The trade-offs are all right with me. But if the legacy we helped give Oregon and which made it twinkle from afar—if it goes, then I guess I wouldn't want to live in Oregon anyhow.

There wasn't a dry eye in the house—including mine—and we raced back to the studio for the eleven o'clock news. It was extraordinarily hard for me to introduce the tape on the air. The impact was powerful—later polling showed that Tom's message turned the tide and the state's urban counties provided the 55 percent vote to reject Measure 6. Tom McCall died of cancer on January 8, 1983.

Bob Straub retired to his beloved farmhouse, but was active in the Garten Foundation, which ran a recycling program employing the mentally handicapped. He spearheaded a waterfront park on the Willamette River in Salem, and a middle school and an environmental center are named for him in his adopted city. He hosted fundraisers for Democratic candidates, among them Neil Goldschmidt, a regular visitor at the farmhouse. Neil later appointed Bob to the Oregon Investment Council that Bob had created.

In the late 1990s, Bob was diagnosed with Alzheimer's disease and, typically, he used it as a teachable moment, encouraging others.

Dixie and I were among about a hundred friends who gathered to celebrate Bob's eightieth birthday on May 6, 2000, and open the Straub Archives at Western Oregon University. We happened to arrive together and, as we walked into the library, Bob shared with me his frustrations. "You never know when it's going to hit you," he said. "One minute you're doing fine and the next you cannot remember where you are." He was good that day, speaking very briefly but greeting everyone and remembering most names—that in itself was unusual; Bob was notorious for forgetting names.

It was his last public appearance. Bob Straub died November 27, 2002. By then, thousands of public employees were benefitting from the investment policies Bob created for their retirement; and we all benefitted from his role in the Oregon Story.

Governor Atiyeh had defended Tom's land-use law when it came under attack and would not have to do so again in his second term. He was totally engaged in trying to get Oregon's economy back on track; he acquired the nickname "Trader Vic" from his frequent travels to build trade. He was also dealing with demands for tax reform, and lingering snippets of the Oregon Story were far from his mind, or the minds of most Oregonians.

Bob Straub and Vic Atiyeh had the first shift in holding the Oregon Story intact; they held off the anti-LCDC forces in 1976 and 1982, allowing the innovative system to establish itself for the long run. Straub convinced the 1975 legislature to pour a lot more money into LCDC, and that was critical. Governor Atiyeh would subsequently play a major role in one of the remaining chapters of the Oregon Story: protection of the Columbia River Gorge.

The issue brought into play two states and their governors and congressional delegations. It was a story made for television cameras and, over a two-year period in 1980 and 1981, the gorge became a priority for my reporting and commentary. The cause fit the Oregon Story model of preserving a precious asset for the benefit of millions of ordinary citizens—and the visuals were wonderful. Even as a teenage immigrant, I was stunned by the powerful beauty of the gorge when we first drove the winding original highway high above the pounding river. It was a white-knuckle drive for flatlanders, one we never forgot.

The farsighted vision of President Franklin D. Roosevelt had saved the gorge from becoming a "Pittsburgh of the West," as envisioned by Portland boomers when Bonneville Dam was built in 1937; they wanted big industries to get power preference, but FDR opted for farmers and small towns that needed electrical service. John Yeon, son of a prominent Portland family and a celebrated Northwest architect, had played a role in saving the gorge from the industrial boomers of the 1930s, and he stayed with the cause all his life. I interviewed him in 1981 on his spectacular rolling acreage he called The Shire, on the Washington side facing Multnomah Falls. At seventy-one, Yeon despaired for the gorge; new developments were already on the drawing board for more suburbs east of Vancouver.

The boomers had discovered real estate. It was only a matter of time before as many houses as the water table could support would be built. Courthouse politicians lined up with the builders. Governor Dixy Lee Ray of Washington and Governor Atiyeh naively hoped local officials would somehow handle the onslaught, perhaps through a bistate agreement; the record of interstate cooperation in the Northwest was not encouraging.

The confrontational and strong-willed Ray rejected a federal role in the Columbia Gorge, and Vic initially sided with her in 1980. Ray was easily the strangest major political figure I ever encountered, a marine biologist whose strong backing for nuclear energy caused President Richard Nixon to appoint her to chair the Atomic Energy Commission. Ray dressed and talked in a masculine manner, and she could be very forceful. She drove Bob Straub nuts when they crossed paths; both were Democrats, at least in name, but there the similarities stopped. Vic was wearing his conservative hat when he joined forces with Dixy.

"For the first time in years, Oregon is following the lead of Washington on an environmental matter," I commented. "The command is 'Backward March' and the troops are in line." Six months later nothing had changed, and I warned, "Conservationists in the

Gorge must wait for changes in governors before they have much realistic hope for their cause."

That's exactly what happened: Atiyeh was basically saved from a serious environmental blunder by the voters of Washington, who rejected Governor Ray in 1980 after a single term and elected Republican John Spellman. Spellman, a quiet, thoughtful man who proved to be a remarkable conservationist, reversed Ray's approach and began talking with his Oregon counterpart about protecting the gorge. This alone was a good sign. The gorge had never been a priority in Olympia—Washington's population and political muscle lives along Puget Sound, whereas the gorge is Portland's eastern portal.

An entrenched or indifferent Washington could prevent any coordination in the gorge—exactly what Skamania County had in mind. A small county with the grandest views of the Oregon shore, Skamania is about 80 percent national forest. Combining forests, dams, and fish hatcheries, federal agencies virtually keep Skamania alive. Yet, as so often happens in government-dependent counties, the natives hated government, if not their paychecks. It was tough country; I went around in late June with Roy Craft, a retired local editor who knew everyone, and got an earful (politely delivered) that made it apparent Skamanians would fight any federal role.

I returned with Jon Tuttle and a tag team of photographers. We produced a five-part series in July 1981 that gave both sides their say. Jon did a masterful job of describing gorge history, and I drew the short straw and positioned myself in the midst of a raucous public meeting in Stevenson, the county seat. Local folk were suspicious of Portland media, as might be expected, but the lightning rod for them was a tall, slender woman named Nancy Russell, who headed Friends of the Columbia Gorge.

Nancy knew the bulwark of opposition was in Skamania County, and she invaded the land of stubborn loggers, fierce defenders of private property, and eager land developers without giving an inch. I watched as she stood her ground against angry shouts, wagging fingers, and occasional threats—her tires were slashed on at least one occasion, and she was given police protection at others. It was no job for the faint of heart. Nancy was neither faint nor retiring.

She told me in 1981: "If the people of Skamania County continue to live in the past, not recognizing what's facing them in the future, then I think this will have to be accomplished over their heads—because I think it's going to happen."

I concluded our five-part series with commentary:

Common ground must be found and it must include an authority that is larger than the sum of its local governments. Counties cannot legally or financially enforce an overall management plan. Yet the Gorge is a series of panoramic views, cutting across property and political boundaries . . .

Management must also span these boundaries and it must include a federal role . . . There must be what Governor Atiyeh calls an arbiter. And there must be a banker as well, working with property owners, elected officials, and neighbors of the Gorge. It can be done. We are all, if you will, "Friends of the Gorge."

Nancy and her friends, many of them influential Republicans in Portland, were a big factor influencing Vic Atiyeh, as was his Washington counterpart. Governor Spellman was willing to compromise, and he opened the door for Vic to reverse himself and support a federal role.

Governor Atiyeh came up with a compromise solution that saved the day. Gorge protectors wanted a national park, a concept that was an anathema to Skamanians. Much of what they knew about the National Park Service came from a professional Sagebrush Rebellion champion named Charles Cushman, who came into the county and scared everyone halfway to death. Hatred for the Park Service was palpable. Smokey Bear was their neighbor, however, and when Atiyeh proposed the Forest Service as the federal partner in the gorge, he neutralized some of the opponents.

Spellman and Atiyeh continued to talk, and the Friends worked political leaders in both states. I stayed on the beat with at least a dozen commentaries plus the news series. Finally, Atiyeh's compromise prevailed and the gorge gang—still minus Skamania—descended on Congress for authorization and money. The maneuvering would continue until 1986.

The political landscape had changed in "the other Washington." Congressman Sid Morrison, a moderate Republican whose large central Washington district included Skamania, sided with gorge protectors, as did all members of Congress from the two states except Oregon Republicans Denny Smith and Bob Smith. It was a heady time for Republicans with Ronald Reagan in the Oval Office, but the Smiths didn't call the shots. Senator Mark Hatfield did; he chaired the powerful Senate Appropriations Committee, and he pressured Reagan's advisors to sign the National Scenic Area Act that Congress drafted, putting the Forest Service in charge.

Reagan didn't want the bill—he opposed any federal reach into states—but he needed Hatfield and also Senator Bob Packwood, who chaired another major committee. The *Oregonian's* man in Washington DC, Jim Flanigan, detailed a full-court press by Hatfield, Packwood, and Washington Senator Dan Evans in the final days before the legislation expired. Most of Reagan's advisors wanted a veto, but he reluctantly signed the measure, and colleagues gave Hatfield the credit. If the bill had expired, gorge protection would have been delayed at least the final two years of Reagan's term, perhaps longer. Skamania County flew its flag at half-staff when the Columbia River Gorge National Scenic Area Act passed.[5]

President Reagan's signature came at the end of November 1986; by that time I had agreed to join governor-elect Neil Goldschmidt's team in Salem. The gorge bill was a farewell gift; it spoke to my love of landscape, open spaces, and special places. Outlooks and open space lured me to the Scottish Highlands time and again; the fjords of Norway were more compelling than a cityscape.

The gorge was not pristine; it was a vital, working area. But it was very special, and I felt as if I had played a part in keeping it that way. I opened my commentary that day, "In this world where so much beauty has been lost to what we call progress, fortune has smiled on the Columbia Gorge." That summed it up.

Many players had put the National Scenic Area Act in place, and it deserved a chapter of the Oregon Story. Another chapter was in progress as well, and in the final half of my seventeen years at KGW, it became a major priority. Portland was reinventing itself, right down Jefferson Street from our studios.

Profile NANCY RUSSELL: STEEL IN A VELVET GLOVE

John Yeon needed younger hands to take the baton after four decades of battling to preserve the Columbia River Gorge. A group of Portland women, many from prominent families, created a small group in 1980 called The Committee to Save the Gorge; Yeon invited them to picnic at The Shire.

Among the group was a striking young woman named Nancy Russell; she was a graduate of Scripps College, but in the language of the time she would have been described as "a housewife" raising four children with her stockbroker husband, Bruce Russell.

When John Yeon looked for support in his decades-long battle to save the Columbia River Gorge from commercial exploitation, he found it in Nancy Russell, who went on to form Friends of the Columbia Gorge in 1981. (Photo Archive, Friends of the Columbia Gorge)

Yeon spotted Nancy's potential and invited the Russells to The Shire to talk about preservation. From that meeting came Friends of the Columbia Gorge, with Nancy as founder, activist-in-chief, fundraiser, and lobbyist. Friends absorbed the Committee to Save the Gorge and among the first Friends were Tom McCall and Bob Straub, Multnomah County Executive Don Clark, and former Washington governor (and future senator) Dan Evans.

Nancy Russell was in love with the Columbia River Gorge. She was a noted wildflower photographer who did an annual exhibit dubbed "Wild Beauty," and she led nature hikes for many years. Nancy stood up to her opponents; she took flak and responded calmly and with controlled passion, a steel fist in a velvet glove. The *Oregonian's* Katy Muldoon described Nancy Russell in a profile shortly before Russell's death in 2008: "This mannerly woman, as cerebral as she was physically strong, as unfussy as she was charismatic, would take to the front lines in one of the Northwest's most hostile, divisive, and long-running land-use wars."[6]

A bumper sticker north of the river read "Save the Gorge from Nancy Russell," but she was not deterred—she believed most people on both sides of the river wanted to save the gorge in some way, and she would not be bullied.

The Russells later bought parcels of strategic property that they converted to public ownership. Nancy Russell acquired Lou Gehrig's disease but friends would drive her to the gorge's back roads so she could view the wildflowers. She died in 2008, truly the gorge's greatest friend.

TEN   Becoming Portlandia

We celebrated my seventy-ninth birthday at an excellent Italian restaurant that my daughter and her husband described as the epitome of the latest "happening" neighborhood in Portland circa 2014: Southeast Division Street. *Division Street?* Anyone whose Portland days were from 1970 to 1989 would certainly not have put Division Street on any such list. Yet as I sipped my Chianti and gazed out at the street scene it finally hit me: We were dining right in the westbound lanes of what had been designated as the Mount Hood Freeway when I arrived in Portland!

In 1970, a neighborhood of blue-collar families and aging but substantial housing was about to be leveled for an eight-lane freeway that wouldn't go anywhere near Mount Hood. The freeway would have ended at I-205 and would have wiped out a neighborhood and belched tons of exhaust fumes and carbon into the atmosphere.

Division a quarter-century later was still a neighborhood of affordable housing, but neat and tidy with clean air and quiet streets instead of acres of pavement, interchanges, noise, and pollution. Young people with babies in strollers, bicyclists, and folks of my generation mingled on busy sidewalks that united rather than divided one of the city's traditional neighborhoods.

Approval of the freeway would have led to more of the same and the whole concept of Portland as a people-friendly city might have been derailed. Stopping that freeway probably contributed more to the future livability of Portland than any other action that took place during my time in the city. It was thought to be inevitable when I arrived in town, but the next five years would see the creation of a most remarkable political movement that would reverse the inevitable. Federal funds for the project were diverted to mass transit and ultimately provided the foundation for the city's light-rail system. When the first MAX train rolled in 1986, it rode tracks laid by the long battle over the Mount Hood Freeway.

Glitzier examples of key Portland decisions in the 1970s and 1980s exist: Pioneer Square, a new Nordstrom anchor store, signature MAX trains, the rebirth of inner Northwest as the Pearl District and, in later years, Portlandia. *Portlandia* was both a controversial sculpture by Raymond Kaskey and, much later, a funky television satire, mostly for the young and hip. Take your choice—the label somehow seems to fit the city; I use it generically here, hoping not to offend friends or foes of either "Portlandia."

Neither version of Portlandia was around in 1970, and the Mount Hood Freeway was a much grittier coming attraction. It had been approved—and funded—by state and federal governmental agencies the year before, and it had strong supporters among labor leaders and Chamber of Commerce types hankering for good construction jobs. Division Street homeowners mostly wanted it to be resolved so they could move on; many supported the project, figuring they might save a few minutes' driving time to downtown. Others saw a buyer for their houses in the freeway's path; some had already been sold to the state highway department. In toney westside neighborhoods, some families actually thought the freeway would go to their favorite ski slopes . . . if not now, eventually.

The 1970s was a decade of citizen activism, and the Mount Hood Freeway was a catalyst for a group concerned about air quality and degradation of neighborhoods. Betty Merten was one, and she later told an interviewer about how she, her lawyer husband Charlie, and others formed STOP, a major citizen group opposing the freeway:

> STOP was formed by several of us—Ron Buel, who had written a book, *Dead End*, about the impact of cars and freeways on American cities; Steve Schell; Jim Howell; and others who were concerned about the maze of freeways that were in the works for Portland, which, if built, would

slice up the city, destroy neighborhoods, reduce livability, create more air pollution, the most notable of which was the Mount Hood freeway that seemed destined to go through southeast Portland. We knew that to be effective on the local level we had to organize, and we had to be visible and focused. STOP was a perfect name for a group committed to stopping the Mount Hood freeway, but the words themselves—Sensible Transportation Options for People—pointed to solutions beyond cars and freeways. We also lobbied the city to adopt disincentives to the auto, like parking lids on new downtown development, and employee incentives to take the bus to work. It was a grass roots group in the best sense. We were focused and informed . . . there were never very many of us but we created a perception of many. We were educated, articulate professionals—young Turks who believed we could overturn a "done deal."[1]

It was my first exposure to the intense focus and organizational skills of Ron Buel, my future colleague at *Willamette Week*. As a *Wall Street Journal* reporter, Ron had gained expertise in transportation matters, and he took that expertise to city hall as assistant to newly elected mayor Neil Goldschmidt in 1972. Ron ran Neil's first campaign, for city council in 1970, and built a cadre of loyalists that included many people I would work with and enjoy for years. Ron was out front early and strong against the freeway; Neil was with him, but feeling his way as he forged a council majority.

Portland in 1970, as I eased into Tom McCall's old job at KGW, was essentially 1950 Portland with urban renewal; it was conservative, stodgy, and controlled by downtown businessmen. Perhaps its most notable features were outstanding parks—the massive Forest Park and the lovely Washington Park with its stunning views of Mount Hood.

I didn't know the neighborhoods, and much of the city east of the Willamette River was terra incognita. I did know several legislators and a few state officials who lived in Portland, and I knew new Councilman Goldschmidt from his campaign work for Bob Straub. My task was to learn the rest of Portland while I continued to cover and explain the Oregon Story, the legislature, and other happenings in a very exciting time. It was also the year of Vortex, the Portland

State protests, and police pushbacks . . . and so much more. Oh yes, and learn how to be on television!

Fortunately, I was young and energetic, with a supportive family and a supportive boss in Forest Amsden, who was also new as station manager. I quickly bonded with Dennis Buchanan, newly installed as assignment editor; we both came from print backgrounds. The Buchanans had good community connections and through them we melded into Portland's increasingly Democratic politics.

Through the 1970s, partisanship was not as strong a factor in Oregon as was strong personal leadership. That was certainly true with governors McCall and Straub, and it was true as well in Portland and Multnomah County. In most local elections, candidates run without party labels, although in large metropolitan areas their political ties are well known. The ability to put together a majority coalition was job one for an executive. Defeating the Mount Hood Freeway required a lot of coalitions, not the least of which was getting city and county governing bodies to cooperate. Rivalries are inevitable in government, but in the big issues of this period progressive leaders worked across jurisdictional as well as party lines.

The groundwork for citizen pushback against urban freeways actually began in 1968 when state highway engineers announced a plan to widen Harbor Drive along the west bank of the Willamette River, to link up with the future Fremont Bridge nearing completion in northwest Portland. Harbor Drive was an ugly, noisy barrier sealing downtown from the river. Governor McCall favored closing Harbor Drive and razing the vacant *Oregon Journal* building to create a greenway park along the riverfront.[2]

In deference to backers of Harbor Drive, the governor appointed a task force to study the proposal, but he was sandbagged by Frank Ivancie and Glenn Jackson, two task force members. They proposed a ten-lane expressway—in total opposition to the governor—and Ivancie was ready to declare victory when the Portland City Club stepped into the debate. The club was the most influential civic organization in the state; presidential candidates sought its luncheon platform every four years, and its research reports were widely quoted by the media. The club went through a prolonged battle over admission of women members during this period—women won— but the publicity didn't negatively impact its clout, and office-holders paid attention.

Neil Goldschmidt, working as a Legal Aid lawyer at the time, was involved in the City Club study and he threw in his lot with a newly formed Riverfront for People (RFP), put together by Allison and Bob Belcher and Jim Howell, neighbors of Neil's in the Irvington area of the eastside. RFP organized a picnic that drew about 250 adults and a horde of their young children; an appealing family image in the era of long-haired hippies. Shortly afterward, with Bob Straub at his side, Neil made one of his first public statements against urban freeways, calling for the closure of Harbor Drive.[3]

An increasingly influential group of young planners, engineers, and architects were beginning to push the envelope in Portland; many were new to the city, urbanites from the East looking for a home that hadn't yet destroyed itself with—among other things— inner city freeways. In the immediate post–World War II era, freeways were all the rage, beginning with President Eisenhower's championing of the interstate highway system.

The concept of multilane roads existed long before the interstate system, but the onslaught was stalled by World War II. The highwaymen continued planning, however. Highway builders such as Robert Moses were planning enormous webs of freeways in major urban areas in the East, and they worked their way west. Moses and a team were in Portland in 1943 and drew up an ambitious plan that included multiple freeways. Oregon highway engineers had also looked at urban freeways and were in accord with Moses' proposals. Local politicians and business and civic leaders supported the aggressive plans.

But by the 1960s, planners and architects working on city planning were not on board; most opposed the idea of both the Harbor

Drive and Mount Hood freeways. Urban planning under the leadership of these young men was becoming a hot topic both in the news and among activists. The City Club report critical of expanding Harbor Drive was very visible proof of this phenomenon.

The combined efforts of the City Club, RFP, and other citizens stopped Harbor Drive in its tracks. Jackson and McCall took it off the table and began working with opponents to plan a waterfront park, eventually named Tom McCall Waterfront Park; it was Tom's original idea but others had to take over the leadership when Ivancie and Jackson pulled the rug from under the governor. It was another example of progressive coalitions replacing traditional power brokers all across the state.

KGW played a role in still another urban freeway debate in 1972; highway engineers proposed a trunk road connecting the new Fremont Bridge to the Northwest industrial area on St. Helens Road. Engineers originally wanted a route that would have taken out a swath of housing along Upshur and several adjacent streets. Station Manager Amsden felt strongly that an alternative, a "Short Yeon" alignment, would protect neighborhoods, although at a somewhat higher cost. In February, he editorialized: "Portland needs close-in housing, on bus lines and near shopping. Northwest Portland's residential area would be damaged by a freeway in the Upshur Corridor. Put the freeway where it is needed—in the industrial area."

City Commissioner Lloyd Anderson, an engineer and planner, led the successful effort for the Yeon industrial location, which was finally decided in 1974. I observed that, as in the beach-highway disputes of a decade earlier, citizens and neighborhoods had a voice in a field that historically had been exclusively for engineers. Anderson was also involved in the closing of Harbor Drive.

There was an enormous amount of jockeying between the old-line highway engineers in Salem and the urban rebels in Portland. Of the city's leading politicians, only Commissioner Ivancie could be counted on to favor more freeways. Goldschmidt was rapidly taking a leadership role against urban freeways and he had the backing of

McCall and Straub. The critical player, however, was often Glenn Jackson. Jackson was adapting to the new rules and would later yield on the Mount Hood Freeway; Frank Ivancie never did adapt.

When the Mount Hood Freeway was funded at federal and state levels in 1969, a group of southeast neighborhood activists formed the Southeast Legal Defense Team to fight the construction. They battled it in court and at city hall. Goldschmidt and Buel at city hall had effective partners at the Multnomah County Courthouse. County executive Don Clark and Commissioner Mel Gordon, the latter an early champion of light rail, were staunch allies in the anti-freeway campaign.

In 1974 both the Portland City Council and Multnomah County Commission withdrew their previous support of the freeway, and Glenn Jackson and Governor McCall joined the opposition. Bob Straub, campaigning to succeed McCall in the 1974 election, was also strongly opposed. His Republican opponent, Victor Atiyeh, supported the freeway and had also been hostile to Tri-Met (the regional transportation agency) as a legislator; the gubernatorial election was critical.

Straub's election sealed the deal and the new governor immediately turned to Glenn Jackson to help lobby Congress and federal highway officials to assure that freeway funds would be transferred to mass transit in the Portland area. Again, Jackson's pragmatism kept him in the game. Jackson knew top federal highway officials personally and he worked closely with Senator Hatfield. Congressmen Les AuCoin and Bob Duncan were important in securing transit funding in the House.

Over the years, the $500 million transfer of federal funds from the Mount Hood Freeway to mass transit in the Portland area became the "father of MAX," the iconic light rail system. I reminded viewers in 1986, when MAX opened, that only $85 million of the transfer funds had actually gone directly to light rail. The vast majority went to improved buses and highway lanes to improve the flow of automobiles. I described the abandonment of the freeway in 1986 as "perhaps the most important environmental decision in Portland in the last 20 years." Certainly it was important well beyond the field of transportation.

The critical highway decisions halting Harbor Drive and the Mount Hood Freeway were in the works as a whole new generation stood on the cusp of an urban renewal; not the official Urban Renewal—Portland had done that a decade before—but a renewal of leadership, ideas, and a concept of urban life to replace Portland's reputation as a city of "quiet old wealth, discreet culture and cautious politics."

That was the description of Portland circa 1970 through the eyes of Neal Peirce, a journalist who went on to become a leading writer on urban affairs. Neal came to Oregon in 1968 while researching a series of books on American states. He sought names of sources he might not have otherwise interviewed; among those I suggested was Neil Goldschmidt, whom I described as a young Legal Aid lawyer with big ideas.

Peirce caught the essence of Portland as the sixties ended; he found that the city had some impressive structures—praising the Forecourt Fountain (now the Ira Keller Fountain), parks, and the new Memorial Coliseum—but, he noted, "sadly, postwar planners permitted an ugly freeway (Harbor Drive) to slice right along the downtown waterfront, decisively separating water and city." He added, in reference to the city's newest office towers:

> Architectural critics have pointed out that virtually all these new mega-structures lack sophistication and create such fantastic parking space demands that vast stretches of the city are given over to parking lots and garages. Where they should bring life to downtown, they tend to do just the opposite with solid marble and concrete street level exposures broken by nothing more romantic than a corporate entrance and a parking garage.[4]

Portland would require a facelift to alter the downtown image Peirce described, and it would be literally in the center of downtown, where a European square would appear, replacing one of the ugly parking structures Peirce described. We called the block Pioneer

Courthouse Square. It was not easy and it nearly didn't happen, but it began in 1970 during an election overshadowed by Vortex and the gubernatorial campaigns of Tom McCall and Bob Straub.

A combination of death and retirement put all four city council positions on the ballot in 1970; Mayor Terry Schrunk was not up for election, but he was ill and exhausted and would not run in 1972. Frank Ivancie, who began his city career as Schrunk's assistant and was considered by the old guard as heir apparent, joined the council in 1966 and built a coterie of supporters based on a law-and-order, anti-hippie agenda. He was challenged in 1970 by Tom Walsh, a liberal Democrat and building contractor, who created his own base of activists. Ivancie dubbed Walsh "king of the hippies" for his youthful following, and narrowly won. Walsh was closely aligned with Goldschmidt, who had an easier time of it against Shirley Field.

Also in the 1970 victory column were two appointees, Lloyd Anderson and Connie McCready, named to council seats vacated by deaths. This would be the council's core as the decade opened. Ivancie was clearly on the right, a combative city hall veteran who often was a voice for the old establishment. Goldschmidt and Anderson usually agreed on major issues, and Anderson was a bridge between business and activists. He and his talented wife Pauline were a formidable pair and easily moved across a variety of social and political circles. Connie McCready was often a wild card; she was a liberal Republican and a former *Oregonian* reporter married to one of the paper's editors. We had things in common and developed a friendship; she was candid and approachable but at times didn't know her own mind.

Taken together, it was the most interesting council in many years; normally boring meetings suddenly generated electricity, and our cameras found their way to the council chambers. Acrimony between council members accelerated when Neil was elected mayor in 1972 and was replaced on the council by the outspoken Mildred Schwab. Television sought out any semblance of action in a dull meeting. We contributed, I suspect, to citizen responses to pollsters: after years of a no-drama council, folks didn't like the infighting.

Lloyd Anderson was a leader in drafting the important downtown plan that would be a cornerstone of the new Portland. Portland State University, just solidifying its place as a major state university in this period, had an ambitious and talented core of planners and urban experts, and the city was in many ways their laboratory. Much of the ultimate product had a PSU stamp on it; certainly that was the case with the 1972 Downtown Plan. The plan grew out of a battle for basic values—parking vs. pedestrian use of a key city block.

Meier & Frank was a Portland icon and the families that owned it were powers both politically and economically; Julius L. Meier was governor from 1931 to 1935. The downtown department store drew customers from the surrounding region and its branch in the new Lloyd Center was hugely popular. But the founders' heirs began warring over the company's future, culminating in its sale to May Department Stores in 1966. Meier & Frank kept its name until 2006 and remained an economic power, but its political clout was diminished.

In 1970 the City Planning Commission rejected Meier & Frank's plan for a twelve-story parking garage on the historic Portland Hotel block that then held an ugly two-story parking structure. Years of sometimes-bitter wrangling resulted as the city debated parking vs. a European-style central square.[5] The European Square idea wasn't new; according to Arnold Cogan, it dated to at least 1959, when he worked as a city planner:

> I had a drafting board right next to a guy named Bob Frasca. And Bob and I worked on a project called Pioneer Courthouse Square—only then we called it the Meier & Frank parking lot. That was one of my first projects. And we worked on the idea—the revolutionary idea—of tearing all that parking down and building an open space in downtown Portland. People thought the idea was somewhere between heresy and communism.[6]

The rejection of the parking garage prompted development of the 1972 Downtown Plan, adopted in the final month of Mayor Terry Schrunk's mayoralty, December 1972. It included Pioneer Square, the Transit Mall on Fifth and Sixth Avenues, and most of the downtown system as it exists half a century later. Adoption of the plan was important, but individual elements then had to be negotiated and developed. Particularly vulnerable were Pioneer Square and downtown housing.

The plan had its first big test just after it was announced but before it was adopted; the *Oregonian* proposed a big new printing plant near its headquarters on Broadway. The plant would fill an entire block right in the middle of the transit mall. It was an outrageous proposal, and I jumped in:

> The Downtown Plan calls for everything that the *Oregonian* cannot or will not place on the site . . . the *Oregonian* is planning a building that was variously described by planners and architects as a fortress and a tomb. It has no street access, is inaccessible, crowds the sidewalk and is a low-density use. It would be, in short, a solid block of concrete wall in a key downtown block . . . The ultimate decision on the *Oregonian* plant will be important, not only because it will be the first test of Downtown Plan guidelines but because if the city cannot gain compliance from a firm that trades in the public interest, it will be difficult to ask compliance from those who trade only in profit and loss.

Oregonian officials took flak from others as well and ultimately built the plant west of I-405, near Lincoln High School. Housing regulations would not be as easily solved, however, and the city council once again was split. I commented:

> There is a basic divide between people who find city life stimulating—their plan is for a city alive day and night. This mix of activity and people sets the city apart from its suburbs—and those who look at a downtown only through the eyes of business. If the latter prevails, Portland can look ahead to a bustling daytime life, but cold, empty canyons of marble and steel after dark. The prospect is sobering for those who have seen it elsewhere. Portland deserves better. But ways must be found to support low-profit activities on high-priced land.

It was a conundrum, but already planners were looking for ways to keep the city core alive after dark with housing, restaurants, small shops, and entertainment venues. Portland was not there yet. In

April 1977, Mayor Goldschmidt lost a major housing proposal in a three-to-two vote when Commissioner Charles Jordan unexpectedly joined Ivancie and Schwab in opposition. Jordan was Portland's first African American councilman, a tall and eloquent young man who came to Portland to work in the Model Cities program. He was appointed to the council in 1974 and normally sided with Goldschmidt.[7] The council was on such a razor edge that I warned of the day when Goldschmidt would move on and his opponents would take over: "If nothing else is made apparent by this vote, it's that progressive forces in the city and downtown should be shopping for a candidate for mayor. Shopping beyond city hall, or this city is in danger of slipping backward into the familiar pattern that has sucked the life from downtowns all across the nation."

Goldschmidt loved to bargain, negotiate, wheel and deal, and the next few months called forth those skills. He had genuine credibility downtown, and business leaders had largely supported his re-election the previous year. He had cajoled Nordstrom into building a classy new store right across Broadway from Pioneer Square, which then invigorated other development. Maneuvering went on behind closed doors, some compromises were made, and a deal was done.

In October Jordan joined in one of the important city votes of the period, a three to two vote that supported downtown housing. Schwab was close to downtown property owners and Ivancie never did get the importance of downtown housing. But the deal was sealed. Once done, the downtown housing part of the package stayed in place. Pioneer Square was about to have its turn on the griddle—and this did, as predicted, come after Neil's departure in 1979 to serve as secretary of transportation in the Carter administration.

The council selected Commissioner McCready to fill Neil's chair, but after two years she proved no match for Frank Ivancie and lost to him in the 1980 election. Some of the old guard marched back into city hall, including Bill Roberts, a key downtown business leader (Lipman-Wolfe department store) and longtime advocate of more downtown parking.

Pioneer Square had never set well with Roberts, but he was forced to bide his time while Goldschmidt was mayor. When Ivancie finally made it to the mayor's office, he didn't wait a beat to go after Pioneer Square. In January 1981 the new mayor sided with businessmen who still hankered for more parking, and he called for "temporary" parking on the Meier & Frank block. That would have crimped a private fundraising campaign to match federal funds for the Square. The federal deadline was rapidly approaching. I had joined the ranks of those advocating a European-style square on the ugly, boarded-up site. I went after the new mayor in commentary filmed directly in front of the abandoned block:

> Fundraising won't work in a divided business community and Ivancie is widening the division. He has no alternative plan of his own, of course. His suggestion of temporary parking on the block is not a plan, only a death sentence for the Square . . . Unless the other Council members assert leadership, they will have only grim choices in the future. One is Ivancie's parking lot. The other is to tear the (parking) structure down, and board the block up until someone comes up with money for the Square. They could even name the hole "Ivancie's Pit"—in honor of its Founder!

I couldn't blame Ivancie for seizing the moment—he had very few of them in the previous decade. Now, his archrival Neil Goldschmidt had moved on, and Frank had the spotlight to himself. But for the umpteenth time, he misjudged public sentiment; Friends of Pioneer Square sold 47,432 personalized bricks and raised $1.5 million to match the federal grant. The square was dedicated in 1984 in a ceremony filled with Pioneer Square friends wandering around with their heads down, looking for their named brick. There's that "friends" label again!

Ivancie was out of sync with the city and the times. Encountering him for the first time, one could come away with the impression of a nice, courteous public official. That image could suddenly change, however, when you saw him publicly berate a hapless city employee at a city council meeting. He could be a bully and was known to intimidate; in political contests he had a nasty edge that eventually hurt his career. He lacked empathy with neighborhood organizers and other activists of the time.

Ivancie's lost causes over the years were a catalog of what made Portland stand out in the last third of the twentieth century. He supported but lost the battles for Harbor Drive and Mount Hood freeways and the Meier & Frank parking lot. He opposed community policing, mass transit, downtown housing, professional planning, and gay rights. That was the platform as he challenged Mayor Goldschmidt in 1976.

Neil Goldschmidt built a citizen network based on issues and personality, and he had a first-rate supporting staff. He worked Portland's business community, which went into his 1976 re-election campaign predominantly in his corner. Ivancie didn't have the organization or the personal appeal to raise big money without large business donations.

After talking to the two men, I wrote a 1975 column for *Willamette Week* that opened with an Ivancie statement that I fully agreed with: "This city is developing quickly into a philosophical fork in the road." Ivancie went on, "When we cut back on flushing the streets because we're moving into another adventure as far as a new program—this is very bad." I certainly didn't value unflushed streets, but it seemed a strange contrast. I wrote: "Neil Goldschmidt's political future is tied to the way people feel about their city, its livability and its future. Ivancie must, of necessity, put his hopes on people who want to return to a simpler approach to government, one based on physical needs and visible services."

The differences between the candidates were staggering. The *Oregonian's* Huntley Collins wrote a full-page story on the race, in which she surveyed twenty-one major issues, concluding that the candidates "can find almost no common ground."[8] Ivancie doubled-down on his tough-guy image in the 1976 campaign, drawing an unnecessary backlash at several points. Memorable was a billboard showing simply a hairy, muscled, and flexed male arm flashing a thumbs-up sign. Women, particularly those of a feminist

They disagreed on almost everything but mayor Neil Goldschmidt (left) and commissioner Frank Ivancie worked together daily on the Portland City Council. Commissioner Connie McCready is at right. (Michael Lloyd Visuals)

persuasion, went nuts, and a lot of men also thought it was in bad taste.

Frank was running a law-and-order campaign, hairy arm and all, relying on statistics that I found inaccurate when I researched them. I expected the race to go into the general election, and was surprised with Neil's decisive win in the primary. "Judging by the votes cast last night in the city, there is a commitment to a planned and creative city here in Portland," I commented. Frank Ivancie never backed down from his 1950s view of city government in his adopted city. Frank had passed up an opportunity to run for mayor in 1972; after that, Neil Goldschmidt simply owned the office for the next six years and during that time virtually all of the new Portland was created.

Several policies of the time must be directly credited to Neil—certainly the revival of downtown with a new Nordstrom's anchor store and Pioneer Square, the conversion of Mount Hood Freeway funds to mass transit, and a renewal of neighborhoods—but in the final analysis Goldschmidt's greatest contribution was to keep Ivancie from the mayor's office until most of the Portland's progressive image was in place. By the time Frank finally achieved his goal in 1980, he had little to offer and the policies of the Goldschmidt era were cemented in place.

Portlandia herself came later, in 1985; Raymond Kaskey's hammered-copper figure was sculpted in a Washington, DC, suburb and shipped to Portland for assembly. Like Cleopatra, *Portlandia* arrived on a much-heralded barge—on the Willamette, not the Nile—and was installed on Michael Graves' spanking-new Portland building. People either liked *Portlandia* or hated her—there seemed no middle ground—I liked her and thought she said something about a city that welcomed the unconventional. Graves' building proved to be attractive on the outside but detested by occupants for an interior that didn't work very well. As for the television show, *Portlandia* touches with humor some of the pretentiousness of Portland in the twenty-first century, but it is what it is—a humorous satire—and not a true picture of a city that grew to become a wonderful place to work and live, thanks in large part to what went on in the 1970s.

A throng showed up to give Neil a sendoff to his job in the Carter administration; KGW did a live broadcast of the event. Neil built his resume and, when Carter lost to Ronald Reagan, took a job as a Nike executive based in Vancouver, BC. He moved between his Portland home and his Vancouver office, keeping his finger on Oregon's political pulse.

Most of the big foundation blocks for Portlandia were in place when Neil left the mayor's office on January 1, 1979; while he was in Washington, DC, and Vancouver, his successors struggled, and a most unusual character moved into city hall in 1985. Neil's departure put Commissioner Connie McCready in the mayor's chair by appointment; she had little time to establish an independent image and lost to a challenge by Frank Ivancie in 1980. Frank earned a good city paycheck for his eighteen years in elective office in Portland, but after all those years of saying "no," he brought no new ideas to his

Portlandia, the controversial sculpture by Raymond Kaskey, nears its destination on the Portland Building in 1985; the work was crafted in a suburb of Washington, DC, and arrived in Portland by barge and the oversize truck seen here, as throngs of Oregonians greeted the new immigrant. (Michael Lloyd Visuals)

office and seldom had a three-person city council majority if he did have an idea. He spent time traveling, especially in Alaska, and the mayor's office seemed atrophied.

Frank hadn't changed from his longtime conservative stance; he was out of step with the new Portland, but challengers inside city hall did not seem eager to confront him in 1984. I surmised at one point that his detractors needed to look outside city hall for a mayor.

Frank didn't see it coming, but his denouement waited a few blocks up Jefferson Street, in the person of a cheery, bearded barkeep who greeted friends with an enthusiastic "whoop, whoop," paddled a canoe while standing upright, and was a lot smarter and quicker than Frank. John Elwood Clark Jr. always went by "Bud,"

Innkeeper Bud Clark poses with the art poster that made him a household name, as he celebrates his 1984 upset over mayor Frank Ivancie. Clark went on to serve two terms. (Oregon Historical Society bb013596)

and his tavern, the Goose Hollow Inn, was already a neighborhood icon and the frequent watering spot of my colleagues at KGW.

He epitomized anti-Ivancie; Bud was a neighborhood guy who rode an old curb-jumper bike, usually clad in hiking shorts and suspenders, and his backers conducted a stealth campaign that surfaced too late for Ivancie to react. Frank's reaction included a brochure headlined, "We all like a good joke, but . . . Portland's future is at stake!" Voters were asked, "Do you want to put a self-proclaimed 'born-again pagan' in the mayor's office, someone whose claim to fame is exposing himself to a downtown statue?"

Well, actually, people did want to do that, and Bud won in the primary election by a staggering 55 to 42 percent margin. The infamous "exposing himself" posters became bestsellers and helped erase a campaign deficit. Bud had posed for the photo in 1978—standing with his back to the camera in what would appear to be only boots, hat, and raincoat pulled open, facing Norman Taylor's statue of a lushly built woman, "Kvinneakt," on the Portland Transit Mall. The poster was titled, "Expose Yourself to Art" and became a national bestseller for photographer Mike Ryerson. What was Bud wearing under the raincoat? Well, he wore shorts and a tee shirt—or so he said; any Scot who has worn a kilt knows to keep quiet when asked.

A poster hanging in my office reads: "To Floyd McKay, who has truly been drinking beer at the Goose Hollow Inn for years. Whoop, Whoop. Bud Clark." A good number of instant "friends of the Goose" had emerged post-election, but Bud remembered his regulars.

Bud Clark's campaign, his warm and genuine character, and his total dedication to neighborhood, culture, and an urban lifestyle was the presage of Portlandia. On a recent visit to the "hood," my feet found their way to the Goose. The posters on the wall, the graffiti in the restroom, and the famous Reuben sandwiches didn't seem to have changed. Bud was not in the house, but his spirit was in the city. Bud was a transitional figure, as if Portland had jumped over Frank Ivancie back onto a track that was laid in the Goldschmidt years.

Neal Peirce, the urban journalist who wrote so critically of Portland in 1970, returned to the city in 1993 and declared a massive turnaround centered on the city's 1972 Downtown Plan. Among his conclusions:

> While most American cities of the 1970s and 1980s saw developers become the driving force, putting forth their proposals, then barely tolerating public input, Portland evolved the idea that *the public's agenda comes first* . . . Portland's 1972 Downtown Plan represented a critical *return to public life*, underscored by investments in such places as Pioneer Courthouse Square, the bus mall and Waterfront Park. In the long run, the Portland approach also turned out to be an extraordinarily healthy one for private business interests. . . Oregon's nationally pacesetting land-use plan, enacted under (Tom) McCall . . . set an ideal context for the 1972 plan and its implementation . . . The state plan's central principle—to maintain the vitality of the urban center and to keep cities from sprawling out onto agricultural and timber lands—provided an expansive context, and one could say ongoing validity, to Portland's efforts. (emphasis original)[9]

Portland's renaissance did owe a great deal to what was happening at the state level—and Portland activists played a major role in those events. The Oregon Story began two decades before Portland's chapter was written, in the pivotal election of 1964 that brought Tom McCall and Bob Straub to state office. That was the year I began covering Oregon politics. By 1986, the last chapter was written and I was closing my reporter's notebook.

I had spent little time with Neil Goldschmidt during his Cabinet and Nike years; he called in June 1985 and wondered if I would join him on a trip to Coos Bay and Corvallis. Neil was thinking about the governorship and needed to see if he still had the chops for a campaign. I could bring a camera.

Neil was actually nervous about resuming campaigning, but he thought the two locations—so very different in every way—would be a good test. Oregon was in need of new energy after eight years of Governor Atiyeh, and Neil talked mostly about getting the sluggish economy moving. Nowhere was that more evident than Coos Bay. I did a documentary in 1986 that I titled "South Coast Blues," about the desperation in Oregon's southwest corner. We used gripping footage of food lines, young people moving out, and an empty deep-water port once filled with log-export ships.

Would a famous big-city mayor play in Coos Bay? Neither of us was sure. Neil was always good in small groups and he was a quick study; at Coos Bay the talk was all about jobs and ways to revive the empty port. Neil was beginning to work around in his mind the community-based strategy he would call "The Oregon Comeback." "If we want to achieve anything, the list has to be short," he cautioned at both stops.

My account of the short trip concluded with, "One of two questions will be answered on this trip. He will find people eager to move and ready to help. The other question—a matter of personal and family commitment—cannot be found downstate. I think he will return home ready and even eager to run—sufficiently so to carry the personal side of the issue." I thought he would run; he was a risk-taker and restless, eager for a challenge. I had no idea how big a risk he was taking; we would learn later, and I deal with that in the Afterword.

Neil announced on July 2, and Norma Paulus on October 28 at an impressive 7:00 a.m. kickoff before a large crowd of her Salem friends and backers. I commented:

> She is the best Salem product since Mark Hatfield began his rise 35 years ago. Like Hatfield, Paulus is an enormously attractive candidate. Pollsters say her personal approval rate is among the highest of any Oregon politician in recent years . . . Paulus is a feminist, but tough, determined and aggressive. She will handle herself in debate and was wise to take the initiative (in calling for debates). The winner in 1986 will know he or she faced the best.

It was the race I had been looking for since Neil and Norma entered political life in 1970, he as a city councilman, she as a state representative. His resume included big-city mayor, cabinet officer, and a short stint as a Nike executive; hers included the legislature and two terms as secretary of state.

Norma Paulus was a good secretary of state; her operation was smoother than those of Tom McCall or Clay Myers, and I had a great deal of respect for her administrative and political skills. From the day she entered the legislature, she was one of the strongest and most effective voices for women's issues. I had no doubt she would be a good governor. As the campaigns rolled forward—featuring really substantive debates between evenly matched candidates—several items began to separate them in my mind.

Neither would repudiate major chapters of the Oregon Story, although Norma's opposition to Willamette Greenway expansion was troubling. I worried about support for urban mass transit—a key plank in Portland's emergence. Governor Atiyeh had not been helpful in key appointments affecting mass transit, and I worried Norma would not reverse them. As a former Salem reporter, I understood the capital city's innate caution and tendency to avoid rocking the boat, and I knew many Salemites would be in a Paulus administration.

Exhausted from a long and difficult campaign, candidates Norma Paulus and Neil Goldschmidt share some thoughts before one of their final debates in the 1986 gubernatorial race, one of the toughest in Oregon history. (Gerry Lewin Photo)

Polling showed the candidates tied at 45 percent each on May 10. Paulus pulled into a commanding 47–39 percent lead on September 14, her peak and Goldschmidt's nadir; undecided voters increased to 14 percent. That was unusual—the number of undecided voters usually drops by September; it was, I commented, a sign that "the jury is still out, and flexible."[10]

Neil put his foot in his mouth shortly before the September poll was taken, describing a debate locale in Bend as "in the middle of nowhere," and the remark caused a lot of pushback in rural areas. But in September, Norma was also leading Neil in the Tri-County area around Portland, where he had to win in November. He was down and very discouraged when I encountered him at one of their seven debates. It was the start of the gloves-off campaign and much tougher campaigning on both sides.

The debates were politics at its best—Neil and Norma went after each other on a variety of issues, sometimes jumping up to insist on a reply, facing each other in attack. They respected each other, and at times humor broke out. In Medford, someone asked if they would appoint persons of the opposite party—even their rival; Neil quipped, "Norma, if you drop out, you've got a job," to which she drily responded that he had just violated state election law.[11]

By mid-October, Neil had reversed Norma's lead and held a 46–43 percent margin. The big change was in the Tri-County area, and I felt the race would now depend on organization and any late stumbles or misfired attacks. I commented:

> What may be happening here is that Paulus has sent her message: the poor girl who made good, the open and honest secretary of state who knows state government. Solid, comforting, Republican in a state that votes Republican. But not very imaginative or very challenging.
>
> Goldschmidt is still getting his message out. It's more complex, much broader. Mayor, secretary of transportation, Nike vice president. The message is more challenging and he is more dynamic. But the level of comfort is lower. It took a long time to establish enough trust so people would hear the message.
>
> That may be happening, and if it is, the Paulus people should be concerned. Paulus will be urged to begin negative advertising—which she has previously rejected. But with her message basically complete and his still coming, she may have to go on the attack.

My analysis was spot-on; she attacked, and he counterattacked, but the ground game went to Neil's organization.

On election night, I declared governor-elect Goldschmidt's 52–48 percent win quite early and was the first to do so, bringing huge cheers from Neil's packed crowd and an acerbic reaction from Norma. Upstairs in Neil's hotel room, I learned later, someone turned to Neil and remarked, "Wouldn't it be great if we could get Floyd in the governor's office?" Several days later, the governor-elect taped a *Viewpoint* show for us, and we adjourned across Jefferson Street for a quick hamburger and coffee at the venerable Leaky Roof. Neil asked me if I would join him in Salem as his spokesman and public liaison. It had been some time since I was offered a job, and I had always rejected politics in favor of journalism.

An important change was taking place at King Broadcasting, however; my boss and mentor for the past sixteen years, Ancil Payne, was to retire in mid-1987. Ancil had supported my work and parried complaints from aggrieved politicians and businessmen. I feared that no successor would ever support me in that manner; television was changing, taking on more entertainment with less serious news and fewer documentaries. I'd been on the beat a long time, but my options in the future seemed limited.

Dixie was not enthusiastic about Neil's offer. I had not shared my concerns about KGW; our kids were almost out of the nest, and we were enjoying a slower pace than during our early Portland years. After a week or so of agonizing, I told Neil I would take the job, if it included a substantial role beyond dealing with my friends in the media. He agreed, and a new chapter opened for both of us.

That was the end of my chronicle of those wonderful years in journalism and the people who made it happen. I addressed our audience for the last time on December 19, thanking viewers for their patience as I was learning a new trade, and for their comments and counsel. In retrospect, the September 4 celebration that heralded the first MAX train in Portland really provided the closure for my time chronicling Portland's renaissance. It was cause for celebration, marking a critical point in the city's transformation as an urban neighborhood. I had immersed myself in much of the Sturm und Drang of creating the transformation, and I was feeling vindicated. As the weekend celebration opened, I posted myself on the new Pioneer Square transit mall and expressed the joy:

> There's a big party down here this weekend, to celebrate MAX. Well, it might also be a celebration of a 15-year transformation of downtown Portland. If you left Portland in 1971 and just returned, you wouldn't recognize the place. A dull, stodgy and decaying downtown has taken on the air of a European city. In 1971, Pioneer Square was an ugly, inefficient parking lot. Nordstrom's was leaving town. Other anchor stores were headed for the suburban malls. Portland was still a fine place to live, but you wouldn't want to visit.
>
> In many ways, rebirth began with Nordstrom's. Newly elected Mayor Neil Goldschmidt pulled out all the stops to keep the store downtown. He got a new store, a sense of can-do and confidence. . . . People began to find downtown interesting again. And finally, we reclaimed our

waterfront. Tom McCall led the drive to close Harbor Drive. The park now bears his name. River Place more recently showed what can be done.

Portland turned itself around in the last 15 years. It was a transformation . . . The visible leaders were Goldschmidt and McCall—the dominant figures of the time. But scores of businesspeople, city planners and ordinary folk played a role.

Anyone who went through that time has a right to party this weekend. And, sure—MAX can come, too!

As I concluded, a gleaming new MAX train trundled by and kids of all ages waved happily from the windows, as was common in the early days of the light rail experience. The sun shone on downtown.

There was little time in the busy, sometimes frantic, years ahead to reflect on the incredible period I had been privileged to share with so many enlightened and dedicated people. There was a long list of Oregon Story accomplishments, but what was its ultimate legacy for our twenty-first century descendants?

Profile TIMBER JIM AND THE REDHEAD

Timber Jim and Bill Walton were transitional figures in the 1970s, bridging the gap between Old Portland, with its logging and Skid Road history, and the dynamic new city, with its hip culture and popular scene. In just three years—from 1975 to 1978—the Portland Timbers and Portland Trailblazers created a new image for the city and helped put it on the national map. We were a Big League city. They were quite different icons, the logger with his roaring chainsaw when a Timber scored a goal and the shaggy-haired, six-feet-eleven redhead who hung out with the Grateful Dead when he wasn't stuffing basketballs through the hoop.

Portland was a minor-league sports town until the persistent sports entrepreneur Harry Glickman gained a National Basketball Association franchise that was named the Trailblazers in 1970. The Timbers joined the North American Soccer League in 1975 and stunned the country by going all the way to the league finals.

Bill Walton and Timber Jim (aka Jim Serrill) weren't on the scene for those franchise openings; they arrived in 1974 and 1978, respectively. The Timbers' amazing 1975 inaugural season built a following that was later dubbed the Timbers Army, one of the most rambunctious crowds in American soccer. The Blazer fan base started slower, as did the team, but it all came together when Walton, Maurice Lucas, and Jack Ramsay combined in 1976.

Ramsay brought a scholarly yet intense coaching style, and Walton and Lucas owned the backboards and forecourt as the Blazers roared to the finals of the NBA. Walton scored twenty points, picked twenty-three rebounds, and blocked eight shots as the Blazers defeated Philadelphia for the NBA title. Portland went wild, there was a huge downtown parade and even traditionalists who debunked Walton as an antiwar hippie had to admit he was quite a player. Lucas, the muscular power forward, was the most prominent of several early Blazers who settled in Portland and were leaders in city causes and events. Walton's career was cut short by injuries, but he became a popular broadcaster headquartered in southern California.

Timber Jim was a real logger, and his chainsaw was wielded like a baton as he cut a slice of Douglas fir to present to a goal-scorer; he climbed an eighty-foot pole and led the cheers with his roaring saw. When he left after his first season to pursue his day job, his "successor," a pom-pom waving bear, was hooted off the pitch. Timber Jim revved up his saw the next year to rousing cheers, and the tradition remained.

We loved the show, and we loved those early Timbers, mostly imports from England, Scotland, and Ireland. Several settled in Portland, and Clive Charles and Bernie Fagan, in particular, played a huge role in bringing soccer to schools and youth leagues. City Commissioner Mildred Schwab, a substantial woman, became Fan One and kicked out the first ball as fans roared their approval.

Portland had become a Big League city at the same time as it was emerging as Portlandia, however that term is defined. It seemed appropriate.

ELEVEN   The Legacy

Settlers and visitors alike were drawn to the Oregon Country by its unrivaled setting, but the rivers and valleys, the mountains and ocean were viewed primarily in terms of economic value. Oregon historian William G. Robbins, in his seminal *Landscapes of Promise: The Oregon Story, 1800 to 1940*, describes the common outlook of nineteenth-century Oregon after arrival of the intercontinental railway:

> The Oregon Country in particular, according to its boosters, was a land abounding in potential, a place where nature's wealth and human technical genius would combine to forge the good society, to provide decent, stable living for coming generations. The future in that view was full with the expectation of improvement, with the hopes that in this special place the next generation would banish want and indigence. That effusive narrative line—pursued in travel and real estate brochures, commercial club and promotional pamphlets, and through regional newspapers—celebrated the seemingly limitless opportunities of the Pacific Northwest. The transcendent vehicle for that transformation was a lush and abundant landscape in which nature would be put to work to benefit mankind.[1]

Oregon's natural resources served the nation in World War II, and the next decade brought a construction and population boom. By the 1960s the "natural" side of the natural resources equation was exhausted. Our iconic Willamette River was a cesspool of industrial and domestic waste, salmon runs were depleted, and three-bedroom houses marched robot-like through strawberry patches and grass fields throughout the Willamette Valley. Mountainsides were stripped of old-growth fir, and erosion was muddying streams. Developers were lusting for building sites on Oregon's beaches.

Great challenges attract great leaders, and great leaders crave great challenges. Time and place and great leaders forge a legacy when fate joins them in common cause. Oregon's natural legacy—the spectacular streams and beaches, the open spaces and clean water and air, the mountains and the Columbia Gorge—were protected in the great achievements of the Oregon Story. Portland's livability was snatched from an unimaginative and sterile asphalt juggernaut and given to new modes of transit more suitable to its sustainable neighborhoods and revitalized city center.

Oregon was still a neighborhood in 1964; people could—and did—walk up to a governor or senator in a public space and express an opinion. State legislators had no aides or spokespeople and answered their own phones and mail. Their campaign costs were a fraction of today's slick media productions. Major employers and nearly all media were owned within the Pacific Northwest; the boss lived in the neighborhood and so did many stockholders. Oregon was their home, not a stop on the way to another high-end suburb in another state.

Scale is important in any endeavor, be it a business, local or federal government, university, or industry. The larger we grow, the more we lose the neighborhood. Oregon's population in 1960 was only 1.7 million people; by 2015 we were home to 4 million, and the neighborhood had become a city.

In 1964, we still retained the "can do" attitude of the war that Americans fought and won, as well as an implicit trust in our elected leaders. We bitched about some of their decisions—and told them so—but we believed them, wished them well, and if it didn't cost too much, we followed their lead. Reporters in general were no different than their audience in this regard. We were all in the same middle-class neighborhood.

The circumstances allowed an unorthodox man like Tom McCall to prosper and an orthodox politician like Mark Hatfield to take unorthodox positions. In the case of the Oregon Story, the challenges we faced were there before our very eyes—or noses; we could smell the Willamette, we needed no further evidence. A new house overlooked our picnic spot at the beach, as we piled a log on the bonfire. Tom used his great gift of rhetoric to tell us—and sell us—on what we already could see with our own eyes.

His leadership was enabled by Bob Straub's vision; Straub was a true big-picture man who thought generations ahead in his visions of the Willamette Greenway, automobile-free beaches, and the purchase of added beach access with a small gas-tax increase. His Oregon Investment Council, discussed in his early campaigns, was a revolutionary change in management of state funds.

The confluence of these men, so easily parodied as a "Tom and Bob Show" (how we journalists love catchy lines!), was unique in Oregon history, and it came at the right time. Bob dreamed big, Tom promoted and cajoled, and we all joined in and had a good time. In a sense, both stood on the shoulders of Dick Neuberger, who had inspired them to dream and act.

Oregonians were ready, in part because we were underutilizing our human resources, in particular a restless corps of young, intelligent, and well-educated urban women. Many came to Oregon in the post-war era with their husbands; they were what we later called "trailing spouses," and their options to use their professional training and interests were limited largely to teaching and administrative tasks.

Many post-war immigrants made a deliberate decision to move to Oregon because of its natural setting, its reputation for good education at all levels, and its manageable size. They became the front lines of many activist campaigns of the era, and by the time the dust settled from all the change, many of the women who had marched, organized, and campaigned were able to take advantage of expanded opportunities for their skills. Half a century later we still have "trailing spouses," but an increasing number are male.

We battled in those days, but generally without rancor; the bitter hatred that seems to pervade twenty-first century American politics was not the norm fifty years ago in Oregon. Disagreements there were in spades, and personal animosity stalked the careers of several prominent leaders. But anger writ large did not define our debates or results.

The media has been criticized for being "soft" on politicians during this period, and some of the charges ring true—in our pursuit of "the issues" we sometimes turned our eyes away from personal or professional behavior that needed exposure. In general, we liked a good-news story as well as a good news story; so did our owners, most of whom also had deep roots in Oregon.

In a similar manner, Oregon industrialists lived in the neighborhood, from Howard Vollum and Jack Murdock at Tektronix to Les Schwab in Prineville. Glenn Jackson, the great conciliator, has no peer today and his company is owned by Warren Buffet. It matters. Jackson and developer John Gray were particularly important to the Oregon Story; they were part of "The Greatest Generation" born before the Great Depression, who rose to prominence in and after World War II. They were approachable by political leaders, who stood on their shoulders as we moved through this era.[2]

Many of the political leaders were themselves of the Greatest Generation and had served in World War II. My own generation— the so-called Silent Generation, born during the Depression and World War II or its immediate aftermath—was shaped by the sacrifices of our parents in those difficult times, and we believed in public service and those we elected to serve. Later generations, born during the Vietnam and Watergate period, were more cynical, less trusting; their experiences with government were vastly different than that of the two prior generations. It mattered.

The Oregon Story was possible because of the people and the way they were able to work together—but this, in turn, was enabled because the challenges we faced were easily understood by citizens and there was general agreement that our natural heritage needed help. Legislators and other leaders were not primarily defined by their parties, and parties and special-interest groups did not pressure them to sign declarations of fealty. The foundation stones of the Oregon Story carried the handprints of Republicans and Democrats and the term "bipartisan" was an assumption, not a shibboleth to batter someone who abandoned the true faith.

The legacy of the Oregon Story is seen in our physical spaces — clean waters, open beaches, trails without litter, urban neighborhoods, and thriving farms and vineyards. These icons were created by not-so-ordinary citizens willing to challenge conventional wisdom and take to the streets or beaches on their own time and their own dime. Neighborhoods, schools, beaches, and rivers prospered from the efforts of activists, predominantly women and often immigrants from other places.

Educated women fueled the generation of activists; educated women are now welcomed in every profession and occupy top political offices. Today's economy demands — and young parents accept — two-parent incomes with all that brings in loss of time to organize and march. Send a check instead; the growth industry of the twenty-first century is nonprofits that organize electronic crowds.

The Oregon Story's roots grew from positive organization for goals that could be uniformly shared. It is important to remember that kitchen-table activists launched the drives that killed the Mount Hood Freeway and the highway on Nestucca Spit. There will be new pressures on beaches, rivers, and farmland; all those "friends of" will need faces at the courthouse and port commission, or the icons will yield to the relentless pressure of the market.

Schools are uniquely situated for activism, given their emotional ties to neighborhoods and families; Portlanders who rang doorbells and organized to pass a critical school levy in 2014 marched in the shoes of those who challenged an insensitive district leadership in 1980. Urban activists facing the new challenge of gentrification and neighborhoods impacted by infill McHouses and apartment towers may seek inspiration in the freeway battles of the 1970s.

Farmers will need to band together again to preserve vineyards and organic farms in the manner that dairies and ryegrass fields were preserved in the past. Protecting farmland and preventing sprawl will be the most difficult part of the Oregon Story to maintain, because Oregon is still a growth magnet and there is much money on the table.

The "brain drain" of bright young people from rural to urban centers has long concerned thoughtful rural families and should concern everyone. Future chapters of the Oregon Story need authors from all parts of the state.

The Oregon Story was built on an important progression of activism. Local people start the process—a beachcomber, a fisherman, a hiker in the Columbia Gorge, a couple with kids in school—and the process widens to neighbors and others of similar persuasion. Political leaders awaken and the circle widens until together they create a movement that legislators and city councils cannot ignore.

Next thing you know, there is an Oregon Story.

Afterword

When I closed my door at KGW in December 1986 to join the Goldschmidt administration, Dixie and I began an odyssey of sorts. In the next five years we would live in six different homes, sometimes separately, as we made our way to a new life in Bellingham, Washington, the nation's far northwest corner and one of the great places on earth. She taught and I wrote and taught and we remodeled two houses as we grew older; it was hectic but worth the strain.

My political stint with Governor Goldschmidt brought hard work, new friends, and gratifying support from old friends, but it was just not my line of work. Privately, I pledged to finish the four-year term but not to continue into a second term. Neil saw me as outside my comfort zone and lacking some of the skills he needed; we agreed to end it after two years, and I left in December 1988. I was finishing my master's degree at the University of Maryland and living in a tiny walk-up apartment near the Washington, DC, school where Dixie was teaching when news reached me of Neil's impending divorce and decision not to seek a second term. The divorce did not surprise me; the strains were apparent to everyone in the office. Neil's withdrawal from politics was more surprising and it wasn't until 2004 that the backstory was revealed.

Others will write the Goldschmidt administration's history, as others have already written the tragic story of Neil's sexual abuse of a young girl while he was Portland mayor. I had no knowledge of that situation, at the time or later, and was shocked and appalled when I read *Willamette Week's* exposé in 2004. There was simply no excuse for criminal conduct that could have meant a prison sentence, had the statute of limitations not expired by 2004.

Neil's imprint on the modern City of Portland is indelible, but he lives out his retirement as a pariah, seldom seen in public in the city he helped become Portlandia. I knew Neil from 1965 to 1990, and the man I knew was a powerful force for the public good, the critical leader in Portland's emergence as an exciting, modern city. He inspired others to go on to leadership positions. Those accomplishments, that inspiration, cannot be taken away and should be recognized by historians along with the tragic flaw in his character that caused him to commit an act that was morally and legally wrong.

Oregon's two Republican senators reached the pinnacle of the Washington power structure when Republicans controlled the US Senate from 1981 to 1987. Mark Hatfield chaired Senate Appropriations and Bob Packwood headed Senate Finance, two of the most powerful positions in Washington. Both faced ethical challenges and Packwood resigned in the face of almost-certain expulsion from the Senate.

Senator Hatfield in 1984 became entangled with Greek arms dealer Basil Tsakos and became the chief booster of Tsakos' quixotic effort to build an oil pipeline across the center of Africa; simultaneously, Hatfield's wife Antoinette received $55,000 for disputed services for Tsakos' wife. Tsakos' pipeline did not seem rational and the Hatfields' explanation did not seem plausible; I said so on the air, drawing enmity from the senator's camp.

The senator was cleared by the Senate Ethics Committee, but Tsakos was secretly indicted by the Department of Justice for bribery. Tsakos' indictment remained secret until after Hatfield's death in 2011; the *Oregonian* obtained FBI files under a Freedom of Information request. Hatfield was named as the bribery target, but not charged.[1]

In 1992, Hatfield was rebuked by the Senate for failing to disclose $42,000 in gifts from friends and lobbyists. He served until 1997, continuing to support Oregon projects and provide an antiwar voice in the Senate. At his death he remained a beloved icon in Oregon political history.

The serial sexual harassment that brought down the career of Senator Bob Packwood in 1995 did not surprise those who knew him well. Packwood had a reputation for hiring young, attractive women and behaving inappropriately with them and others. Many of us chalked it up to boorishness after a few drinks; apparently it was more. The Senate Ethics Committee unanimously voted to expel him from the Senate for improper sexual conduct, soliciting jobs from lobbyists for his estranged wife, and tampering with evidence in the case. He resigned on September 7, 1995, three years after the *Washington Post* ran stories exposing his history of forcing himself on women associated with his office or his campaigns. His elective career at an end, he opened a successful lobbying practice and lives in semi-retirement in Portland's most exclusive neighborhood. His reputation remains besmirched by the sexual misbehavior, but he changed the way politicians view campaign strategy and—ironically, perhaps—advanced the national discussion of feminist issues.[2]

As I wrote this text, governor John Kitzhaber resigned his office to face the consequences of a romantic affair that over-ran his duty to Oregon voters. It was a sad time for the many who believed in him, including this writer who first met the young physician in 1978. The book is yet to close on Kitzhaber but he, also, leaves a record of permanent contributions to his state.

I have chosen in this work to discuss those who played a part in the Oregon Story—including myself— in historical terms, describing them as I saw them at the time. Those among us who have fallen from grace also deserve to be remembered for contributions to the greater good in better times. There are lessons and counsel that may be extracted from the fall of those we chose to lead, but they are for another time and a different forum.

As I left my longtime home in 1989, my natural instinct was to return to a different form of journalism, where I could share the lessons of three decades and continue to write in an environment not dominated by daily deadline pressure. Politics behind me, I prepared for an academic career; I had taught a few classes at Linfield College, my alma mater, in the 1970s, and found it satisfying. My Linfield BA was three decades old, however, and my Nieman Fellowship at Harvard didn't grant a degree. I was fifty-five years old, a white male in the age of affirmative action.

A wonderful transition intervened. In 1984, I had spent two months at the East-West Center in Honolulu, an institution founded in the 1960s to improve relations with Asian nations. I was a Jefferson Fellow, a program for journalists from the United States and Asia, and my grant included a month in Asia. The position of director of the Jefferson Fellowships came open on an interim basis just as I left politics, and I spent seven months in Hawaii in 1989. The East-West Center was great for decompressing, but it interrupted my search for an entry into teaching, a world that demanded a graduate degree.

Finding a graduate program wasn't difficult; my journalistic career made me a wonderful catch as a teaching assistant. I finished my master's at Maryland in ten months and in the spring of 1990 I was hired for a teaching position at Western Washington University in Bellingham.

Western's small program is generally regarded in the industry as the best of Washington's professional journalism programs. We had no graduate program and stressed news essentials. I was also hired in part because my two years with Neil gave me administrative and political experience; the department would need a new chair in three or four years. I served eight years as chair. In addition to my fulltime faculty work, I commuted to the University of Washington in Seattle for my PhD, focused on media history. Dixie taught at a middle school in nearby Mount Vernon, and later was a consultant at a private school for the learning disabled in Vancouver, BC, just across the Canadian border.

Writing was still in my blood and over the years I wrote frequent opinion pieces for the *Bellingham Herald* and the *Seattle Times*.

Opinion editor Jim Vesely hired me in 2003 to write two columns a month for the *Times* and I did so for five years. In 2008 I moved to an Internet start-up, Crosscut.com, opened by well-known Seattle journalist David Brewster. I retired from Western in 2004, so I had more writing time.

This publication is my second full book; my biography of my *Statesman* editor, Charles A. Sprague, was published in 1998. I also wrote an annotated bibliography of Pacific Northwest media history and several articles for history or journalism journals. Writing is in my bones, I guess.

Moving around as we did, one loses touch with old friends in the process of making new ones, but our children continue to live in Portland and we feel as if we have dual-state citizenship. The Pacific Northwest is really the best place on earth. Our four grandchildren share that sentiment!

Acknowledgments

Reporting the Oregon Story was the highlight of my professional career, as I matured from a very naive "cub reporter" into a time when I interacted on a daily basis with the leading figures of a state that was becoming an exciting and exhilarating place to work and live. Civility and tolerance marked our politics and media, and friendships across political barriers and media competition flourished.

We found our own mentors in those days; none were assigned to young reporters feeling their way. In my newspaper days, the tutelage and examples of H. P. "Red" Hornish in Springfield and newsroom colleagues Tom Wright, Conrad Prange, Don Scarborough and Wes Sullivan in Salem—and the inspiration provided by Charles A. Sprague—were pivotal in my career and life. At KGW, Ancil Payne and Forest Amsden supported and counseled and Dennis Buchanan guided me into my new city. A hardy band of talented photographers were special companions and guides. Portland friends and mentors are too numerous to mention, except for the remarkable Professor Don Balmer of Lewis and Clark, whose knowledge of the players and understanding of the Oregon system was unrivaled.

This work is largely based on my personal reporting and observations; it lacks (for better or worse) the deep archival research of the academic writing I did in my later career. Although I conducted no formal interviews, several longtime friends and associates helped me recall people and events and some read draft chapters. They know who they are, and how grateful I am for their help.

Although I did not delve deeply into archival documents, an extensive search for photographs to illustrate my text brought me into close contact with archivists across the state. The Oregon Historical Society is always vital in any aspect of Oregon history, and archivist Scott Daniels provided extraordinary support and expertise; OHS Executive Director Kerry Tymchuk also provided important help and encouragement.

Among the many archivists who helped, special efforts were made by Western Oregon University's Jerrie Lee Parpart, the University of Oregon's Bruce Tabb and several colleagues, as well as informal archivists who have access to collections of photographs. Among them were Paul Kenney of KGW, Gail Wilhelms of the Dorchester Conference, Drew Vattiat of the *Oregonian*, Tom Fuller and colleagues at the Oregon Department of Transportation, and Stan Hall of Friends of the Columbia Gorge. Professor Peggy Watt and Karen Smith of my old department at Western Washington helped greatly with scanning photographs.

Newspaper photographers, often friends from those days, captured many of the images in this book, and credit is given where known. But the extraordinary skill and dedication to Oregon history of Gerry Lewin is quite remarkable; his trove of first-rate images is a treasure, and working with him a great pleasure.

Mary Elizabeth Braun of Oregon State University Press put the idea of this book in my mind and her enthusiasm and good words kept me going. The sensitive and perceptive editing of Micki Reaman is most appreciated, as is the assistance of Marty Brown and Tom Booth. They kept me on target and contributed ideas and support.

Finally, the contributions of my immediate family have always been essential in my life, beginning always with Dixie and extending to our children, Karen and David, Karen's husband Edward (Ted) Wolf—a fine writer who gave me valuable feedback and ideas—and grandchildren Andrew and Amanda McKay and Laurel and Lydia Wolf. In good times and trying times, we have always pulled together, celebrated victories and confronted challenges. I have been blessed.

Notes

CHAPTER ONE

1   I describe that era in "Green Beans, Green Cash: Alderman Farms' Post–World War II Teenage Workforce," *Oregon Historical Quarterly* Vol. 111 (Fall 2010), 372–388.

2   My biography of Sprague, *An Editor for Oregon: Charles A. Sprague and the Politics of Change* (Oregon State University Press, 1998), contains details on the *Oregon Statesman*.

3   Brent Walth, *Fire at Eden's Gate: Tom McCall and the Oregon Story* (Oregon Historical Society Press, 1994), 96–111.

4   Charles K. Johnson, *Standing at the Water's Edge: Bob Straub's Battle for the Soul of Oregon* (Oregon State University Press, 2012), 76–89.

5   Although Jack Capell is always listed as one of the "original team," he worked part-time for the first two years, delivering a weather report two or three times a week while keeping his job at the Weather Bureau. He went full-time in 1958.

CHAPTER TWO

1   The documentary is available at the KGW-TV web page: http://legacy. kgw.com/search/pollution%20in%20paradise/.

2   Johnson, 95–107 and 134–138.

3   Governor Tom McCall's official portrait in the capitol, by Henk Pender, is based on the beach heroics of 1967. The Dutch-born Pender immigrated to Oregon in 1965.

4 A program in the OPB series *Oregon Experience*, "The Beach Bill and Nestucca Spit" (2007) covers the Beach Bill and the beach-highway battle. Available at http://www.opb.org/television/programs/oregonexperience/segment/the-beach-bill-/.

5 Current wild and scenic rivers may be found at: http://www.gorp.com.

6 A program in the *Oregon Field Guide* series at OPB examines the current Greenway: http://watch.opb.org/video/2339333429/.

CHAPTER THREE

1 Robert Eells and Bartell Nyberg, *Lonely Walk: The Life of Senator Mark Hatfield* (Chappaqua, NY: Christian Herald Books, 1979), 23.

2 Mason Drukman, *Wayne Morse: A Political Biography* (Oregon Historical Society Press, 1997), 311–317 and 437–441. See also A. Robert Smith, *The Tiger in the Senate: The Biography of Wayne Morse* (New York, Doubleday, 1962), 370–379.

3 "Ghosts of Tonkin" is a play written by Steve Lyons; it played in Portland and Springfield, and in Seattle and Bellingham in 2014–2015.

CHAPTER FOUR

1 Floyd McKay, "The 'Kaffeeklatsch' Constituency," *The Nation* (Feb. 17, 1969), 205–207.

2 Walth, 214–217, describes McCall's Vietnam trip.

3 Richard Oulahan and William Lambert, "Lax Laws and a Powerful Clique Invite the High Rollers to Swarm In," *Life*, Feb. 3, 1967, 59–74.

CHAPTER FIVE

1 Dorothy McCall's two books are *Ranch Under the Rimrock* (1968) and her autobiography, *The Copper King's Daughter* (1972), both published by Binford and Mort, Portland.

2 Richard A. Clucas, Mark Henkels, and Brent S. Steel, editors: *Oregon Politics and Government: Progressives versus Conservative Populists* (Lincoln: University of Nebraska, 2005), 108.

CHAPTER SIX

1 Walth, 232–239 and 448–449, discusses Sam McCall's drug issues, including the Jackson fund. Johnson, 161, describes Bob Straub's reactions.

2 Oregon Public Broadcasting's *Oregon Experience* series "Vortex I" (2010) includes photographs and interviews.

3 Walth, 174.

CHAPTER SEVEN

1 Paul Koberstein, "Trojan: PGE's Nuclear Gamble," *Willamette Week*, March 9, 2005.

2 Daniel Jack Chasan, *The Fall of the House of WPPSS*, (Seattle: Sasquatch Publishing, 1985).

3 Betty Roberts. *With Grit and By Grace: Breaking Trails in Politics and Law, a Memoir* (Oregon State University Press, 2008), 147–158.

4 *The Business Journal*, June 23, 1986 and *Oregon Business*, October 1985.

CHAPTER EIGHT

1 Ernie Bonner's interview with Cogan is just one of several available at http://www.pdx.edu/usp/planpdxorg-interviews-planning-participants. The site is a treasure trove of history of planning in Oregon, particularly Portland. Bonner was a former City of Portland chief planner.

2 Holbrook's books can only be found in used-book aisles, but Brian Booth's anthology preserves many gems: *Wildmen, Wobblies & Whistlepunks: Stewart Holbrook's Lowbrow Northwest* (Oregon State University Press, 1992).

3 Laura Jane Gifford, "Planning for a Productive Paradise," *Oregon Historical Quarterly* 115 (Winter 2014), 470.

4 Walth, 390–396. See also McCall's autobiography, *Tom McCall: Maverick* (Portland, Binford and Mort, 1977), 237–256.

5 Walth, 325.

6 Doris Kearns Goodwin, *The Bully Pulpit: Theodore Roosevelt, William Howard Taft and the Golden Age of Journalism* (New York: Simon & Schuster Paperbooks, 2013), 203–211.

7 Oregon's current bicycle program is at http://www.oregon.gov/ODOT/HWY/BIKEPED/Pages/index.aspx.

CHAPTER NINE

1 Johnson, 177–183.

2 Drukman, 460–461.

3 Sy Adler, *Oregon Plans: The Making of an Unquiet Land Use Revolution* (Oregon State University Press, 2012), 103–119.

4 Adler, 151–169.

5 James Flanigan, "Hatfield led late lobbying to get Reagan to sign gorge bill," *Oregonian*, Nov. 24, 1986.

6 Katy Muldoon, "Guardian of the Gorge," *Oregonian*, June 15, 2008.

CHAPTER TEN

1 Ernie Bonner, interview with Betty Merten, http://www.pdx.edu/usp/planpdxorg-interviews-planning-participants .

2 The *Oregon Journal*, founded in 1902, was an afternoon paper usually backing Democrats. It was purchased by S. I. Newhouse, owner of the *Oregonian*, in 1961 and closed in 1982.

3 Tim DuRoche, "A Riverfront Park Runs Through It," Metroscope. Available: http://www.pdx.edu/sites/www.pdx.edu.ims/files/ims_mscape1ow-inriverfront.pdf.

4 Neal R. Peirce. *The Pacific States of America* (New York: W. W. Norton, 1972), 188–222.

5 The Portland Hotel was the city's grandest lodging from 1890 until the early twentieth century. The deteriorating icon was purchased in 1944 by Meier & Frank and razed in 1951 for parking.

6 Ernie Bonner, interview with Arnold Cogan, available: http://www.pdx.edu/usp/planpdxorg-interview-arnold-cogan.

7 Portland has a commission form of government, in which the mayor's vote is only one among equals.

8   Huntley Collins, "Goldschmidt and Ivancie: 'Poles apart'" may be too narrow a distinction," *Oregonian*, April 12, 1976.

9   Neal R. Peirce and Robert Guskind. "Portland's 1972 Downtown Plan: Rebirth of the Public City," in *Breakthroughs: Re-creating the American City* (New Brunswick, NJ: Center for Urban Policy Research, 1993), 74–75.

10   Polling data is from Bardsley & Haslacher, a Portland firm, published in the *Oregonian* during the election cycle.

11   Governor Goldschmidt actually appointed Norma Paulus twice to top jobs: shortly after taking office in 1987, to the Northwest Power and Conservation Commission and later as superintendent of public instruction.

CHAPTER ELEVEN

1   William G. Robbins. *Landscapes of Promise: The Oregon Story, 1800 to 1940* (Seattle: University of Washington Press, 1997), 179. Of particular importance to this discussion are pages 179–204.

2   I avoid lists in this work, knowing that inevitably there will be omissions, but such a list would surely also include Gerry Frank in Salem, Aaron Jones in Eugene, Ken Ford in Roseburg, the Naito and Schnitzer families in Portland, and the retailer Fred Meyer. So many others, so little space . . .

AFTERWORD

1   Jeff Mapes, "Mark Hatfield was named as bribe target in secret 1985 indictment of Greek arms dealer, newly released FBI documents show," *Oregonian*, June 2, 2012. Available: http://blog.oregonlive.com/politics_impact/print.html?entry=/2012/06/newly_released_fbi_documents_s.html.

2   The complete report of the Senate Ethics Counsel is contained in *The Packwood Report: the Senate Ethics Counsel on Senator Robert Packwood*, published in 1995 by Times Books (New York), with a foreword by Helen Dewar of the *Washington Post*.

Additional Reading and Viewing

Abbott, Carl. *Portland: Planning, politics, and growth in a twentieth-century city*. Lincoln: University of Nebraska Press, 1983.

_____. *Greater Portland: Urban life and landscapes in the Pacific Northwest*. Philadelphia: University of Pennsylvania Press, 2001.

Adler, Sy. *Oregon Plans: The Making of an Unquiet Land Use Revolution*. Oregon State University Press, 2012.

Booth, Brian, editor. *Wildmen, Wobblies & Whistlepunks: Stewart Holbrook's Lowbrow Northwest*. Oregon State University Press, 1992.

Burton, Robert E. *Democrats of Oregon: The Pattern of Minority Politics, 1900-1956*. University of Oregon, 1970.

Clucas, Richard A., Mark Henkels, and Brent S. Steel, editors. *Oregon Politics and Government: Progressives versus Conservative Populists*. University of Nebraska, 2005.

Drukman, Mason. *Wayne Morse: A Political Biography*. Oregon Historical Society, 1997.

Eells, Robert and Bartell Nyberg. *Lonely Walk: The Life of Senator Mark Hatfield*. Chappaqua, N.Y.: Christian Herald Books, 1979.

Gifford, Laura Jane. "Planning for a Productive Paradise," *Oregon Historical Quarterly* 115 (Winter 2014), 470-502.

Hatfield, Mark O. *Not Quite So Simple*. New York: Harper & Row, 1968.

_____. *Conflict and Conscience*. Waco, Texas: Word Books, 1971.

Johnson, Charles K. *Standing at the Water's Edge: Bob Straub's Battle for the Soul of Oregon*. Oregon State University Press, 2012.

Karnow, Stanley. *Vietnam: A History*. New York: Viking Press, 1983.

Kirchmeier, Mark. *Packwood: The Public and Private Life from Acclaim to Outrage.* New York: Harper Collins West, 1995.

Lansing, Jewel. *Portland: People, Politics and Power, 1851-2001.* Oregon State University Press, 2003.

_____ and Fred Leeson. *Multnomah: The Tumultuous Story of Oregon's Most Populous County.* Oregon State University Press, 2012.

Marsh, Tom. *To the Promised Land: A History of Government and Politics in Oregon.* Oregon State University Press, 2012.

McCall, Dorothy Lawson. *Ranch Under the Rimrock.* Portland: Binford and Mort, 1971.

McCall, Tom with Steve Neal. *Tom McCall: Maverick.* Portland: Binford and Mort, 1977.

McKay, Floyd J. *An Editor for Oregon: Charles A. Sprague and the Politics of Change.* Oregon State University Press, 1998.

Neal, Steve, editor. *They Never Go Back to Pocatello.* Oregon Historical Society, 1988.

Peirce, Neal R. *The Pacific States of America.* New York: W. W. Norton, 1972.

Peirce, Neal R. and Robert Guskind. "Portland's 1972 Downtown Plan: Rebirth of the Public City," in *Breakthroughs: Re-creating the American City* (New Brunswick, N.J.: Center for Urban Policy Research, 1993), 52-83.

Roberts, Barbara. *Up the Capitol Steps: A Woman's March to the Governorship.* Oregon State University Press, 2011.

Roberts, Betty with Gail Wells. *With Grit and by Grace: Breaking Trails in Politics and Law, a Memoir.* Oregon State University Press, 2008.

Robbins, William G. *Landscapes of Promise: The Oregon Story, 1800 to 1940.* Seattle: University of Washington Press, 1997.

_____. *Landscapes of Conflict: The Oregon Story, 1940-2000.* Seattle: University of Washington Press, 2004.

_____. *A Man for all Seasons: Monroe Sweetland and the Liberal Paradox.* Oregon State University Press, 2015.

Smith, A. Robert. *The Tiger in the Senate: The Biography of Wayne Morse.* New York: Doubleday & Co., 1962.

US Senate Select Committee on Ethics. *The Packwood Report: The Senate Ethics Counsel on Senator Robert Packwood.* New York: Times Books, 1995.

Walth, Brent. *Fire at Eden's Gate: Tom McCall and The Oregon Story.* Oregon Historical Society, 1994.

_____. "No Deposit, No Return: Richard Chambers, Tom McCall, and the Oregon Bottle Bill," *Oregon Historical Quarterly* 95 (1994), 278-99.

Wingard, George. *Footprints: The Oregon State Legislature in the '70s.* Eugene: Grand Prix Press, 1990.

ADDITIONAL VIEWING: VIDEO

Oregon Public Broadcasting, "Oregon Experience" DVD Recordings:
Tom McCall, 2013.
Wayne Morse, 2012.
Rajneeshpuram, 2012
Vortex I, 2010.
The Beach Bill and Nestucca Spit, 2007.

Index

A

Abell, Ron, 85–87
Aerosol ban (1975), 4, 186–187
Agnew, Spiro (Ted), 97–98, 132, 172, 174, 181
Ahslen, Ralph, 112
Amsden, Forest, 109, 110, 120, 198, 216, 218, 251
Anderson, Lloyd, 142, 218, 221–222
Appling, Howell Jr., 25, 26, 31, 70
Atiyeh, Victor, ix, 9, 122, 151; campaign for governor (1974), 189–190; Columbia Gorge protection, 207–209, 219, 232, 233 election as governor (1978), 200–203; as governor, 204, 206
Atkeson, Ray, 152
AuCoin, Les, 219

B

Baker, Doug, 109
Bateman, Allen, 195, 196
Bateson, Cornelius, 34,169
Bazett, Sidney (Sid), 49–50
beach bill (1967–1969), x, 48–52, 57, 58, 102, 120, 128, 130, 142, 163, 176, 190, 198, 200
beach highway controversy (1965–1969), 41–47, 133

Belcher, Allison and Bob, 217
Belton, Howard, 21, 25–27, 31
Benner, Richard, 196
Berkman, Craig, 104–106
Bergstein, Leonard (Len), 191–192
bicycle bill (1971), 144, 186
Biggs, Joan, 124
bipartisanship, 3, 7, 51–52, 53, 129, 148–149, 159–161, 174–175, 216, 242–243
Blanchard, Robert, 156–157
Boe, Jason, 151, 162–164, 173, 174
Boise Cascade mill, 185
Branchfield, Ed, 129
Brinkley, David, 112
Brown, Walter (Walt), 185–187
Browne, Elizabeth (Betty), 161
Buchanan, Dennis and Maryanne, 165, 216, 251
Buel, Ron, 121–122, 214, 215, 219
Bullitt, Dorothy, 15, 125, 127
Burns, John, 115
Burns, Joseph E., 131

C

California Proposition, 13. 122, 202
Calley, William, 72–73
Cape Kiwanda, 42, 45, 152
Capell, Jack, 15, 35, 36,111, 121

Chambers, Richard, 142–143, 149, 151, 152
Charles, Clive, 238
Clark, Donald (Don), 212, 219
Clark, John Elwood Jr. (Bud), 229–231
Cogan, Arnold, 169, 222
Coleman, Elsa, 149
Collins, Huntley, 226
Compton, James, 111
Corbett, Alfred (Alf), 21, 23–25
Corbett, Alice, 105
Craft, Roy, 208
Craven, Tom, 119
Cronkite, Walter, 4, 14, 15, 83, 126
Cross, Travis, 33, 69, 70, 78–79, 145
Curry, Ann, 111

D
Dargan, Tom, 198
Davidson, Mike, 131
Davis, Robert (Bob), 139, 192
Day, L. B., 168–169, 175, 183–185, 194
"death with dignity," 154
Democratic Party, 5–6, 65–68, 99–100, 115–116, 122, 144, 149, 155, 162, 190
Demoforum, 155
Denehy, Tom, 159
Dorchester Conference, 89–91, 106, 154–155, 180
Drinkwater, Terry, 170
Duncan, Robert (Bob), 80–82, 84, 85, 151, 219; personality, 67–68; Vietnam and 1966 US Senate campaign, 64–65, 67–70
Drukman, Mason, xi

E
Earth Day (1970), 149–150
East-West Center, x, 248
energy shortages (1973–1974), 178–180
Equal Rights Amendment (ERA), 160–161
Evans, Dan, 210, 212
Eymann, Richard (Dick), 174

F
Fadeley, Nancy, 175–176
Fagan, Bernie, 238
Falconer, David, 140
Flanigan, Jim, 210
Ford, Cynthia, 162
Fowler, Stephanie, 116
Frasca, Robert (Bob), 222
Friedman, Ralph, 171
Friends of the Columbia Gorge, 147, 208, 212
Friends of Pioneer Square, 225

G
Glickman, Harry, 237
Godfrey, Ed, 109–110, 116–117, 119, 141
Goldschmidt, Neil, 127, 142, 162, 173, 197, 205, 210, 215, 221; campaign for governor (1986), 232–235; 237, 245–246; opposition to urban freeways, 217–219; Portland City Council and mayor, 221, 224, 226–228
Goodwin, Alfred T. (Ted), 52
Gordon, Mel, 219
Gray, John, 195, 242
Green, Edith, 6, 12, 23, 81, 159–160
Grenfell, Ralph and Elizabeth (Betsy), 55, 163
Guildemeister, Al, 158

Gulf of Tonkin: Senate resolution, 62, 66; 2014 stage play, 67

H

Hallock, Ted, 143, 154, 174–176
Hand, Beulah, 161
Hanneman, Paul, 142–143
Hansell, Stafford, 53–54, 131
Harbor Drive (Portland), 216–218, 220, 237
Harms, Edward (Ed), 18, 168
Harvey, Paul, 19
Hatfield, Antoinette Kuzmanich, 20, 33, 69, 77, 114, 246
Hatfield, Mark O., xi, 2, 6–8 210, 219, 233; early opposition to Vietnam and 1966 campaign for US Senate, 61–66, 68, 70; governor, 19–20, 26, 28, 31–32, 34, 54–55, 169; national politics and 1968 prominence. 70–72, 76–77, 84–85, 93–94, 96–99; personality, 33, 61–64, 69–71, 77–79, 173; Tsakos affair, 246–247
Hay, William, 48, 51
Hayes, Denis, 149
Heffron, Norm, 107, 108, 109
Hesburgh, Theodore, 74
Hoffer, Eric, 115, 197
Holbrook, Stewart, 171–172
Holmes, Robert (Bob), 19–20, 66
"Holy Land, Bloody War: The West Bank," 123
Hornish, Harrison P. (Red), 10, 20

I

initiative and referendum, 157–158
Ivancie, Francis (Frank): campaign for mayor (1976), 226–227; mayor of Portland, 224–230; Portland City Council, 142, 216, 218, 221, 224

J

Jackson, Glenn, political influence and power broker, 40–41, 66, 135, 162, 170, 173, 195, 197, 242; role in beach highways, 41, 43–45, 58; role in Portland freeways, 216, 218–219
Jackson, Henry (Scoop), 132, 160
James G. Blaine Society, 171
Jarvi, Don, 180
Jaycees, 92, 104, 145
Johnson, Charles, xi
Johnson, Eric, 112
Johnson, Ken, 25, 197
Johnson, Lee, 51, 102–103
Johnson, Lyndon B., 14, 61–62, 65, 68, 81, 83, 94–96, 113
Jordan, Charles, 224
journalism, the craft, 4, 8–9, 14–17, 18–19, 28–30, 34, 35–37, 38–39, 43–44, 49–52, 72–79, 92–93, 107–112, 116–127, 135, 138, 140–141, 170, 188, 192–193, 197–198, 218, 235–236, 242
Joy, Patricia, 120

K

Kafoury, Greg, 152
Kaskey, Raymond, 228, 229
Katz, Vera: activism, 151, 164–166; Speaker of the House, 160, 162
Kennedy, John F., 4, 14–15, 62, 109
Kennedy, Robert, 83, 84, 165
KGW television, xi, 5, 15–16, 23–24, 30, 35–37, 50, 74, 77, 92, 107–128, 140–142, 149, 156–157, 179–180, 198–199, 204, 211, 215, 218, 228, 230, 235–236, 251

Kitzhaber, John, 160, 162–163, 166, 173, 247
Kramer, Matt, 49, 52

L

LaGrande, Dan, 116
LaMear, Doug, 15, 16, 35, 111
Lesser, Harold (Hal), 112
Linfield College, 10, 76, 248
Lollis, Keith, 74
Lucas, Maurice, 238

M

MacArthur, Scott, 171
Mackin, Catherine (Cassie), 112
Macpherson, Hector Jr., 149, 174–175, 183
Mahoney, Thomas (Tom), 163
Marbet, Lloyd, 151–152
Martin, Roger, ix, 200–201
McAlmond, Phil, 85
McCall, Audrey Walker, 24, 33, 134
McCall, Dorothy Lawson, 112–114
McCall, Thomas William Lawson Sr. (Tom), xi, 1–3, 53, 83, 90, 100, 142, 144, 154, 183, 185, 186, 188–189, 194–196, 197, 200, 216–219, 231, 237, 240; beach bill, 50–52; campaign for governor (1966), 35, 40–48; campaign for re-election (1970), 128–132, 135–140; campaign for re-election (1970) and nerve gas issue, 130–132; campaign for re-election (1970) and Vortex rock festival, 136–138; campaign for secretary of state (1966), 21–24; final campaign (1978), 200–202; highways on beaches, 40–41, 44–46; journalism career, importance of television, 15–17, 24, 30, 35–39, 50, 108, 197–199; land use and tax measures (1970–1974), 169–170, 174–178, 200, 205; personality, 22–23, 29–30, 33, 56, 57, 79, 94, 112–114, 129, 130, 133, 135, 171–173, 188; relationship with Hatfield, 32–33, 56, 79, 93; relationship with Glenn Jackson, 41, 43; relationship with Straub, 3, 7, 8, 31, 39, 55–58, 128, 197, 216; Vietnam views, 93–97; Willamette River cleanup and Greenway, 54–57
McCall, Thomas William Lawson Jr. (Tad), 74, 94
McCall, Samuel Walker III (Sam), 134–135
McCall, ZeeZee, 74
McCarthy, Eugene (Gene), 99, 100, 181
McCarthy, Steve, 196
McCready, Connie, 142, 221, 224, 227, 228
Mcintire, Don, 159
McKay, David, 11, 84, 115
McKay, Dixie Johnson, 163, 165, 180, 193, 197, 206, 236, 245, 248
McKay, Douglas, 15, 24, 139
McKay, Karen, 11, 84
McLennan, Janet, 43, 58–60, 149
McLeod, Mike, 123
McPhillips, B. A. (Barney), 152–153
Measure 6 (1968 gas tax), 52–53, 58, 130
Measure 6 (1982 repeal LCDC), 204–205
Meier, Roger, 104

Meier & Frank block, 222, 225–226. *See also* Pioneer Courthouse Square
Merten, Betty and Charles, 149, 214
Montgomery, F. F. (Monte), 49, 51, 101
Morgan, Howard, 6, 65–68
Morrison, Sid, 210
Morse, Wayne Lyman, 54, 91, 102, 160; campaign for re-election (1968), 83–89, 92, 93, 102; political role (1954–1966), 6, 11, 27, 32, 66, 68–69, 94, 165; post-Senate, 191, 201–202; role in 1966 campaigns, 65–66, 68, 70; Vietnam views, leadership, 7, 61–62, 67, 73, 94–96, 100
Moses, Robert, 217
Mosser, John, 54, 129, 192
Mount Hood Freeway, 9, 81, 149, 189, 197, 213–216, 219–220, 226, 227, 243
Murrow, Edward R., 14, 31, 107
Myers, Clay, 101–102, 151, 178, 189–190, 200, 233

N
Nehalem Bay estuary, 45–47
Neuberger, Maurine Brown, 11–13, 64, 161
Neuberger, Richard L., 6, 11–13, 27, 32, 68, 69, 171, 241
Nieman Fellowships (Harvard), 22, 70, 84, 92, 108, 112, 148
Nixon, Richard, 74, 83, 93, 95–99, 109, 119, 132, 135–136, 159, 178, 180, 207
North Dakota, 9, 27, 84, 161, 167
nuclear power (Trojan plant), 132, 152–153
Nunn, Warne, 145

O
One Thousand Friends of Oregon, 147, 195–196
Onthank, Karl, 55
Operation Red Hat, 1970, 130–133
Oregon Environmental Council, 148, 149
Oregon Historical Society, ix, xi
Oregon Journal newspaper, 52, 109, 216
Oregon Mystique, 1, 27, 200, 205
Oregon Public Broadcasting (OPB), x, 146
Oregon state agencies: Board of Control, 31–32, 61; Energy, 196; Highway Commission, 40–41, 44–45, 130, 162, 217: Investment Council, 103–104, 205, 241; Land Board, 31, 55; Land Conservation and Development Commission (LCDC), 194–96, 200, 204–206; Legislature, 13, 33–34, 47, 48–52, 53–54, 56–57, 102, 115–117, 128–130, 142–144, 154, 160–162, 166, 169–170, 174–177, 185–187, 196–199, 206; Sanitary Authority, 54, 130; State Capitol, 18–19, 29, 164; State Fair, 27–28, 185
Oregon Statesman, 5, 11, 14, 16, 18–20, 34, 43–44, 76, 84, 107–108, 127, 161, 249
Oregonian, 86, 118, 121, 133, 140, 210, 212, 221, 223, 226, 246

P
Packwood, Robert (Bob), 176, 182, 191, 210, 246–247; campaign for US Senate, 1968, 80,

83–89, 93, 101; Dorchester Conference, 89–91, 106, 154, 178; personality, 89, 91–93; role in Republican campaigns, 102–104, 147

Paulus, Norma, 57, 152, 160, 161, 162, 191; campaign for governor, 1986, 233–235

Page, Ancil, 102

Payne, Ancil, 24, 50, 71, 102, 108, 110, 111, 117–118, 120, 123, 126–127, 198, 235–236

Peirce, Neal, 220, 231

Phillips, Ray, 158, 202

Pihas, John, 146

Pioneer Courthouse Square, 222–223, 231. *See also* Meier and Frank block

Pollution in Paradise, documentary, 38–39, 50, 54

Porter, Don, 122

Portland City Club, 88–89, 216–218

Portland Downtown Plan, 222–223, 231

Portland Planning Commission, 222

Portland Rose Festival, 119

Portland Public Schools, 149, 156–157

Portland State University, 194, 222

Portlandia, the statue, 214, 228–229

Portlandia, the television program, 214, 228

Preppernau, Charlie, 193

Property tax measure six (1978), 202–203

Prophet, Matthew, 157

R

Ramsay, Jack, 238

Rand, Dewey, 25

Ray, Dixy Lee, 207–208

Reagan, Ronald, 93, 95, 124, 210, 228, 124–126, 171, 174, 179

Redden, James (Jim), 51, 105, 151, 179, 189–191

Reporters' Shield law, 30

Republican Party, 64, 68, 101, 106, 134, 149, 154, 188–189

Richmond, Henry, 195–196

Rinke, Ken, 52–53

Ritter, Milt, 119

Riverfront for People (RFP), 217–218

Robbins, William, 239

Roberts, Barbara, 11, 29, 159, 160

Roberts, Betty, 11, 143, 151, 160–162, 173; campaigns of 1974, 189–191

Roberts, William (Bill), 224–225

Rockefeller, Nelson, 95, 97, 130, 181

Romney, George, 62

Roosevelt, Franklin D., 12, 207

Roosevelt, Theodore (Teddy), 12, 185

Ross, Richard, 15–16, 35–36, 75, 109, 111, 119, 140, 198

Russell, Nancy, 149, 208–209, 211–212

S

Sanderson, William, 118–119

Scenic Waterways Initiative, 1970, 53–54

Schell, Steve, 194, 214

Schmidt, Ronald (Ron), 29, 33, 131, 133, 144–146, 178, 192, 200

Schrunk, Terry, 221, 222
Schwab, Mildred, 221, 224, 238
Senate Bill 100, 174–176, 194
Sensible Transportation Options
    for People (STOP), 214–15
Skamania County, Washington,
    208–210
Smith, Denny, 210
Smith, Elmo, 90
Smith, Ivan, 15–16, 35, 111
Smith, R. P. (Joe), 131–132
Smith, Robert (Bob), 49, 128,
    142–143, 169, 179, 210
Smith, Steve, 193
Snell, Earl, 70
Solomon, Gus, 52
Spellman, John, 208–209
Sprague, Charles A., 5, 18–19, 43,
    61, 101, 107–108, 127, 249
Springfield, Oregon, 17–18, 168,
    193
Springfield News, 10, 17–18, 20,
    126, 168
Stacey, Robert, 196
Stathos, Don, 105, 144, 185–186
Stop Oregon Litter and Vandalism
    (SOLV), 143
Straub, Patricia Stroud, 39, 114–
    115, 193
Straub, Robert (Bob), ix, xi, 3, 6–8,
    9, 11, 17–18, 31, 45, 50, 55,
    58–59, 79, 102, 103–104, 114,
    129, 168, 173, 206, 207, 212,
    215, 216, 217, 219, 241; cam-
    paign for governor and beach
    highway controversy (1966),
    34–35, 38–45; campaign for
    governor (1970), 130, 134–135,
    139, 145, 150, 170; campaign
    for and election as governor
(1974), 188–193, 219; campaign
    for re-election (1978), 202–203;
    campaign for treasurer (1964),
    25–28; gas tax initiative (1968),
    52–53; as governor (1975–
    1979), 183, 186, 188, 196–197,
    199–200, 206, 219; personality,
    17, 27–28, 30, 39, 114–115,
    190, 203, 205–206; Willamette
    Greenway, 55–57, 129–130
Sullivan, J. Wesley (Wes), 43
Sweetland, Monroe, 6

T
Taxation proposals, measures,
    52–53, 121, 129, 158–159, 176–
    178, 202–203
Thornton, Robert Y. (Bob),
    102–103
Timber Jim (Jim Serrill), 237–238
Tompkins, Joseph (Joey), 16–17,
    116–117
Tri-Met, 121, 197, 219,
Tsakos, Basil, 246
Tuttle, Jon, 119, 122, 208

U
Udall, Stewart, 45
Upshur Corridor, Portland, 218

V
VanLeeuwen, Elizabeth (Liz), 57,
    149
Vanocur, Sander, 135
Vernon, Doug, 122
Vietnam War, 4, 6, 7, 8, 14, 36, 58,
    61–69, 71–73, 75–76, 79–83,
    85, 88, 91, 94–96, 100, 102,
    130, 132, 135, 149, 152, 153,
    155, 242
Volpe, John, 94, 96
Vortex Festival, 136–138

W

Walsh, Tom, 142, 221
Walth, Brent, xi, 145, 184
Walton, Bill, 237–238
Washington Public Power Supply
  System (WPPSS), 153
Watergate scandal, 30, 98, 153,
  178, 181, 242
Webb, Wendell, 4, 14, 18
Wednesday Club, US Senate, 76
West, Oswald, 47–48
Westerdahl, Edward (Ed), 133,
  136, 139, 144–146, 200
Western Washington University, x,
  248–249
Whitehead, Dorothy Blosser, 115
Willamette Greenway, 55–57, 129,
  149, 150, 182, 189, 196, 199,
  233, 241
Willamette Week, 122, 152, 215,
  245
Williams, Larry, 148, 149
Willner, Don, 53–54
Wingard, George, 175
Wright, Marguerite Wittwer, 19,
  82
Wright, Thomas G., Jr. (Tom),
  19–20, 251
Wyatt, Wendell, 159–160

Y

Yeon, John, 207, 211–212
Youngstown (Ohio) State University, 76–77

FLOYD MCKAY was a prominent political reporter for the *Oregon Statesman* in Salem, and news analyst for KGW-TV in Portland. For his work as a reporter and producer of documentaries, he won the DuPont-Columbia Broadcast Award, the "Pulitzer Prize of Broadcasting." He was a Nieman Fellow in journalism at Harvard University and taught journalism at Western Washington University. He holds a PhD in media history from the University of Washington. He's the author of *An Editor for Oregon: Charles A. Sprague and the Politics of Change.* McKay lives in Bellingham, Washington.